I0612989

Peter Henderson

Practical Floriculture

A Guide to the successful Cultivation of Florists' Plants for the amateur and

professional Florist

Peter Henderson

Practical Floriculture
A Guide to the successful Cultivation of Florists' Plants for the amateur and professional Florist

ISBN/EAN: 9783337106195

Printed in Europe, USA, Canada, Australia, Japan

Cover: Foto ©ninafisch / pixelio.de

More available books at **www.hansebooks.com**

PRACTICAL FLORICULTURE;

A GUIDE TO THE SUCCESSFUL CULTIVATION OF

FLORISTS' PLANTS,

FOR THE

AMATEUR AND PROFESSIONAL FLORIST.

BY
PETER HENDERSON,

AUTHOR OF "GARDENING FOR PROFIT," "GARDENING FOR PLEASURE," "HAND
BOOK OF PLANTS," "GARDEN AND FARM TOPICS," "HOW THE FARM PAYS," ETC.

NEW AND ENLARGED EDITION.

ILLUSTRATED.

NEW YORK:
ORANGE JUDD COMPANY,
1899.

CONTENTS.

(3)

PREFACE TO FOURTH AND GREATLY ENLARGED EDITION.

It is eight years since the last edition of "Practical Floriculture" was published. Great strides have been made in Floriculture in this country, even in that short time, particularly in the growing of Roses, Bulbs, and other prominent classes of plants for winter flowers, in all of which we have endeavored to give as plainly as possible the details of the most approved methods as practiced in the vicinity of New York City, where at the present time, a higher degree of perfection is believed to have been attained than in any other section of the country, or, perhaps, in any part of the world. London, Paris, and other large European cities may yet excel us in the variety and in the greater care of plants grown for sale, but by careful observations they seem to be now far behind us in the methods of producing the leading kinds of winter flowers grown for sale.

Although prices for both cut flowers and plants are even less than when the last edition of this work was written, the improvement in green-house structures, together with improvements to lessen the labor of culture, have kept the business of commercial floriculture, so that all things considered, it is quite as profitable as it was ten or twelve years ago. There are now believed to be over 10,000 florists in the United States, a large per centage of whom, if not making colossal fortunes, are making comfortable livings in a safe and pleasant business.

PETER HENDERSON.

(7)

PRACTICAL FLORICULTURE.

CHAPTER I.

HOW TO BECOME A FLORIST.

I am often asked the question if it is necessary in order to become a florist to enter some large establishment for a few years, or whether it is possible to learn from reading only. I reply, if it can be afforded, it will be best, by all means, to serve at least two years in some well-conducted establishment—one that has been long enough established to have made the business a success, for the best index of ability in any business is success. I have said, if it can be afforded, as for the first two years, unless a youth proves himself unusually smart, he will not likely receive more than enough to pay his board, for he is simply an apprentice under instructions, who has come with the design of leaving when he has acquired a knowledge of the trade, and just at the time when he begins to be of use to his employer.

But to those to whom it would be inconvenient to place themselves thus under instructions, a knowledge of the business could be unquestionably obtained from books, particularly if actual practice were followed conjointly with the reading. There are now thousands of my patrons (about one tenth of whom are ladies), located in nearly every State of the Union, who have worked themselves into the florists' business exclusively by reading and their own practice, having had no opportunity for other instruction. In not a few cases some of these have got ahead of what are known as professional gardeners, those who have had no other experience than that received in private gardens in Europe, which by no means fits them for the American style of commercial floriculture. The increase of a taste for flowers for the past thirty years has been truly wonderful. A gentleman who has a turn for statistics in this peculiar line, informed me that he had begun to procure information from all parts of the country of the numbers engaged in the trade, together with the capital employed. He said that his investigations for this locality, taken in the rough, extending in the radius of ten miles from the center of New York City, proved that the number of florists' establishments was about 500, and the capital used in stock and structures upwards of $6,000,000. If the number of establishments is nearly correct—and there is no reason to doubt it—I am certain that the value is not overestimated, as we have at least half a dozen establishments where the capital used in stock and buildings must be nearly $100,000 each. And this, too, in New York and its suburbs, where the taste is lower than it is in either Boston or Philadelphia. In those places, no doubt, their excellent Horticultural Societies have done much to refine the tastes of the people, and it is to be regretted that neither New York nor its adjacent cities, with over two millions of people, have, until quite recently, had a Horticultural Society, and even that at the date I write, 1887, it is not to be compared with either that of Boston or Philadelphia.

GARDENING AS A BUSINESS—HOW TO BEGIN.

In response to continued inquiries from those who wish to engage in gardening as a business, I propose in this chapter, to give briefly, yet comprehensively, such advice and instruction as my long experience, together with my intercourse and correspondence with hundreds engaged in the various branches of gardening, enable me to offer. I find that the persons who desire to begin gardening as a business, are generally such as have had their tastes turned in that direction by being amateur cultivators. Their gratuitous distributions of slips, seeds, or roots, to sometimes not over-grateful recipients, starts the idea that "what is not worth paying for is not worth having" is as true of garden products as of other things, and that they had better sell than give. As selling means business, the question then is, how to best begin the business to make it pay. My advice to all such inquirers is, to keep away from large cities, unless they have a large capital and a thorough practical knowledge of the business. The beginner with limited means, and more limited knowledge of the business, would be quite unable to compete with those who have been long established, and such are to be found in nearly all cities of 100,000 inhabitants, or over. On the other hand, in cities of 5,000, 10,000, 15,000, or 20,000 inhabitants, the business may be begun, and profitably carried on, with but little capital and a moderate amount of knowledge at starting. How to start is the all important question. In my work on commercial gardening—"Gardening for Profit"—I have given advice on the culture of vegetables and fruits as a separate and distinct branch of the business. Further experience has led me to believe that it would often be of great advantage to the beginner in small towns to undertake the cultivation of small fruits, flowers, and vegetables combined. In a town of, say, 5,000 inhabitants, the profits from the sale of flowers alone would hardly be enough to warrant a beginning, while an acre or two of well-grown fruits or vegetables in addition would make quite a respectable business. We will suppose, then, that a frugal man, able and willing to work hard, has a capital of

$1,500 to $2,000; let him select not more than two acres, either on a lease of, say, 10 years, or by purchase, as near to the business part of the town as practicable. The soil should be of a quality that has borne good crops of Hay, Corn, Potatoes, or other farm produce. Do not be induced to go far from the business center of the town, because land is cheap there; it is better to pay $100 rent per acre for, say, two acres, a mile from the center of the town, than to buy land at that price three or four miles distant for such a purpose. It is a fact beyond all question, that whenever fine specimens of fruit, flowers, or vegetables are offered for sale, a demand is created that did not before exist, and would not then have existed unless these articles were placed before the eyes of the people. Presuming, then, that the one or two acres is secured, if a dwelling-house, stable, or other buildings are to be erected, let them be placed, if practicable, on the northeast corner, so that the part of the land to be cultivated, or where greenhouses are to be erected, be not shaded. If flowers are to be grown, of course a greenhouse or some place where plants can be protected (see Greenhouse Structures) is indispensable, and the proper construction of that is a matter of importance. Perhaps the most appropriate size for a beginner is one twenty feet wide by fifty feet in length, which may be heated either by smoke-flues or hot water circulating in iron pipes. At present prices the house twenty feet wide would cost, if heated by flue, about $9 per running foot; if by hot-water, $15 per running foot. The details of construction are given in other chapters of this work. This greenhouse, having an area of 1,000 square feet, should produce a crop of flowers and plants, when once properly stocked, which should sell at retail for at least $1,000 each year. The stock of plants to begin with, purchased from any wholesale florist, would cost from $100 to $200, according to kinds. The annual cost of fuel, labor, etc., after it is in running order, should not exceed $300 per year. It will be seen that the profit on the investment is good, if the work is mainly done by the owner; but a glass structure of this size would not pay to hire a man to work it, though it would be large enough at first for the wants of an ordinary population of 5,000. But such a population will buy far larger amounts in fruits and vegetables, and will probably buy three times as many and give more for them if fresh and home grown, than they would for those that are packed and shipped from a distance. In fruits, Strawberries hold the most prominent place, and a quarter of an acre will contain, at two feet apart each way, about 2,500 plants. If these are planted by August 1st, from plants layered in pots in July, the ground having been properly prepared, at least 1,000 quarts can be gathered as the first crop; this is a low estimate, the best cultivators claiming to gather one quart per hill of the large fruiting kinds. Next in importance in small fruits come Raspberries, Blackberries, Grapes and Currants, with which another quarter of an acre might be stocked. This would leave, if there were two acres at the start, an acre and a half to be devoted to vegetables. Of this, one-eighth of an acre might be devoted to Asparagus, and the same amount to Rhubarb, Beets and Onions, Cabbages, Cauliflower, and Lettuce, and to Celery; Cucumbers and Melons, Tomatoes and Beans, may each have a quarter of an acre, while one-eighth of an acre may be devoted to other things not provided for. The cultivation of this quantity of land with such crops, together with the care of greenhouse, would require the labor of two active men during the summer months, and probably at some part of the time, three, but in winter, one man could easily do it all. One horse would be sufficient for cultivating and carting manure, etc., but the first plowing of the land in spring should be done by two horses, so that the work may be done deep and thoroughly.

As to the cultivation of fruits and vegetables, it is
not my object in this volume to give detailed directions
"how to do it;" for these reference may be made to my
work "Gardening for Profit," new edition published in
1887.   I merely wish to show that in small towns the
combined culture of fruits, flowers and vegetables can
be more profitably carried on than the culture of either
by itself.   My first attempt at commercial gardening
was a combination of the business of market gardener
and florist, and even for the great market of New York
I believe it was more profitably conducted than if each
had been run separately, for on wet or stormy days, when
they could not work in the open vegetable grounds, the
men were turned into the greenhouses, where their labor
was just as profitable and valuable as in the open field.
But while arguing for the benefits to be derived from
this combination of the several departments of a kindred
business, let it be distinctly understood that it must be
done at one place, so that all can be under the eye of
the owner.

   Thirty years ago, after the successful culture of a garden of some ten acres, combined with quite an extensive
greenhouse business, my ambition led me to think that
if I made $3,000 a year from ten acres, I might as readily
make $9,000 from thirty acres, so I undertook the culti-
vation of two other places, each some ten acres in extent,
but about a mile apart.   A trial of three years showed me
that I had made a serious mistake, for I found that I was
actually making less from my thirty acres than I had
made from my original ten, and yet I had experience,
capital, and, I believe, as much energy and business
capacity as the average of mankind.   Had the thirty acres
been all in one spot, the result might have been different,
but it is probable that the profits would not have been in
the same proportion, as if ten acres only had been cultivated.   This lesson to me was a salutary one, and I never

hesitated to state my own case to any one who informs me of his intention of attempting to carry on gardening in two or more different places at once.

CHAPTER II.

THE PRICES OF NURSERY AND GREENHOUSE PRODUCTS ABROAD AND AT HOME.

While the price of labor is from one-third to one-half more in this country than in Europe, nearly all the products of the nursery, greenhouse or garden are sold lower here than there—not merely lower, but in a majority of cases at less than half the price. In nursery stock, I have the authority of Ellwanger & Barry, of Rochester, N. Y., for stating that, in many leading articles in fruit trees, the difference in prices in favor of this country are as follows: In England, Standard Apple trees are quoted at $18 per 100 ; the same quality are sold here at $12 per 100.   Dwarf Pear trees there sell at $35 per 100 ;. here at $15 per 100.   Standard Pear, Plum and Cherry trees average in England $18 per 100 ; here $15 per 100. Apricots and Nectarines are sold for about the same price here and in England, but Peach trees, which are sold here at an average of $70 per 1,000, are sold there at $150 per 1,000.   The general assortment of ornamental trees and shrubs shows a corresponding average in favor of lower prices here.   In greenhouse or bedding plants, the difference in favor of our lower rates here, is even greater, both at wholesale and retail.   Carnations, or Pinks, which are quoted in England as specially low at $20 per 100, are sold here at $12 per 100.   Ferns sold here at $6 per 100, are offered at $8 there; Tuberoses and Gladioluses that are now sold here at $2 and $3, are quoted there at double these rates (in fact, their supply of Tuberoses is now obtained from us), while, to take the average of bedding or greenhouse plants, that may average here $6 per 100 to the trade, are offered to us by the wholesale English houses as specially low at $8 per 100.

Owing to the unusually dry weather a few years since, nearly all our stock Fuchsias were destroyed, so that we had to import from London ; the price paid was $25 per 100, the very same quality that we sell at $12 per 100. In sales at retail, particularly for new plants, the prices paid in Europe are fully four times more than we charge here. For example, a new Rose, when first offered, is sold in London at £1 1s. (about $6) the plant ; here, the first sales of the same plant are at from $2 to $3 each. New Fuchsias or Geraniums are rarely sold in London at less than $2 each ; here we think we are getting well paid if we get one-fourth of that sum. In addition to the greater price paid for the article itself, they invariably saddle us with the expense of boxing and packing, often no small item, which is rarely charged by our florists. The wonder is, that Europe can ever sell to us at all, particularly when it is known that at least one-half of the imported plants are lost by injury sustained in transit. The question arises, how can our nurserymen and florists sell so much lower, and make the business pay—for that they do make it pay quite as well as European growers do, there is but little doubt. The answer to this is, the known fact that the high cost of labor has long ago forced us to use our ingenuity in simplifying our work. What we do with the plow, most of the English gardeners still think it necessary to do with the spade. What we do with our horse or hand cultivator, they still do with the hoe, and often a very primitive sort of hoe at that. Where we use stakes and labels that are made by machinery, they, in many cases, yet make them by hand, when a single one actually costs as much in labor as do a hundred when made by machinery. When it comes to the manual operations, necessary in the propagating and growing of greenhouse plants, the same waste of labor is apparent. Our average propagator will take off, make and set in bench 2,000 cuttings per day ; at the rate I saw the propagators of two of the leading establishments in London working, when there a few years ago, I doubt if the average was 500 a day, and when we tell them that some of our crack workmen can place 10,000 rooted cuttings in pots in ten hours, they honestly think it false, for probably not more than one-half of that number has ever been done in the same time there. I do not wish to be understood as saying that the English gardener cannot move as rapidly as the American can, but custom there clogs his hands with unnecessary work, to accomplish the object desired. The other day a man of forty years of age presented himself to me, with credentials from a long-established Edinburgh firm, stating him to be an experienced propagator and cultivator of plants. To test his capabilities, I handed him a lot of Rose cuttings to prepare, every one of which he cut at an eye or joint, in the approved orthodox style of a half a century ago ; all propagators of experience here have long known that this is not only a great waste of materials, but a still greater waste of time, and we never do it unless in particular cases that very rarely occur. I might mention scores of similar operations which are performed abroad in a manner which seems to us as primitive as this.

Those who have studied the subject, tell us that from the specimens of the "stone period," at the Smithsonian Institution at Washington, there is reason to believe that it took some thousands of years for our "rude forefathers" to discover that the handles could be better fastened to their hammers of stone, by drilling a hole through them, than by lashing them to the handles with thongs ; and it is a matter of not very ancient history, that in parts of the South of Ireland, the plow was attached to the horses' tails, and that a great row was the consequence when some meddling innovator suggested a change. It appears that mankind, in all ages, is naturally conservative, and it takes years, sometimes centuries, to get out of old ruts. If, while paying for labor one-third more, we can sell our garden products here nearly one-half lower than they are sold in Europe, the conclusion is inevitable, that we have learned how to make our labor more effective than they do.

The adage, that "A prophet is not without honor save in his own country," is true in this matter as in many others; for we find that most Americans having horticultural tastes, when visiting Europe buy largely there, their plants costing them twice as much for half dead trees or plants, as they would pay at home for healthy ones. It is often the case, especially with fruits, that the varieties purchased are utterly useless for our climate. For example, the Jargonelle Pear, Ribston Pippin Apple, and Keen's Seedling Strawberry, still hold a first place in the English gardens, while experience has shown them to be worthless here. So with many ornamental trees; beautiful as are the varieties of English Holly and Rhododendrons, hundreds of Americans have poured down anathemas on the heads of European nurserymen for selling them as "hardy," plants that the frosts of our Northern States, or the hot sun of the South, utterly destroyed the first season.

CHAPTER III.

THE PROFITS OF FLORICULTURE.

It is much easier to estimate the profits of the products of the soil, be they in fruits or vegetables, than to define by any certain rule what the profits of our greenhouse floriculture are. In fact, we can only approximate to it, because the conditions in which the operations are carried on at different places, or the different articles grown, make anything like a general average for the whole country impossible. But, as we have heretofore done, we will confine ourselves to the district of New York, which may be taken at the present time as a fair representation of the whole country.

The capital required in starting this department of horticulture I consider need not be so much as in that of either nursery, vegetable, or fruit growing, and the chances of moderate success I believe, from my observations, to be far greater. I say moderate success, for the chances of making a colossal fortune in this are by no means so good as in the regular nursery business, while to offset this the chances of failure are less, and the business is pleasanter and less exhaustive to follow. I have hardly ever known a man who has started in the florist's business to fail, unless he brought failure on himself by his own imprudence ; while I have known scores to fail in the vegetable and nursery business, from causes entirely beyond their control. A frugal man, with a knowledge of the business and $1,000 capital, may safely start in this vicinity, or in any vicinity where there is a town of 10,000 inhabitants of average intelligence and culture. But the difficult question with all at starting is, how best to make that $1,000 available. Of course expensive buildings, such as we describe in some of the chapters on greenhouse structures, are beyond his means, and something cheaper must be adopted. (See chapter on Cheap Greenhouses). The general principle on which these greenhouses are formed is in all respects the same, and the beginner with limited means, instead of erecting three houses, need erect only one, which should not be more than fifty feet long and of a width of eleven feet in the clear. The proportions of height, etc., will be found in the drawing on page 77. The sides may be formed of cedar or chestnut posts planked up to the required height, having a lining of tarred paper between the boards. In this way, at present prices, a structure of this kind, with flue, benches and all complete, need not cost more than six or eight dollars per running foot, or $300 or $400 for a house of fifty feet. But something else will be needed besides the house, and sunken pits or cold frames should be erected parallel with the east side of the greenhouse and connected with it. A portion, say half, of these should be excavated to the depth of two feet, and used as a sunken pit for Roses, etc.; the cold frame portion, which is not sunken but made level with the soil, can be used to grow the hardier sorts of flowers, as Pansies, Daisies, Pinks, etc. I here again repeat that the Rose, unless grown to force for winter flowers. is easily injured by fire heat, which it must necessarily receive if placed in the greenhouse, in which are grown a variety of plants that require fire heat.

These pits and cold frames should be covered up carefully, either with shutters or mats, during severe weather in winter, and care taken that all water is thoroughly drained off from them. The sunken pits and cold frames of twenty-five feet each will cost, say, $100, which, together with the purchase of stock and coal to last through the winter, would make the expenditure from June to November, $600 or $700, leaving $300 or $400 for expenses in winter, or until sales open in spring. If the plants have been handled with even average skill, the sales should by June give a profit of at least fifty per cent. on the capital invested, supposing the plants to be sold at the average retail rates.

I am not prepared to say what the profits on the capital invested are when business is done on a large scale, the articles grown, the manner of selling, the economy of management, being so varied that in this, as in all other occupations in life, we have all degrees of success. But the broad fact is beyond question, that the profits of the business will compare favorably with the general run of business in which the same capital is invested.

One fact, very flattering to our florists in this country is, that although our plants on an average are sold lower than they are in England, and our new plants at less than one-fourth of the prices obtained there, the business is more profitable here than there. Why is this? the reader may doubtingly ask. Simply that our necessities with regard to labor compel us to apply our common sense to the work, and we cut loose from many of the established rules with which many of the English florists are yet stupidly trammeled.

In two of the London establishments in 1872, having each about 100,000 feet of glass, the average number of hands employed during the year was fifty. The same quantity of glass would be worked here in a style quite equal to theirs, as far as the quality of the plants goes, with less than one-third of that number. I am informed by a gentleman who was for many years connected with one of these English establishments, that the profits did not exceed ten per cent. of the sales. I am afraid that the smallest operator of us all here, would soon quit the work if it gave no better results.

For the past fifteen years, cut flower growing, particularly the growing of Rose-buds in winter, has been more profitable than the growing of plants, and is so even at the date of writing. While plant growing for market has probably averaged a profit of thirty per cent. on the investment, Rose growing may have averaged forty or fifty per cent., and, in consequence, the structures for Rose growing and other cut flowers for winter are increasing much more rapidly than those for plant growing. This will lead to the natural result, an over-production, and my advice to beginners in all small cities and towns is, to begin a general florist's business, adding cut flowers to it if need be, but do not risk all your capital on any one specialty— at least, not until you have proved beyond question that you can make such specialty profitable.

What is true of the florist's business I believe to be equally true of the nursery trade, and it is much to be doubted if that business anywhere in all Europe is so simply, yet profitably, carried on as it is in the great nurseries of Rochester and Geneva.

CHAPTER IV.

ASPECT AND SOIL.

The aspect of the flower garden, when choice can be made, should be towards the south, or southeast, and if sheltered by hills, or belts of timber, from the northwest, many plants and trees can be safely grown that could not otherwise succeed without that shelter. Such a situation also permits operations to be begun earlier in spring, and continued later in the fall, in some locations making the season from two to three weeks longer than if the aspect had been to the north or northwest.

The soil in flower gardening, as in all horticultural operations, is the basis of success, and is of even more importance than aspect or location; and whether it is the man of wealth, looking for a site upon which to build, and surround his home with a flowery landscape, or the working gardener about to become florist, and venturing his hard earnings in a first essay in business, let him first be certain that old " Mother Earth," in the spot about to be chosen, is in such condition as will reward his labors with success. Soils are so varied that it is difficult indeed to convey to the inexperienced by description what the proper character should be. To say to the uninitiated, that the best soil for all garden purposes is a sandy loam, not less than ten inches deep, conveys very little information, unless he is first made to understand what a sandy loam is. The subsoil, or stratum of earth immediately underlying the top soil, or loam, usually determines the quality of the soil. If it be gravelly, or sandy, then the top soil will almost invariably be a sandy loam ; but if the subsoil is of putty-like clay, then the top soil will usually be of the same nature, and be what is known as clayey loam. One great advantage usually in soils having a gravelly or sandy subsoil is, that the water passes off freely, rendering the expensive operation of draining unnecessary, while in all soils with clayey subsoil, draining must be done, and thoroughly, or failure will certainly be the result. Those most to be avoided are what are known as "thin soils ;" these may be either of sand, gravel, or clay, being in many places little more than " subsoil," without its stratum of loam. No process of manuring or cultivation can ever bring such soils into a condition to compete with those naturally good; for be it remembered that manures answer only a temporary purpose, and exert no permanent change in soil. Our richest market gardens, when left untilled, relapse into their normal state in three years. Thus it is in many parts of the Southern States, that plantations are said to be "worn out" in a few years, while in fact it is simply the supply of food to the plants that has been exhausted, the organic matter formed by decaying leaves or sods having been expended by the crops.

Supply this want by fertilizers, and you again have the land in its primitive fertile condition; but this must be continued, or the crops will again show indications of the soil being "worn out," but quicker, of course, on a thin soil than on a deep one. Hence the importance of selecting, when a choice can be had, a deep soil, with a subsoil of sand or gravel.

CHAPTER V.

THE PREPARATION FOR NEW AND THE RENOVATION OF OLD LAWNS.

It may be questioned whether or not the subjects of Lawns or Landscape Gardening, come under the province of the florist; it may not in his own business directly, but hundreds of florists are appealed to every season by their patrons for information on this matter, so that even the brief directions I am able to give, I know will be welcomed by many.

The preparation for the lawn is usually preliminary to the laying out of the flower-beds in grounds having pretentions to the modern style of gardening. It is the foundation of all subsequent operations, and if imperfectly done, it can hardly ever be remedied afterwards.

We not unfrequently see, after a dwelling costing, 5, 10, 20, or 30,000 dollars is erected, that the grounds surrounding it are left to the tender mercy of some ignorant pretender to grade and put in shape. The educated, intelligent architect's duties, in many cases end with the completion of the building, and the "garden architect" —likely some pretentious laborer—is installed to grade for the lawn, and a common consequence is, that the beauty of the place may be forever marred — for this matter really often requires as much intelligence and good judgment, as the construction of the dwelling itself. One of the first conditions of a perfect lawn is, that the land be drained properly either naturally or artificially; if the subsoil is sand or gravel, so that water can quickly pass through it, then there will be no need for artificial drains, but if there is a stratum of adhesive clay for a subsoil, then drains at every fifteen or twenty feet are indispensable. As the formation of the lawn is the foundation of all subsequent operations, it is imperative that it be carefully done; for if badly done at first, it cannot be changed or altered, unless to the great detriment of trees or shrubs that have been planted, or flower beds or walks that have been laid out.

The first thing to be done is, to get the ground shaped to the desired grade, taking care in grading that when hills and rocks are removed, sufficient subsoil is also removed to be replaced with top soil, so that at least five inches of good soil will overlay the whole in all places, and where trees are to be planted, there should be twice that depth of good soil. When the grading is finished, if the nature of the ground requires it, drains should be laid wherever necessary; then the whole should be thoroughly plowed, a subsoil plow following in the wake of a common plow, until it is completely pulverized. A heavy harrow should then be applied until the surface is thoroughly fined down; all stones, roots, etc., should be removed so that a smooth surface may be obtained. We have used, with great effect and saving of labor, a comparatively new implement known as the "Disc Smoothing Harrow," which fines and levels the land equal to a steel rake; and whenever large areas are in preparation for lawns, or in fact for any field culture, requiring a fine, smooth surface, this implement will be found to be of great value.

When the seed is sown, a light harrow, such as
the "Disc Smoothing Harrow," should be again applied, so as to sink the seed two inches or so in the
soil, and after that a thorough rolling given, so that the
surface is made as smooth and firm as possible.   In the
latitude of New York, the seed may be sown any time
during the months of April and May, and will form a
good lawn by July or August if the preparation has been
good, or in about one hundred days from the time of sowing.   If sown in the hot months of June or July, a
sprinkling of oats should be sown at the same time, so
that the shade given by the oats will protect the young
grass from the sun.   Lawns are very often sown during
the early fall months (September being the best) with excellent results. For small plots, of course, digging, trench-
ing and raking must be done instead of plowing, subsoil-
ing and harrowing, and the surface after sowing should be
patted down with the back of a spade or rolled down with
a roller.   On sloping banks, it is often necessary to use
sod, as the rains wash the soil off before the grass seed
has time to germinate.   It is sometimes even necessary,
in sodding very steep banks, to use wooden pins, eight or
ten inches in length, to pin the sods in place, to prevent
them from being washed down by excessive rains before
the grass roots have had time to fasten in the soil.   In
small yards, sodding is often done so as to get immediate
results ; but in all such cases great care should be taken
to see that the sods used are of the proper quality, otherwise it is much better to wait a few months for the lawn
seed to produce the lawn.

TO GET A LAWN ON A SLOPING BANK.

Unless under very favorable circumstances, it is exceedingly difficult to get a growth of grass from the seed
on a bank sloping at an angle of even fifteen degrees, be-

cause a heavy shower of rain on the sloping bank would
run off the fresh soil before the young grass had formed
enough roots to mat it sufficiently to hold it in place.
To remedy this, the following plan will be found to be
most effective: To an area of twenty by fifteen feet—
300 square feet—or in that proportion, be the area large
or small, take two quarts of lawn grass seed and mix it
with four bushels of rather stiff soil, to which add two
bushels of cow-manure. Mix the whole with water to
the consistency of thin mortar. This mixture is to be
spread on the sloping bank, first having scratched the
surface of the bank with a rake. It should be applied as
thinly as will make a smooth and even surface—in short,
just as plaster is spread on a wall. The grass seed will
rapidly start and quickly make a sod of the richest green,
its smooth, hard surface preventing its being furrowed
out by the rains. It will be necessary, until the grass
has fully covered the surface, to keep the plastered bank
covered with hay or straw to prevent the plaster from
drying or cracking. If the weather is dry a watering will
hasten its growth ; if sown at a season when the temperature will average seventy degrees, a green sward will be
obtained in fifteen days. By this method, using orchard
or other strong growing grasses, no cheaper plan could be
adopted to keep up railroad or other embankments.

As a guide for the proper quantity of seed required to
form a perfect lawn (sown in the usual way, after the
ground has been properly prepared, as already described),
we may state that one quart of lawn grass seed is sufficient to sow an area of twenty feet by fifteen feet—300
square feet—or to cover an acre, four bushels will be required. It should be borne in mind that, in order to produce the best results, grass seed for lawns should be sown
twice as thickly as if sown for hay. In fact, if very rapid
results are wanted, a lawn will be much quicker obtained
by using three times more seed per acre. In a lawn of about

an acre in extent, which we made lately, six bushels of lawn grass seed was sown on the 25th of April, harrowed well in with the ordinary farm harrow, then rolled firmly with a heavy farm roller. The result was that by July 1st, or about sixty days from the date of sowing, a perfect lawn was obtained, having had to be twice mowed over by machine previous to that date.

The question of fertilizers for the lawn is an important one. If the soil is naturally a deep, rich loam it is not necessary that any manure at all be used the first season of sowing, although in every case it would be an advantage, and is really essential if the soil is poor or light. Perhaps the best way to apply well-rotted stable manure is to spread it thick enough to cover the ground after plowing or digging, and then harrow or rake it in, but when cost is of no special object, the best plan to insure permanency for the lawn is to use, as above, from 2,500 to 3,000 pounds of coarse, ground bone per acre, or in that proportion over lesser areas, as the bone decomposes slowly. This quantity, harrowed or raked in deeply, would insure a "velvet lawn," under ordinary circumstances, for six or eight years without further application of manures.

When the land has not been fertilized before sowing, it is necessay to use some top dressing of manure each season to keep up the fertility of the lawn, and nothing is better for this purpose than to spread over it late in the fall (November or December), short stable manure, enough to partially cover the surface. This should be allowed to remain on until such time as the grass shows signs of starting in the spring, when the rough portion of the manure should be raked off and a heavy roller applied, so that the surface of the lawn be rendered smooth and firm for the mower. If the top dressing of stable manure has been omitted in the fall, fine bone dust and nitrate of soda in equal parts, or any good brand of "lawn enricher," mixed with finely sifted coal or wood ashes, in equal parts, may be sowed on the lawn, about as thick as sand is usually strewn on the floor, and rolled down, or where the soil is light or sandy, clay or marl, broken fine and sown on while dry, will be found excellent to encourage the growth of grass.

Mowing should be begun in spring as soon as the grass is two or three inches high, and continued every seven or eight days until the cessation of growth in fall. If the lawn is gone over with a mower once a week, the clippings are best left on, as the sun quickly shrivels them up so that they never appear unsightly; but if mowing is delayed two or three weeks, then the grass must be raked off, which should always be done with the regular lawn rake, as the ordinary toothed rake injures the grass.

It sometimes happens that the soil contains seeds of perennial plants, such as Dandelion, Dock or Thistles, which seriously interfere with the beauty of the lawn. When such occur, there is no other remedy than the slow process of cutting them out with a knife; it is not necessary to take them out by the root. If the "crowns" of these perennial weeds are cut just below the surface, they will not grow again. It is a common belief that the seeds of these weeds are in the grass seed. This is rarely the case; they are generally wafted from adjoining lands and will often lie dormant, if buried deeply in the soil, for years, until the preparation of the soil for the lawn brings them near the surface.

To Renovate Lawns.—Lawns that have become worn out by neglect or other causes, and where it is not convenient or desirable to renew them by plowing up, may be greatly benefited by running a light harrow over, if the surface is large, or by a sharp, steel rake for smaller areas, after stirring the surface by such means judiciously, so as not to too severely hurt the roots. Lawn grass should be sown over the surface after harrowing or raking in about half the quantity advised for new lawns.   After sowing, the surface should be harrowed or raked over, and firmly rolled or beaten down ; but if spurious grass or other weeds have got possession of the lawn, then this way of renovation would not be satisfactory, and it had better be plowed under and sown afresh, in the manner already given for the formation of the lawn.

CHAPTER VI.

LAYING OUT THE FLOWER GARDEN.

In the vicinity of New York, the taste displayed in this matter is certainly not very flattering to us ; compared with that shown in the suburbs of London or Paris, we are wofully behind.   Our city merchants annually build hundreds of houses, the cost of many of which range from $10,000 to $50,000 each, but the flower garden surrounding the house is in nineteen cases out of twenty left to the tender mercies of some ignoramus who styles himself a "Landscaper," and who generally manages before he is through to make the proprietor appear to be utterly devoid of taste, if not utterly ridiculous. A worthy of this stamp held kingly sway as a "Landscaper" in the vicinity of New York a few years ago, and has left behind him some wonderful specimens of his art ; he was great on "Sarpentine" walks, as he called them, and had a true artist's horror of straight lines.   It would have been useless for Euclid to have attempted to demonstrate that the nearest distance between two points was a straight line.   Terry knew better than that, and curved accordingly.   One of the most marked of his efforts was made in behalf of a "shoddy" king, who had built a splendid mansion in about the middle of a four-acre lot. The carriage drive, entering at each side of the plot, was made in his best "Sarpentine" style, but the centre approach, a six-foot walk for pedestrians, started at a point in the centre of the block, and was twisted like a corkscrew until it reached the hall door. The portly owner submitted like a martyr for awhile, but eventually snubbed Terry's science, obliterated the walk, and got a more expeditious, if less artistic method of getting to his home ; his dogs and children, having less reverence for Terry's art, had long before taken the initiative. But this is only telling what not to do, which perhaps is as necessary as to tell what to do in the brief space that this subject can be treated of in this work. The following remarks and drawings are by the late Eugene A. Baumann, Esq., of Rahway, N. J., whose ability as a practical landscape gardener was perhaps second to none in this country, as the thousands of acres of tasteful grounds laid out by him in this and adjacent States, during the past twenty years, will attest.

CHAPTER VII.

DESIGNS FOR ORNAMENTAL GROUNDS AND FLOWER GARDENS.

DESIGN FOR A CITY OR VILLAGE LOT.

Figure 1 gives a plan for a city or village lot of 100x200 feet, fronting south, but without stable or carriage-house.

The dwelling at 1 is supposed to be without area, or entrance to the basement and cellars from outside, but with the water-table, or first floor, raised above the ground some five feet, and the earth from the foundations and cellars employed for a terrace, rising about two and a half feet above the ordinary level, which is understood to be some two feet above that of the public road.

This plan is entirely in the geometric style, or with straight walks exclusively, as we think that, considering everything, this arrangement is the most suitable for small lots.

What, indeed, is the best use to which to put so little room ? Fruit trees, vegetables, and large pieces of lawn are not what are here required ; fruit and vegetables the proprietor may procure at the market cheaper than he could raise them ; lawns, or grass plots, would not be accessible for any amusement or exercise in damp or rainy weather. Therefore I consider well-made walks, that may be dry in the afternoon of a rainy day, much more needed for the promenade of persons, who, having been busy all day, require some exercise and fresh air in the evening. Fine shrubbery, flower-beds, and shade are also required.

In a planting of the right sort, it requires not much depth to form good belts to protect the place against the cold winds, or sometimes against cool neighbors.

A large display of flowers does not require a very large space of ground, and if plenty of flowers should be wanted, as is generally the case, their quantity may be increased by a judicious selection of flowering shrubbery.

For a more sheltered, shady walk, I should, in such a place, suggest a well-built arbor, covered on the top with out-door grape-vines, and on the side towards the house with fine flowering climbers, or those that have good and durable foliage, such as Climbing Roses and Honeysuckles, the Clematis, Akebia, Viginia Creeper, Bittersweet (or *Celastrus scandens*), Chinese Wistaria, etc., as permanent plants, which may be trained so as to cover the whole front ; and then, for variety, of a dwarfer habit and covering the lower parts, the Madeira Vine, Canary-bird Plant, and *Adlumia*, or Allegheny Vine. Some of the new *Cucurbitaceæ*, the broad-leaved Periwinkle, Ivies, and a number of other sorts may be recommended.

I intend, in progressing with the explanation of the

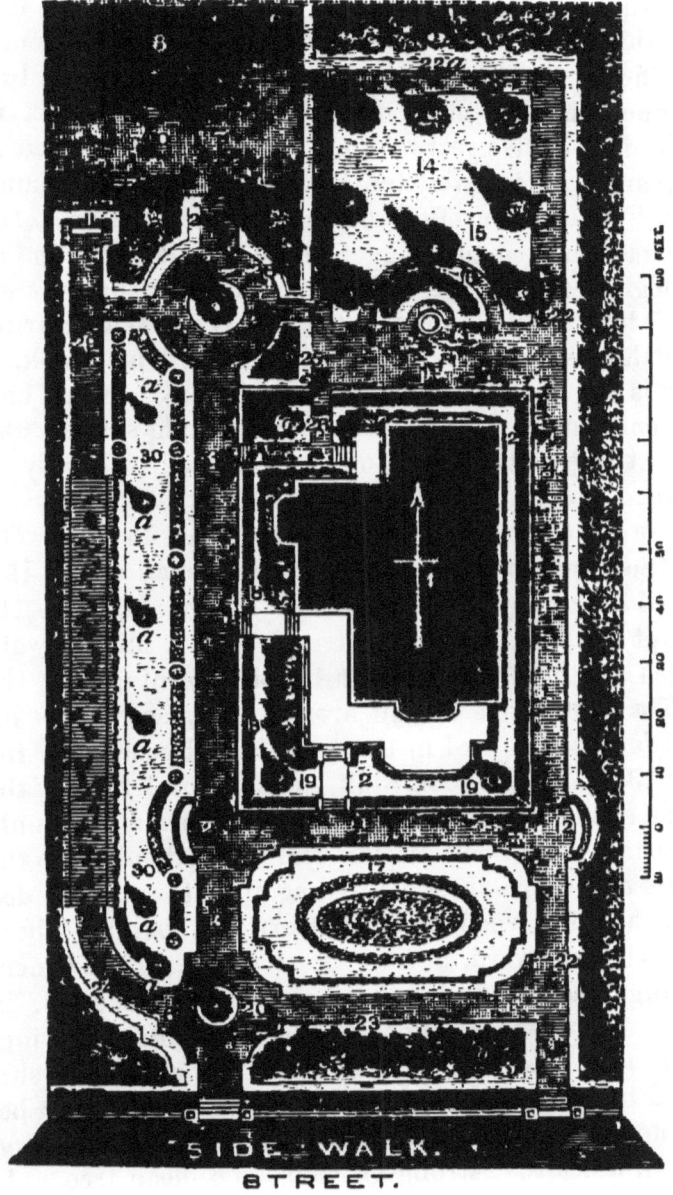

Fig. 1.—DESIGN FOR A VILLAGE LOT.

numbered objects of this plan, to give a list of such trees and shrubs as are required on a small place. It is a point which ought always to be considered, that trees and shrubs fit for a large place are not exactly suited to a small one, whatever may be their appearance or effect in the first four or five years ; the mistakes are only seen in after years. Fortunately for the generality of the "landscapers," before the effect of their work is shown, the owner has removed to a bigger house, or the planting has been neglected, and the trees have died, or the " landscaper" has found employment far away out West, caring very little how his *chefs d'œuvre* in the East may look.

At 2 is the terrace, with the embankment. Small embankments ought to be of the most simple shape ; any fancy outlines in the slope, on a small scale, will only be seen when the grass is freshly cut short, and they are therefore of no use. 3 is the main approach to the dwelling. (See scale for width.) At 20, in a small circle, it is intended to employ a fine bush of *Pyrus Japonica*, to interrupt the view from the street. 4 is a smaller walk intended for the use of the family, but forming with the walk 3 a continuous circuit around the place. 5 is intended for a small yard in the rear of the house, with the well at 13. 6, a six-foot walk, passing underneath the arbor ; a shady place in summer. 7, the arbor, with only spare room enough left in its rear for attending to the climbers and grape-vines planted against it. 8, intended to be a shed for wood and other articles, besides a hen house, with hen-yard, at 10. 9, an office. 11, a bench, or resting place. 12, benches, or even stone seats, in recesses. 14, a grass plot, to be used for a drying ground, and also as a play-ground for children, surrounded by seven deciduous shade trees, which might be, in preference, the Silver-leaved Maple (*Acer dasycarpum*), a healthy, strong-growing, and clean tree. At 15, for variety of foliage, a Weeping Willow. 16, a hedge-row of Siberian Arbor-vitæ. 17 is a flower bed, with an outside border made of the small-leaved, trailing Juniper, or *Juniperus procumbens.* This magnificent plant, which, in small beds, forms the densest glaucous-green carpet, may be easily trained for a border by planting small young plants at eight and ten inches apart, and then guiding the main leader with small wooden pins in the direction of the border. It offers something entirely new in color and shape, and it is to be regretted that it is so little in use.

A second border, immediately around the flower-bed, affording a greater contrast in color, would be the small Tom Thumb Arbor-vitæ—a very precious novelty, too, on account of its very dark foliage.

At 18, on the northwest side of the house, there would be a very favorable location for a group of Rhododendrons and other so-called North American evergreen shrubs.

At 19 may be placed two single bushes of *Calycanthus floridus,* or Sweet-scented Shrub, or, still better, two large vases or pieces of statuary.

At 21, a circle, to be decorated with a Purple Beech, or a good specimen of the Kilmarnock Willow.

At 22, all along the eastern boundary, a row of Norway Spruces, Balsam Firs, and American Arbor-vitæ, in the rear, planted at sufficient. distance from each other to permit a second row in front of them (alternating), about four or five feet from the side of the walk.

In this front line ought to be employed Siberian Arbor-vitæ, Irish and Swedish Junipers, Golden Arbor-vitæ, Upright Yews, *Retinispora ericoides* and *Podocarpus.*

At 22 *a,* in the rear of the play-ground, there ought to be the following shrubs, in three rows : for instance, in the rear, the Venetian Sumac, *Cercis Siliquastrum,* and *Cercis Canadensis,* Double White and Red Flowering Thorns, American Mountain Ash, etc., etc., but no larger trees.

In the second row there might be planted (alternately) the Purple Hazel (or Filbert), the Silver-Bell (*Halesia tetraptera*), some Philadelphus, Euonymus, and Rose of Sharon.

In the third row, still smaller sorts, closing down to the edging, such as the Purple Barberry, *Hypericum Kalmianum, Daphne Mezereum,* Cotoneasters, *Prunus Sinensis,* and *Prunus triloba.* Herbaceous plants, like Peonies, Iris, Phloxes, etc., etc., may be added, too, to great advantage.

At 23, the group near the front fence must be stocked with such shrubs as will prevent outsiders from disturbing the privacy of the place, but low enough to allow the inmates to see the street from the piazza, or first floor.

The following plants may best answer, viz. : *Spiræa Reevesii fl. pleno, Spiræa prunifolia,* and *Spiræa callosa, Deutzia crenata fl. pleno, Cratægus Pyracantha* (near each gate), and in front of these, towards the house, *Hypericum Kalmianum, Deutzia gracilis, Spiræa Fortunii,* and some herbaceous plants. 24, a corner group, ought to be filled in the rear with one or two *Cladrastis tinctoria,* better known in nurseries as *Virgilia lutea,* and in front of these there should be some five or six *Æsculus macrostachya,* a shrub of a remarkably fine effect.

At 25 and 26, the two small groups could be employed for Hydrangeas. 27 and 28 require, to hide the henyard, some taller shrubs of the following sort : the Californian Privet, some Lilacs, and the Golden Elder (*Sambucus nigra aurea.*)

The small border, 29, may be employed for some espaliers of Pears, Apricots, or Medlars.

30 is intended for flower beds, arranged in the most simple way, and which ought to be filled in the fall with Dutch bulbs for the spring season, and in summer with fine selected bedding plants, of very distinct colors, but each separate color in one strip ; or with annuals, like *Portulaca, Phlox Drummondii, Nemophilas,* etc., etc.

At *a*, in Div. 30, there may be some Magnolias, a *Cercis Japonica*, and one *Berberis macrophylla* or Japonica.

By mentioning exactly all the sorts of trees and shrubs that I might employ, I do not intend to say that the laying out may be a failure by employing other sorts, as corresponding varieties in size and foliage will answer just as well, but it will be noticed that I have mentioned no trees of large size, except along the eastern boundary and the play-ground. Indeed, of what use would it be to employ Sugar Maples, Elms, Norway Maples, and Sycamores, which, after a few years, would cover up half the width of the place, and leave no room for good shrubbery and flowers ; allow no sun in the place, and even

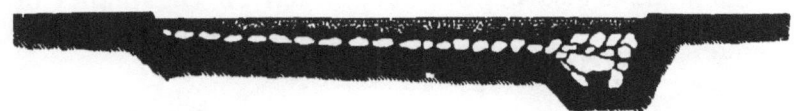

. Fig. 2.—SECTION OF ROAD WITH SINGLE DRAIN.

prevent the turf from growing under their shade ? It would be as sensible as to place in a small drawing-room a table, of which the four corners would touch the four walls.

In the selection of the right kind of plants is the whole secret of the art.

The walks in such a regular garden must be as well graded as possible, and on the same level as the turf, which ought not to overreach them more than one inch or one inch and one-half. Very narrow walks, unless the grass is frequently clipped, often look like ditches.

To establish such walks, if there is any drainage required, the digging out of the soil before stoning ought to be as clearly defined and done as well as the dressing of the top.

The best way to dig them out is, in general, for single drains, according to the diagram, figure 2, and where

double drains are required, I generally recommend the
following system, shown in figure 3.

It will be seen by the first diagram that the bottom of
the ditch represented in the cut is an inclined plane, running downwards from one side of the walk toward the
opposite side of the drain, which I figure here simply as a
stone drain.   The stoning is to be laid upright, and
never flat, on the hardened bottom of the ditch or dug-
out trench; if laid flat, the stones will never bind together, but if upright, they will soon become tight by the
intrusion of the gravel that has to be put on top of them.

The depth of the trench depends very much on the
quality of the subsoil, and has to be regulated by it, and
so with the ditch for the drains.

Such walks also depend very much on the quality of

Fig. 3.—SECTION OF ROAD WITH DOUBLE DRAINS.

the soil, and very often, indeed generally, on the facility
of procuring the materials.

In some places I have seen walks and roads made by
simply scratching off three or four inches of light top soil,
beneath which was gravel several feet deep.   Such a road
may be dry, but is very noisy, tiresome, and movable.

In other instances I have seen walks made by opening
ditches over four feet deep, only for the sake of burying
rocks and saving the soil found in digging; these form
very fine drains, and help to clear the land of boulders
and rocks, as is the case on top of Orange Mountain, N. J.

The second diagram (figure 3) shows the section of a
walk or drive requiring more drainage.   The bottom,
between the two drain ditches, forms a curving line, on
which, if well placed, the stones will soon form an arch,
and give the road all the qualities required.

The depth here is not as much regulated by the quality of the soil as by the width of the drive or roads. The more convexity given the bottom, the better for the absorption of the water by the drain, which ought to be at least twelve inches deeper than the extremity of the curve, whilst the top of the curve must remain at least six inches below the top of the road or drive.

Frequent raking, to remove the larger gravel or pebbles, and more frequent rolling during damp weather, are necessary for new walks.

If good clay is at hand, a thin coat of it may be put between the coarse and the fine gravel on top.

Gutters made of flagstone, or simply paved, will be needed only where there is a great descent and a large accumulation of water above, or sometimes even where the ground is very light and sandy, although the surface may slope but very little.

In uneven grounds, drives and walks are to be made in the same manner, but their finish and beauty will never depend upon themselves, nor upon the way in which they are laid down. An additional, correct grading of the grounds, right and left, so as to bring the sod everywhere at equal height over the gravel, and then a careful grading of the grounds three, four to six feet off the margin, where the soil rises or falls, is indispensable in such cases to make a finished drive.

The staking out of such uneven walks, and the regular distribution of the grading, to avoid unsightly ups and downs, is a matter of taste and practice, ruled by the shape of the land and the direction of the walks.

DESIGN FOR A FLOWER GARDEN.

We give in figure 4 a design for a regular flower garden, intended for the ornamenting of the foot of a terrace, built in front of a large villa.

The terrace is intended to be of a heavy stone work, about three feet above the ground, with a projection in

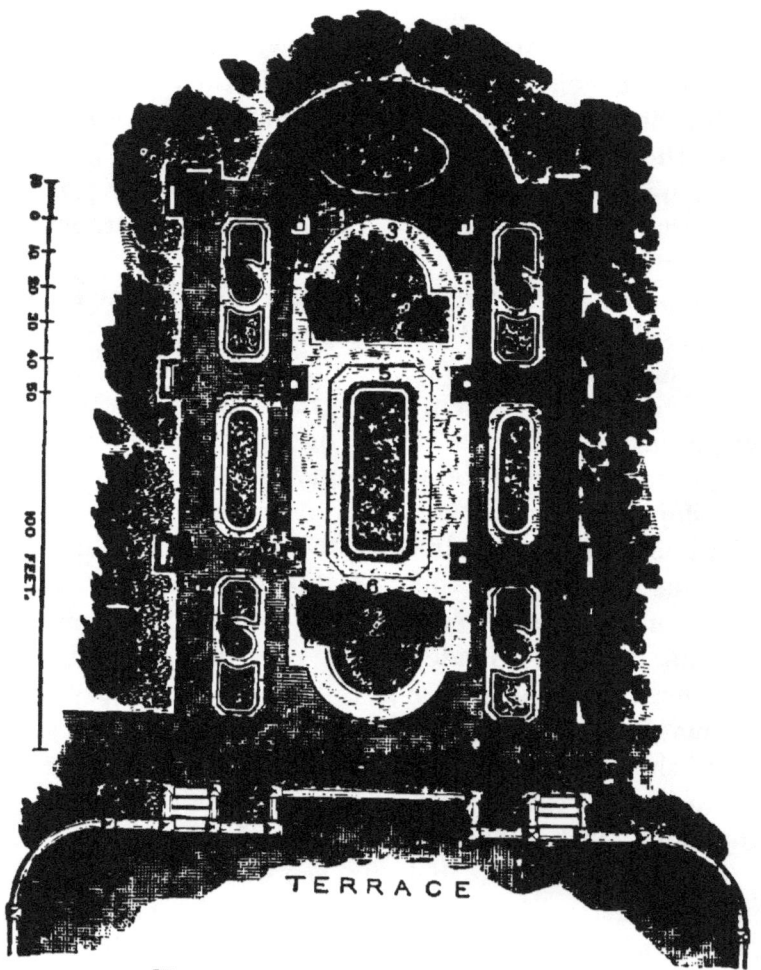

Fig. 4.—DESIGN FOR A FLOWER GARDEN.

the middle and two steps on each side, leading to the main walks of the flower garden.

Such an arrangement, often seen in English villas, or in English designs, belongs only to large pleasure grounds, and may be considered as the real "dress ground."

This design has been expressly made with the view of keeping in order cheaply.

The lawn, or what is to be kept in sod, is as much as possible in regular straight lines, easily mowed with some of the patent lawn mowers.

The walks are wide, as, starting from the bottom of the terrace, they will be overlooked the whole length from the top, and would appear scanty if not of liberal dimensions.

The place is intended to be kept as private as possible—a sort of open-air saloon—by a belt of selected shrubbery, and shade trees in its rear.

At 1, there are seats indicated in several recesses cut into the shrubs, the seats to be of heavy timber, as stone would be rather too cool, and iron or rustic work not looking architectural enough.

At 2, there are pedestals for pieces of statuary, or vases or large specimen plants in painted boxes.

At 3, 4 and 6, groups of Roses, bedding-out plants of broad, showy foliage, or flowering shrubs, such as Hydrangeas, which continue long in bloom.

At 5, the center piece, there is a large flower bed for Scarlet Geraniums, Feverfew, etc., surrounded by a border of Irish Ivy, kept in line, so as not to exceed twelve to eighteen inches in width.

Such borders of Ivy, if employed in the right place, and well kept in order, are a magnificent ornament to a garden, and, according to their location, may be kept three and four feet wide. A very little covering in winter will keep the foliage, of the right sort, in very good order.

In the large squares, plainly sodded, that are in the gardens of the Louvre and the Tuileries, at Paris, there is no other ornament but such borders of broad-leaved Ivy, established at three to four feet from the walks, and left running about two to three feet wide; and they make, with the dark green against the lighter turf, a most agreeable contrast.

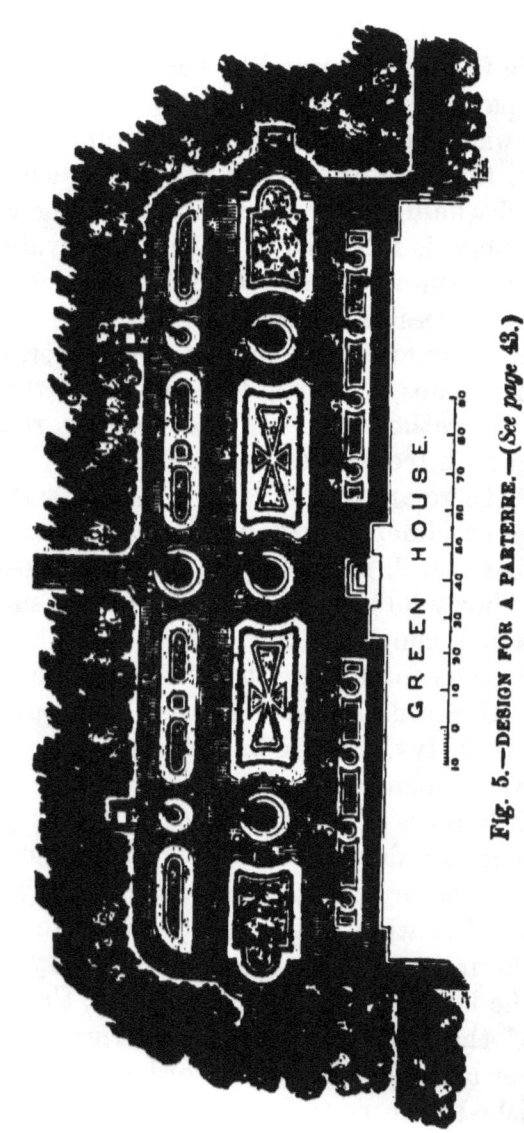

GREEN HOUSE.

Fig. 5.—DESIGN FOR A PARTERRE.—(See page 43.)

At 7, on the floor of the terrace, and protected by the

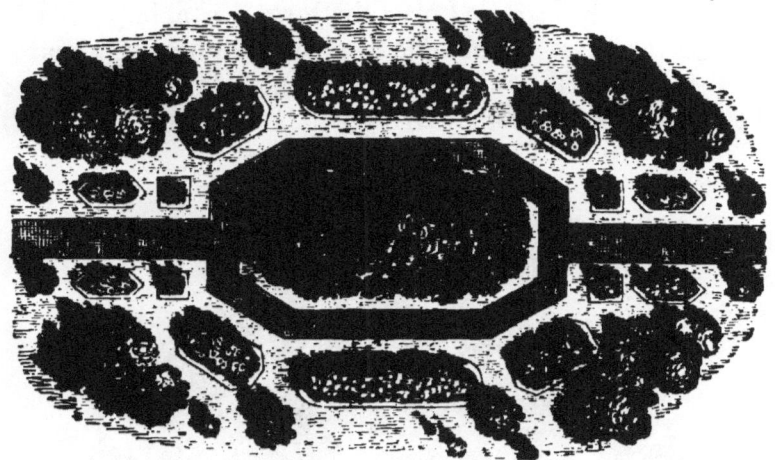

Fig. 6.—DESIGN FOR A FLOWER BED IN A WALK.—(*See page* 45.)

shade of the balustrade, there will be a very good location for hardy Rhododendrons, and similar shrubs.

DESIGN FOR A PARTERRE.

The design (figure 5) represents a parterre to be

Fig. 7.—DESIGN FOR A FLOWER BED IN A WALK.—(*See page* 46.)

established in front of a large greenhouse, or conservatory, and bringing together, in one single spot, all the flower beds generally scattered over the lawn, on a large place. For privacy, it is surrounded by a belt of flowering shrubs.

Two principal flower beds, at 1 and 2, are intended to be surrounded by a small evergreen border, kept for itself,

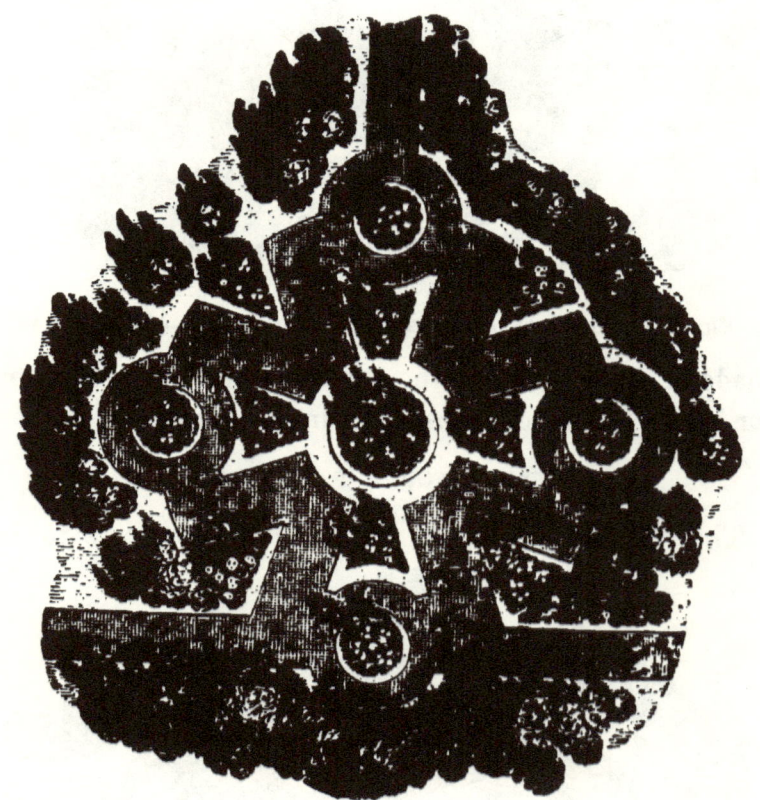

Fig. 8.—FLOWER BEDS AT THE JUNCTION OF WALKS.—(*See page* 46.)

and not to be considered as an edging ; small edging-box might answer best.

At 3, there are recesses for statuary, behind which the foliage ought to be of the darkest kind, to contrast with the white statuary, and make that conspicuous.

At 4, similar recesses for seats of heavy timber.

At 5, in front of the greenhouse, alternating with the flower beds, are simple, upright growing evergreens, symmetrically planted, such as Irish and Swedish Junipers, *Taxus erecta, Podocarpus Japonica, Retinispora,* etc.

At 6, single specimens of shrubs of medium size,

Fig. 9.—FLOWER BEDS AT THE TERMINUS OF A WALK.

remarkable for their flowers, fragrance, or fine foliage; for example, *Deutzia crenata flore pleno, Pyrus Japonica, Cratægus Pyracantha,* or the *Prunus triloba.*

FLOWER BEDS IN WALKS, OR AT JUNCTONS OF WALKS.

Figure 6 (p. 43), and the three following illustrations, are designs for introducing ornamental planting where

opportunity offers along the course of a walk. In figure 6, the walk divides and passes each side of a bed of
choice shrubbery, while the opposite sides of the walk are
planted with some of the select shrubs already named, or
others. By the judicious use of flowering shrubs, and
the low-growing evergreens, very fine effects may be produced. In figure 7, is a similar but more elaborate plan,
which allows of the introduction of flowers in masses ;
such an arrangement would be very appropriate for a
Rose garden. In figure 8, we have a design for ornamenting the point at which two walks unite at right angles.
The planting may be of Ivy, Trailing Juniper, and other
low-growing evergreens, upon a ground-work of well-
kept grass, or flowers may be introduced. In figure 9,
we have a bit of ornamental flower garden at the terminus
of a walk. What has been said of the selection of shrubs,
etc., in describing the larger designs, will be a sufficient
guide in carrying out these smaller plans.

CHAPTER VIII.

PLANTING OF FLOWER BEDS.

Much difference prevails in the modes of planting
flower beds, some holding to the promiscuous intersper-
sion of the different plants, others to the ribbon or carpet
style of planting, now so general in Europe. If the promiscuous system is adopted, care should be taken to dispose
the plants in the beds so that the tallest plants will be at
the back of the bed, if the border is against a wall or
background of shrubbery, the others gradating to the
front, according to height. In open beds, on the lawn,
the tallest should be at the centre, the others grading

down to the front, on all sides, interspersing the colors so as to form the most agreeable contrast in shades. But, for grand effect, nothing, in our estimation, can ever be produced in promiscuous planting to equal that obtained by planting in masses or in ribbon lines. In the grounds of the Crystal Palace, near London, and at the Jardin des Plantes, in Paris, wonderful specimens of this mode of planting are to be seen. The lawns are cut so as to resemble rich green velvet ; on these the flower beds are laid out in every style that art can conceive ; some are planted in masses of blue, scarlet, yellow, crimson, white, etc., separate beds of each, harmoniously blended on the carpeting of green. Then, again, the ribbon style is used in the large beds, in forms so various that allusion can here be made to only a few of the most conspicuous. In a circular bed, say of twenty feet in diameter, the first line towards the grass is blue Lobelia, attaining a height of six inches ; next comes the famous Mrs. Pollock Geranium, occupying a space one foot and one-half wide and nine inches high, with its gorgeous leaves and flowers ; then, against that, is a line of Mountain of Snow Geranium, with its silvery white foliage and scarlet flowers, backed by the maroon-colored *Coleus Verschaffeltii* ; the center being a mound of scarlet Salvia. Another style is a fringe for the front, of the fern-like, white-leaved *Centaurea gymnocarpa* ; back of that is the Crystal Palace Scarlet Geranium ; then *Phalaris arundinacea picta*, a recent style of Ribbon Grass ; next, *Coleus Verschaffeltii*, and, in the center, a clump of Cannas, or Pampas Grass.

During a visit to Europe in 1872, I went to the celebrated Battersea Park, the most interesting, in a horticultural view, of the many parks in the neighborhood of London. A feature peculiar to Battersea Park is the subtropical and alpine planting, both of which, as here done, were to us a novel feature in landscape gardening. It was interesting to see how common and rough looking plants were made to produce such wonderful effects when grouped and contrasted in the subtropical arrangement. The plants were mainly Cannas, Japanese Maize (striped), Wigandias, Bocconias, Solanums and many of the tall-growing sorts of Amaranths. These were grouped on beds of every conceivable form, some clearly defined in

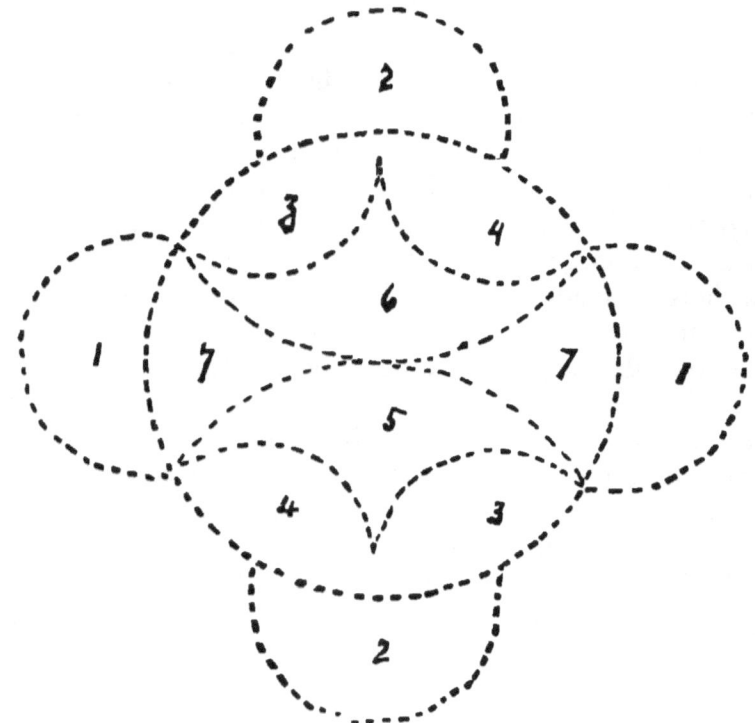

Fig. 10.—A CARPET BED.

1. Echeveria Secunda.
2. Sempervivum Californicum.
3. Echeveria Rosea.
4. Echeveria Extensa.
5. Yellow Alternanthera.
6. Yellow Alternanthera.
7. Crimson Alternanthera.

the broad lawn, some skirting the edge of a clump of trees. others planted in and among the trees and shrubbery as undergrowth, giving the impression, when looking at it under the roofy shade of trees, that you were viewing an undergrowth of the tropics rather than a piece

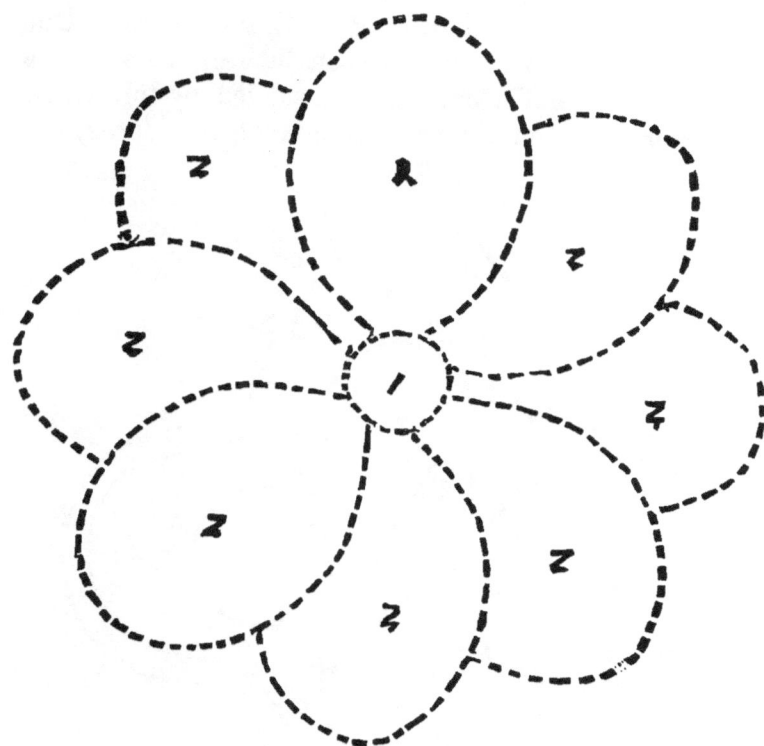

Fig. 11.—DESIGN FOR BED.

1. Scarlet Salvia.   2. Coleus Verschaffeltii.

All lines in the figure to be edged with Yellow Coleus, or reversed if so desired.

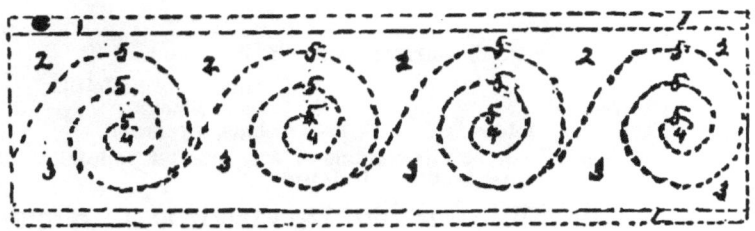

Fig. 12.—DESIGN FOR BED.

1. Alternanthera, Crimson.   3. Lobelia, Blue.
2. Alternanthera, Yellow.   4. Coleus, Golden.
5. Achyranthes, Crimson.

The Coleus and Achyranthes to be pinched low.

of the most artistical planting of an English park.   One
particular spot, which will not soon be forgotten, was a
ravine of considerable extent, well shaded by tall trees,
where were planted immense plants of tree ferns, the

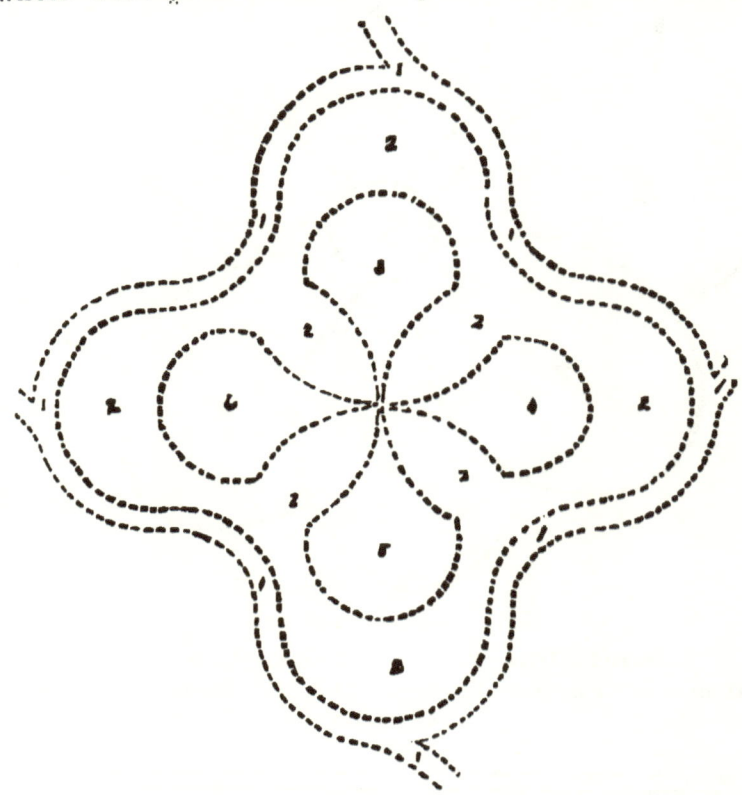

Fig. 13.—DESIGN FOR A BED.

1. Walk.   4. Coleus, Verschaffeltii.
2. Grass.   5. Coleus, Black.
3. Coleus, Golden.   6. Coleus, Firebrand.
Or 3, 4, 5 and 6 can be alternations of crimson and yellow
Alternantheras if desired.

stems covered with Lycopodium, so exactly as to resemble what would be their condition in nature.   Behind
these and against the blue sky stood out strongly some
gigantic Palms, so that we had here again a glimpse of
what an Australian or Indian forest might be.   In

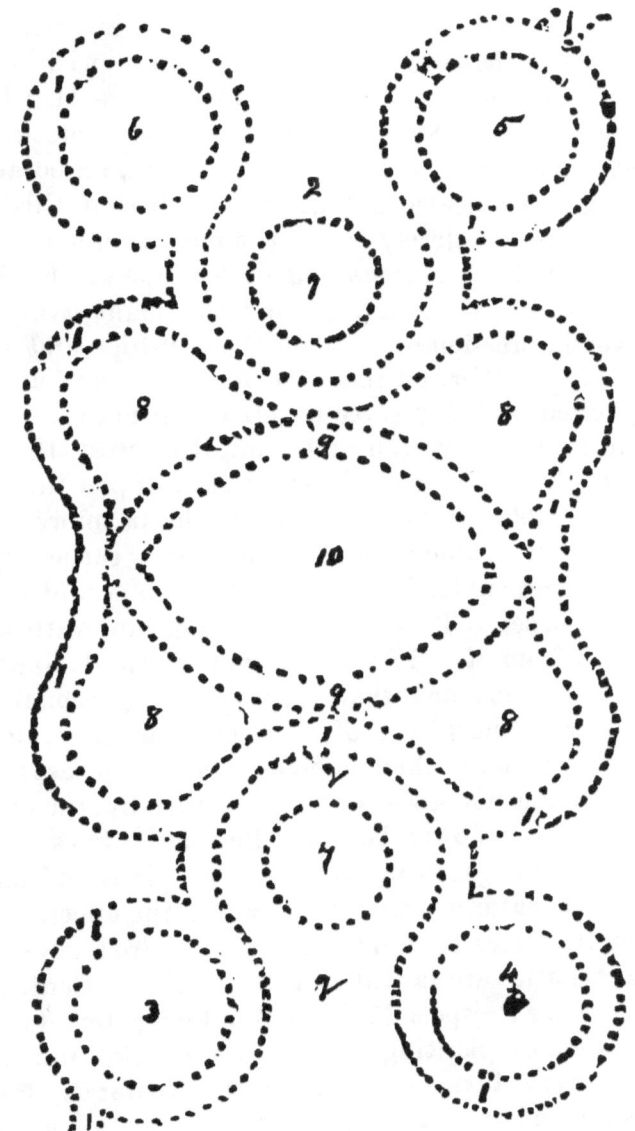

Fig. 14.—DESIGN FOR BED.

1. Gravel Walk.
2. Grass.
3. Double Alyssum Tom Thumb.
4. Double Alyssum Tom Thumb.
5. Double Alyssum Tom Thumb.
6. Double Alyssum Tom Thumb.
7. Geranium, Silver Leaf.
8. Geranium, Happy Thought.
9. Centauria Gymnocarpa.
10. Scarlet Geranium.

direct contrast to these was a hill, a miniature Alp, planted from base to nearly the summit with alpine plants of the rarest kinds, among which were largely interspersed Sedums, Sempervivums, and other succulents, in rarity and variety sufficient to give joy to a botanist's heart. On the peaks and in the crevices of this little hill, was planted closely one of the most common native plants of Britain, *Antennaria dioica*, one of the Everlastings, having white foliage, and this plant easily conveyed the impression of snow on the hill-tops and in its gullies. Altogether, on this little mound of half an acre, were planted probably three hundred distinct species.

Then from this mound of botanical interest, the first turn brought us to a very different style of planting—the massing or ribbon style, or what would be more appropriately (as it is done here) called the "carpet style," for it often resembles just such patterns as would make a beautiful carpet. This style is meeting now with much opposition from Mr. Robinson, editor of the "Garden," and many others; but whatever may be objectionable to those whose conceptions of gardening are beyond this rectangular system, there is no denying the pleasure that it gives to the masses—as was apparent by the crowds admiring those flower beds at Battersea Park, many persons being engaged in sketching the plans and taking notes of the varieties used to produce the effect. This Park of Battersea contains only two hundred acres. Its natural beauties are far inferior to either our Central, of New York, or Prospect Park, of Brooklyn; but its judicious system of planting, which gives novelty and freshness at every turn, conveys to the visitor a lasting impression of pleasure that the plain, monotonous shrubbery and lawn of our New York parks can never give. The public parks in Britain or Ireland are the best schools of taste in floriculture the people have to model from; and so it should be with us, but with the few extremely limited attempts that have been made at the Central Park, New York, the past few years, there has been no ornamental planting of a public character in the vicinity of New York. Some fine examples of this

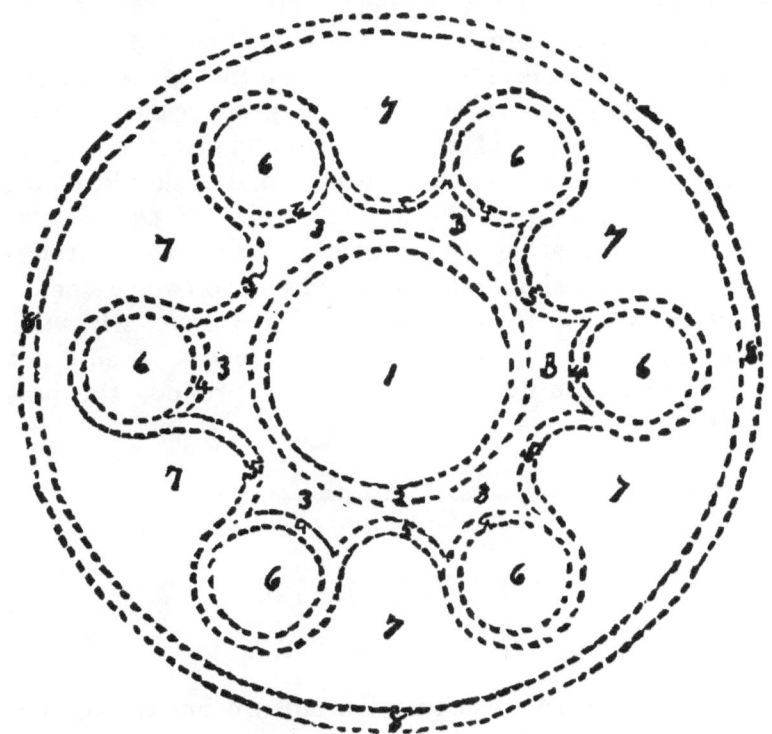

Fig. 15.—DESIGN FOR BED.

1. Coleus Verschaffeltii.
2. Stevia Variegata.
3. Coleus, Firebrand.
4. Stevia Variegata.
5. Achyranthes, Maroon.
6. Coleus, Black.
7. Coleus, Golden Bedder.
8. Achyranthes, Crimson.

All kept pinched even.

kind of gardening may be seen in the public parks in Washington, D. C.; Chicago, Ill.; Allegheny City and Philadelphia, Pa.; Boston, Mass., and even Albany, N. Y., where the effects of massing may be studied to advantage. But even as we write (1886), neither in Central Park, in New York City, or in Prospect Park,

Brooklyn, has there been anything done at all to compare with that done in the far less imposing parks in the cities already named.

The designs on the preceding pages for massing in colors, from the " Book of Plans," recently issued by Geo. A. Solly & Son, of Springfield, Mass., will be found useful. Of course, there is nothing arbitrary in the use of the different plants here recommended to produce effects; that is entirely a matter of taste and judgment in the operator. The distance apart in which plants should be set for effect varies with the kind and size of the plants. Coleus, Achyranthes, Geraniums and the other strong-growing kinds should be set from ten to twelve inches apart each way, while Lobelias, Echeverias, Alyssum, Alternantheras, and all low-growing plants, should not be set wider than five or six inches to produce the best effects.

CHAPTER IX.

SOILS FOR POTTING.

I rarely pick up a work on floriculture but the matter of soils is treated of in such a way as to be perfectly bewildering to amateurs, if not also to professional florists. One authority gives a table of not less than nineteen sorts! Whether these authorities practice as they preach is very questionable ; some of them I know do not, but why they should thus write and mystify those they attempt to teach, can only be ascribed to a desire to impress their readers with the profundity of their knowledge on such subjects. Now, what is the effect of such instructions ? Our amateur cultivators are disheartened, as such combinations of soils are to them perfectly impracticable. The private gardener, perhaps, falls back on his employer, and ascribes the unhealthy condition of his plants to the effect of his not being able to procure such and such soil, which, he says, is necessary to some class of plants, and excuses his failures thereby. The young florist, beginning business in some country town, with restricted means, and with limited knowledge of what he is undertaking, looks upon this august authority in despair, and his heart sinks within him when he knows that no silver sand is within a thousand miles of him, and he is told, without qualification, that it is necessary for his propagating bench, or as an ingredient in his potting soils. He begins without it, and as he will possibly make some failures, these failures are laid at the door of the soil or sand that he has been obliged to use, while the chances are, twenty to one, that they were not. Not the least satisfaction I have in writing this book is, that of being able to attempt the simplification of many of our operations to such an extent as to put the means of doing the work within the reach of every one. Not the least simple of these operations is the preparation of our potting soil. We have, we may say, only one heap—a big one at that— but it contains only two ingredients, rotted sods, from a loamy pasture, and rotted refuse hops from the breweries, or, in lieu, rotted cow or horse manure, in about the proportion of two of the sods to one of the hops or manure. The sods are cut during the spring or summer, and laid, with grassy sides together, so as to decompose, and the heap is repeatedly turned until it becomes friable. The rotted refuse hops (one year old), or rotted manure, is then added, either at once or when the soil is wanted for potting. For small pots—from two to four inches—we run it through a sieve of one-half inch meshes, which thoroughly incorporates the parts ; for larger pots, it is not necessary to run it through a sieve, unless, perhaps, for the sake of thoroughly mixing, it may be quicker to

run it through a screen or sieve with a one or one and a
half inch mesh. If the loam is rather clayey, we use
more hops or manure ; if rather sandy, less than the proportion named.   From this mould-heap the soil is taken
from which all our plants are grown and flowered ; we
make no exceptions, unless in the case of the few fine-
rooting plants, such as Heaths, Ferns, Gloxinias, Caladiums, Azaleas, Epacris, etc.   In potting these, we use
about two-thirds of the decayed refuse hops to one of
loam ; if the hops are not attainable, leaf mould from the
woods will do, in lieu of the hops, for this purpose. Our
general mould-heap supplies the soil, alike for Bouvardias, Begonias, Carnations, Camellias, Chrysanthemums,
Daphnes, Dracenas, Dahlias, Fuchsias, Gazanias, Garde-
nias, Geraniums, Hyacinths, Liliums, Lantanas, Petunias,
Pansies, Roses, Tuberoses, Violets, Verbenas, etc., etc.
Whether plants show vigorous growth under this universal application of soil to their varied natures, our thousands of patrons, who will be readers of this book, can
attest. If any of the disciples of the old school doubt this,
let them come and have ocular evidence of the fact.
Our location is within half an hour's walk (or fifteen minutes' ride) of the city of New York ; our gates and doors
are always open ; visitors are free to go and examine as
they choose.   They will see our mould heap looming up
like a miniature mountain : they will see hundreds of
thousands of plants, natives of every clime, deriving their
luxuriant growth from this one source.   While ignoring
the necessity of special varieties of soil for special families
of plants, I do not mean to say that plants may not be
grown as well by the use of such compounds as by ours ;
but I claim that, as a whole, they can be grown no better,
and that the advice to use these combinations is bewildering to the amateur, or inexperienced gardener, troublesome in its practice, and of no benefit whatever in its
results.   In proof of this, I have, on many occasions, re-

ceived all kinds of plants from a dozen different growers in different parts of the country, hardly two of whom use the same soil, but all grow them well. So in the vicinity of New York, where the soil is varied at the different points, as much as soil can be ; yet we see growers using very different compounds with equally good results, showing, as has long ago been satisfactory to me, that special soils have less to do with the healthy growth of plants than the proper application of temperature and moisture. In cities having paved streets, we find the sweepings to be a most valuable ingredient, which may be used to advantage in lieu of refuse hops, manure or leaf-mould.

CHAPTER X.

TEMPERATURE AND MOISTURE.

Many young gardeners and amateurs flounder befogged, attributing failure of crops in the garden, or want of health of plants in the greenhouse, to bad seeds, uncongenial soil or fertilizers, when it is much oftener the case that the cause is of a totally different nature, and entirely within their control. A temperature at which seeds are sown and plants grown must be congenial to the nature of the kind, else success cannot follow. In a temperature at which a Portulaca will vigorously germinate, a Pansy seed would lie dormant, or, at least, show a sickly existence, and *vice versa.* Nearly half of the Corn and Lima Beans sown annually, perish by being sown from two to three weeks too early, by the impatience of our embryo horticulturists. On the other hand, the cold-blooded Carrot or Turnip seed all but refuse to germinate in the sultry days of July. Seeds of Calceolarias, Cinerarias and Chinese Primroses will germinate more freely if sown in greenhouse or frame during the cool months of March, April or May, in our climate, than if delayed until June or July, the time it is usually done in the colder climate of England. It has been our own practice for years to sow in these months ; but if by chance it has been omitted, we prefer to delay sowing till September, rather than to sow in midsummer. Many failures are attributable to want of knowledge of this fact, and they are, without question, laid to the charge of the seedsman.

The same necessity of accommodating the temperature to the nature of a matured plant, exists even to a greater extent, than it does with the seed ; and one of the main causes of want of success in cultivating plants under glass is, want of knowledge of the proper temperature, or from carelessness in keeping a temperature unsuited to the growth of the plants. In ordinary greenhouse collections, the fault is oftener in the temperature being kept too high than too low, for it is much easier, requiring far less watchfulness by the person in charge, to keep up a high temperature. The injury done by this is gradual, and will not, like the action of frost on the plants, show in the morning. In consequence of this, we often see the greenhouse containing Camellias, Azaleas, Pelargoniums, Carnations, etc., etc., sweltering in midwinter under a continued night temperature of sixty-five degrees, when their nature demands fifteen degrees lower.

We too often see collections of hot-house and greenhouse plants intermingled, and attempts made to grow them together, which must result in failure to one or the other. The temperature to grow, in healthy condition, Coleus, Bouvardia, or Poinsettia (hot-house plants), would not be likely to maintain Verbenas, Carnations, or Geraniums, long in a healthy state. The same rules follow as to the propagating house, showing the necessity, even in a greater degree, of observing the requirements of their different natures. Coleus, Bouvardia, Begonia, and Lantana, root in a bottom heat of seventy-five degrees, with atmospheric temperature of sixty-five degrees, in ten days; at twenty degrees lower they will not root at all, but will perish. Although cuttings and plants of a more hardy nature will root in some conditions of growth at this temperature, yet we prefer, to insure plants of vigorous health, that Verbenas, Carnations, Geraniums, Roses, etc., be rooted in a temperature at least ten degrees lower, both in bottom heat and temperature of the house.

The subject is one that relates to so many varieties and different conditions of organization at the different seasons of growth, that it is impossible to convey to the inexperienced what these varieties and conditions are; but my object is to impress upon young or inexperienced readers what I have long believed to be an important truth—that the supplying the proper conditions of temperature to plants under glass, according to their different natures and conditions, has as much, or more, to do with their welfare, than any other cause; and that often when ascribing the unhealthy state of a plant to uncongenial soil or defective drainage, or the " damping off " of some favorite cutting, to the way it was cut, or the sand in which it was put, the true and sole cause of the failure was nothing more than condemning the plant or the cutting to an atmosphere uncongenial to its nature.

Thus far, we mainly allude to temperature. Serious injury is often done to plants from a want of, or excess of, moisture. The old gardener with whom my first essay in gardening was made, used to define the difference in dryness in plants as " dry " and " killing dry " " dry " was the proper condition that the plant should be in, when water was applied, the surface indicating dryness by becoming lighter, but no flagging or wilting; but woe betide the unfortunate that allowed a plant in charge to become in the condition of " killing dry;" this, in his eye, was an unpardonable offence. "Killing dry" was, to some extent, really killing, in such a collection as we grew, which consisted largely of Cape Heaths, Epacris, Azaleas, and other hard-wooded plants, which are easily killed outright by allowing their tender, thread-like rootlets to become dry; unlike soft-wooded plants, such as Geraniums, Fuchsias, or Roses, they have less recuperative powers, so that a "dry" that would kill a Heath or Azalea would have only the effect to stagnate the growth of a Geranium, and bring the tell-tale yellow leaves that are certain to follow whenever such plants have suffered for a lack or excess of moisture. Although the effect of drying is, for the time being perhaps, less marked in a hard-wooded plant than in a soft-wooded one, yet the ultimate effect is much more fatal. To the unpractised eye, a Heath or Azalea that has been injured by drouth may appear all right, while it has gone beyond recovery. The old gardener before alluded to used to make his dead Heaths do excellent service in assisting him in some severe jokes played on his less experienced brethren. Specimen plants of Heaths were scarce, and, in some sorts, very valuable, and if he succeeded in making a present of one of these dead plants to one of his less-knowing friends, it used to keep him in good humor for a week.

No plant should ever be allowed to flag or wilt for want of moisture, neither should it be watered until the necessity for water is shown by the whitening of the surface of the soil, particularly if in dull weather, or if the greenhouse is kept at a low temperature. As a rule, with greenhouse plants kept in a night temperature of forty-five degrees, with a day temperature of sixty degrees, watering twice a week from December to March will generally be sufficient; on the approach of clear weather, with higher temperature in April and May, they will require daily attention.

Our practice is to water during winter with the common

rose watering pots, giving the plants water sparingly, or otherwise, as required. But as spring opens, we go at the operation more expeditiously, using a one and a half inch hose, through which the water is forced by a force pump, or through pressure from the city water works. To the end of the hose is attached a heavy sprinkler. In all districts where there is no hydrant-water, the force pump makes a good substitute, though, of course, entailing double work. Most of our large florists, in the vicinity of New York, who are out of the range of city water works, use windmills to raise the water from wells to elevated tanks, so as to get the necessary pressure, and thus do away with the necessity of the force pump. When practicable, we prefer to water or syringe plants early in the forenoon (say from 9 to 11 A. M.), although it is by no means imperative to do so.

Two rules are laid down by nearly all writers that I have read on floriculture, in reference to the water to be used for plants ; one, that it must be rain, or, at least, "soft" water ; the other, that the water should be of the same temperature as the atmosphere in which the plants are growing.

To both these dogmas, I beg to respectfully enter my protest. Such dogmas are handed down from one to another, without one in a hundred of those who hold them, having either the opportunity or inclination to test their truth by experiment. My greenhouses, at Jersey City, for a dozen years, were entirely watered from a deep well of hard water, winter and summer, which might average in temperature forty degrees ; most of my greenhouses, now on Jersey City Heights, were watered from cisterns inside the greenhouses, from rain-water caught by the roof, for some ten years, and for the past dozen years we have used the city water, yet we have never been able to see that our plants have been in any way different under these three different conditions of watering.

If any one will take the trouble to reason for a minute, he will understand why there is no necessity for this equality of temperature between the water and the soil. If we plunge a thermometer into the soil of a plant in the hot-house, it may indicate, say, eighty degrees ; if we pour a pint of water at forty degrees into the soil, the tempera-ture will not be forty degrees, but about the mean between forty and eighty degrees, say sixty degrees. Now, if the soil remained for any length of time at sixty degrees, it might be, to some extent, injurious ; but it does not. In ten minutes it will become of the same temperature as before it was watered, or nearly so, by the absorption of heat from the atmosphere of the house. It is the duration of extremes of temperature that does the mischief ; place a plant of Coleus in a temperature of thirty-three degrees for forty-eight hours, and it will be almost certain to die, while it would remain as many minutes without injury. Let a dash of sun raise the temperature of your hot-bed to one hundred degrees, or over, for ten minutes, and it will not seriously injure the contents, but an hour of this temperature might destroy all the plants.

We pour ice-water into our stomachs at a temperature of less than forty degrees, with impunity, because but a few minutes suffices to bring it to the temperature it meets with there ; did we swallow a sufficient quantity to keep the stomach at the temperature of ice-water for any length of time, fatal results may follow.

Although I am emphatic against the necessity of water being of the temperature of the house, where the application of water is generally used, yet I admit that if preference can be given without trouble, give it to the warmer water. I also agree that in cases such as forcing of Lily of the Valley, or for tropical cuttings or seeds just germinating, that water should be used of the tem-perature of the house.

A point indispensable in our hot and arid climate is, that all plants in the greenhouse should stand on close benches, overlaid with sand or ashes, or some such material. This keeps moist and prevents the plants from suffering, if any omission occur in watering. We know that the practice in many places is entirely different from this, the plants being stood on benches of open slat-work. No plant can be kept healthy in such a place, unless with at least double the labor of watering necessary with those standing on sand. This, like many other of our mistakes, is copied from the mode pursued in England, where a colder, moister, and less sunny climate may make it a necessary practice.

For this reason, also, we prefer to use benches, or tables, instead of the stair-like greenhouse stage, which is now almost discarded. However, an exception to this rule is necessary in growing Roses or other plants in large pots or tubs for winter flowering, where complete drainage is necessary. They should, in all such cases, stand on slatted benches ; if placed on sand or ashes, it would stop the free passage of water from the holes in the bottoms of the pots or tubs. If placed on such benches, the pots or tubs should be raised an inch or so on pieces of wood to admit of free drainage.

CHAPTER XI.

THE POTTING OF PLANTS.

The first operation of potting is, when the rooted cutting is transferred from the cutting-bed to the pot. Almost without exception, plants of every variety, at this stage, should be placed in a two-inch pot ; occasionally some of the coarser-growing Geraniums may require the three-inch size, from the fact that the roots are too large for the two-inch pots; but there are few exceptions of this kind. The great mass of plants, when in the condition of rooted cuttings, do much better in the smaller size, for the reason that the smaller mass of soil in the two-inch pot allows the moisture to pass off quicker, and thereby prevents the soil from becoming sour, or sodden, which would be the case, more or less, if the cuttings had been overpotted in a three or four-inch pot. The operation of potting cuttings is very simple, and, in florists' establishments, is performed with great rapidity, average workmen doing three hundred plants per hour, though expert working florists should do five hundred per hour. We have quite a number of men who can do this with ease. The pot is filled to the level with soil, a space made with the finger, in the center of the soil, of sufficient size to admit the root, which is placed in the opening thus made; the soil is closed in again by pressing with the thumbs close to the neck of the cutting, which firms the soil around the root; a smart rap is struck the side of pot with the hand, which levels the surface of the soil, and the operation is done. After the plants are placed in pots, they are shaded from two to six days by covering them with paper while the sun is shining on them, care being taken to keep the paper moist by sprinkling. For nearly all the commoner kinds of bedding plants, such as Roses, Verbenas, Heliotropes, etc., cuttings in these two-inch pots, if stood on tables, which are covered with an inch of sand, and occasionally moved, to keep the roots from pushing too far through into the sand, will keep in a healthy condition from one to two months, at the cool season of the year, from January to May; but when the pots get filled with roots, the plants should be shifted into larger sized pots, to keep them in good health. When plants are required to be grown as specimens, or of larger size, for sale in spring, they must be repotted at intervals as the condition of their growth demands; for example, to grow a Fuchsia to a height of six feet, and three feet in diameter, a pot of at least twelve inches across the top and twelve inches in depth would be necessary ; but it would not do to jump from the two-inch cutting pot to this size at once ; three or four different shifts are necessary to attain this end ; these shifts should be made, as a general thing, not greater than from a two-inch size to a three-inch, and so on. I know that, a few years ago, considerable agitation was made in favor of what was termed the " one shift system," and fine specimens were exhibited by its advocates, to show its advantages. There is no question that, in the hands of a careful and experienced man, it can be done, but it must necessitate much closer watching in watering, involving much more labor than the trouble of the safer plan of repeated shiftings. The time to shift a plant from a smaller to a larger pot is shown by the roots beginning to mat around the outer surface of the ball. It is not necessary to shift when the first roots touch the side of the pot; let them curl pretty well around the ball, but they must not be allowed to remain long enough to become hard or woody. They must be of that condition known to gardeners as " working roots," a condition not very easy to describe, unless to say that the appearance of such roots is white, soft and succulent. We think that the mode of shifting a plant from a smaller to a larger pot would soon suggest itself to the operator, even though he had never seen it done ; but it is a little ludicrous to see the various absurd methods sometimes resorted to by our amateur friends to attain this very simple end. One proceeds with a knife and inserts it all around the sides of the pot, and thus scoops it out ; another favorite way is to break the pot with a hammer. I have known many of our lady amateurs to practice these methods, who, no doubt, know well how to turn a pudding or a jelly out of a form, but who did not think that the ball of earth enveloping the roots of a plant could be turned out of a flower-pot in the same way. In most cases the slightest tap on the edge of the pot is sufficient to turn out the ball of earth. Soil, in depth according to the size of the plant, should be placed in the bottom of the pot, the ball placed in the center, and the soil packed moderately firm in the space between that and the sides of the pot, either by the fingers or by a piece of wood, made of suitable size for the purpose. When plants are first potted off, or shifted, they should be stood with the pots touching each other, if the diameter of the plant is less than that of the pot; but, as they begin to develop growth, the plants should be spread apart, according to their size or development of foliage, to allow the air free circulation about the outside of the pots. The effect of this is most marked in the greenhouse, and teaches us a lesson as to the great necessity of the admission of air to the roots in all our operations, whether under glass, or in the open field. If we pot off a lot of Fuchsias, Geraniums, or other large-leaved plants, with the pots touching each other, and place them in a temperature of sixty degrees, in eight or ten days they will have grown so as to cover over the whole space, so that the pots can hardly be seen. Examine those in the center of the lot, and it will be found that the roots that have reached to the side of the pot are few and feeble; but move a portion of the pots so that a space of an inch or two is made between them, to give the air a free circulation around the pots, and in six days after it will be found that strong and healthy roots will have been emitted by those that have been given the additional space, while the others, left standing close, have made little or no progress in root formation, and but a slender and weakly upward growth. The roots in the open field, could we see them in their unbroken state, as we can in turning out a plant from a pot, would show the same differences in vitality under corresponding circumstances.

It has often been a matter of surprise to many amateurs, and even professional gardeners, how it is that such extraordinary vigor and health are obtained in the plants grown by many New York florists, in pots that seem to be entirely inadequate in size for the support of such vigor. This is done by a practice not generally known outside of this vicinity. When a plant shows by the condition of its roots that it requires a supply of fresh soil for its support, instead of shifting it into a larger pot, it is taken out and the soil washed clean from the roots, and either placed back again in the same pot, in fresh soil, or in one of only a single size larger.

This washing the soil from the roots, instead of shaking it off, has the advantage of leaving all the fibres or working roots intact, while by shaking the soil from the ball, the most valuable parts of the root are injured. Plants thus grown are particularly valuable for distant shipment, as a strong-rooted and vigorous plant is obtained without the necessity of shipping a heavy weight of soil.

For many years we have sent to our patrons in the trade thousands of plants annually, every particle of soil being first washed from the roots ; the plants, in all cases, arriving in as fine order as if they had been sent with the ball of soil around them, and saving at least nine-tenths of the freight.

This practice, however, is not good, unless the season is early enough for the plants to have time to become established in the pots, and it is not prudent to do so later than March. If the weather is hot, more care is necessary in shading the plants until they have begun to take root in the new soil.

CHAPTER XII.

DRAINAGE IN POTS.

Many years ago, in some of my first writings on the subject of drainage in pots, I admit to having taken rather too radical ground against the practice, because, in those days, almost everybody used to " crock " or drain the very smallest pots. The absurdity of this soon became apparent to me, as I found that, with hardly an exception, for plants in pots up to the size of four inches, it was worse than useless to drain ; and as all my practice, up to that time, had been with pots but little larger than four inches, I rather rashly jumped to the conclusion that, in our warm, dry atmosphere, the European practice of crocking all sizes of flower pots might be wholly dispensed with here ; but added experience showed that even in our dry atmosphere, flower-pots of five inches in diameter and upward, in which are grown Roses or other plants with roots sensitive to moisture, had better be crocked or drained, particularly if to be grown in winter. It is not pleasant to admit an error, particularly when promulgated in print for the "instruction" of others ; but it is better to make what amend is possible, by making the acknowledgment, than to continue to stick to opinions before given, when there is reason to believe these were formed in error.

DRAINING IN FLOWER POTS.—If the pots are over five inches in diameter, charcoal broken into pieces from one-half to one inch in diameter, I prefer to every other kind of drainage ; this should be in depth from one inch to four inches, according to the size of the pot to be drained, an extra quantity being necessary if the plant is being shifted into a pot too large ; then ample drainage is indispensable to admit of the quick escape of water. This drainage, so called, is not alone of use as a means for the rapid escape of water, but also for the admission of air to the roots, which brings in another important matter in connection with the drainage in pots, the necessity of standing them on some rough material (when solid benches are used in the greenhouse, or when placed in the open air in beds), such as gravel or cinders; for if placed on sand, soil, or anything that will close up the orifice in the bottom of the pot, all the drainage placed in it will avail nothing. It is far better to use no drainage at all, and stand the pots on a rough surface, than to use the drainage and place the pots on some material that will close the outlet. If, however, the bench is formed of slate, or boards that have been cemented over, so as to form a smooth surface, there is no necessity for placing any gravel or other rough material under the pots, as such a surface will allow the water to pass from the pots more freely than if anything, such as gravel, were placed under them. For very large pots slatted benches are best.

CHAPTER XIII.

EXPERT GARDEN WORKMEN.

In my long experience with workmen, I have observed that, other things being equal, the man who could move his hands quickest, was almost certain to be the man most successful in life. Rapid movement of the hands in such light operations as writing or typesetting, argue quick mental decision, and if such a mind is well-balanced, its possessor is more likely to distinguish himself than he who moves more sluggishly. Now, two-thirds of all garden operations—particularly those of flower gardening—are as light as either writing or typesetting, and for many years I have taken great pains to stimulate my workmen to rapidity of movement in all our light work, and it is astonishing what the gain in labor has been in this particular. The average work of a man planting Cabbage or Lettuce plants, when we began market gardening, did not exceed 2,000 a day; now, and for many years past, a man, with a boy to drop the plants, will set 6,000 a day, and one of my old foremen, John Scarry, has repeatedly planted 10,000 in a day. In the lighter work of our greenhouses rapid movement is even of more importance, and the rivalry among our workmen for distinction in this matter is of great benefit to themselves as well as to us.

Four years ago the acknowledged "Champion" in all our force of seventy hands, was a young Irishman named James Marvey, who died in 1883 at the age of thirty-two. He had been in my employment for nearly twenty years and had ever distinguished himself for rapid and neat workmanship, for, some years before his death, he had repeatedly potted 10,000 cuttings, in two and a half inch pots, in ten consecutive hours, and had attained on one occasion the extraordinary number of 11,500 in ten consecutive hours. I paid him for years $5.00 per day, and always considered him one of our cheapest workmen, because, not only did he earn all he got, but his example fostered a spirit of emulation among our other employees, valuable alike to themselves and to us.

CHAPTER XIV.

COLD FRAMES.—WINTER PROTECTION.

Many of the plants used for the decoration of the flower borders in summer, may be kept through the winter in what are termed cold frames, or sunken pits.   These are formed by excavating the earth about two feet deep and of a width to suit the usual six-foot sash, and of such length as may be required.   The sides of the pit are boarded up, on the front or south side, to a height of eight or ten inches, and at the back or north side, some six inches higher, to give the necessary slope to carry off the water from the sashes and to better catch the sun's rays.   Thus formed, the frame will measure about three feet deep from the sash in front and about three feet and one-half at the back.   Or, if the work is desired to be permanent, the sides may be built of brick instead of boards.

Above all other considerations, the place where the pit is built must be free from standing water, and if not naturally dry, must be so drained as to carry off the water. A good plan is to cement the bottom of these pits, which tends greatly to keep the bottom dry.   We adopt this plan in all our sunken pits, having the bottom so formed that all water is carried off from the front or lower side. Whenever practicable, the situation should be warm and well sheltered, as such a position will save a great deal in winter covering.   In such a pit, tender Roses can be kept in the best possible condition, better, in our opinion, than in any greenhouse.   If kept in pots (which is the best way to keep them), the pots should be plunged to the rim in sawdust, leaves, tan-bark, or some such light material. Besides Roses, the plants embraced in the following list may be wintered over with safety in this latitude, pro-

vided that care is taken to admit light and air, whenever
the weather will permit. The pits must be thoroughly
covered up at night with mats and shutters ; this, if well
done, will keep the plants from freezing injuriously in
any district where the thermometer does not fall more
than ten degrees below zero.

Azaleas,	Pentstemons,
Antirrhinums,	Verbenas,
Carnations (Monthly),	Stock Gilliflowers,
Camellias,	Wallflowers,
Fuchsias,	Roses of all kinds,
Geraniums,	Pinks, (Florists').

Plants to be kept over in frames should be potted at
least a month previous to the setting in of cold weather ;
all had better be well established in pots before the
middle of November, and until that time the plants
should be fully exposed to the light and air, by the entire
removal of the sashes, unless on unusually harsh and cold
days.   From the middle of November to the middle of
March but little watering will be required. In cases of
severe snow storms, the pit may remain covered up, if
the weather is cold, for two weeks at a time, without
exposing the plants to the light, and Roses, Camellias, or
Azaleas, in a dormant state, may remain even a month ,
but, as before said, whenever practicable, admit light and
air.   For outdoor protection of Roses, see chapter devoted
to them.

Many plants may be saved in a dry, cool cellar.   The
plants that can be best kept during winter in the cellar
are : Carnations, Fuchsias, Geraniums, Roses, Lemon
Verbenas and Dahlia roots.   If the plants are to be lifted
from the ground, cut away all strong growing shoots ; in
the case of Geraniums or Fuchsias, cut them well in, and
plant them in shallow (six-inch deep) boxes of soil,
keeping them exposed to the open air as late as the
weather will permit.   This can be best done by taking

them into some shelter at night and exposing them to light and air during the day; this will harden them to endure their winter quarters in the cellar. Once placed in the cellar, if cool and moist, as cellars usually are, no water should be given until they are again moved out to the light in May. Remember that thus immersed in the dark cellar in their dormant state, water or moisture will injure them beyond recovery, unless they have become unusually dry.

Shallow cold frames are used for keeping Pansies, Carnations, Daisies, Forget-me-nots, Primroses, Auriculas, etc., over winter. They are formed by using a ten or twelve inch board for the back and a seven or nine inch board for the front of the frame, which should be of a width that can be covered by a six-foot sash. All of the plants above named, will keep safely over winter without other covering than the sash, but if wanted for early flowers, it will pay well to cover at night with shutters, or, better, with straw mats. There has been recently introduced a thin, light fabric, which has been named "protecting cloth," which, after April 25th, answers all the purposes of sashes in this latitude. When all danger of severe freezing is past, and at a time when greenhouses get crowded with bedding plants, such as Geraniums, Verbenas, Roses, or other plants that can be grown at a low temperature, the covering with this cloth will answer quite as well as sashes—in fact, in inexperienced hands, better, for there is no danger of the frames being too much heated when so covered, as is the case with sashes, if ventilation has been neglected. "Sashes" formed of the protecting cloth can be made for twenty-five or thirty cents each, as the cloth can be bought for nine or ten cents per yard, and all that is necessary is to tack it on to a light frame and you have a cover as useful during the months of May and June as a glass sash would be, costing ten times as much. We have also found this covering of the protecting cloth sash to be an excellent covering for Pansy and other seeds sown in the fall, as it keeps the ground moist, preventing it from drying up by the sun and air, and giving just the amount necessary for the germination of seeds ; but it should not be used to cover anything in this latitude from the first of December to the middle of April, as it would not answer in severe weather.

CHAPTER XV.

THE CONSTRUCTION OF HOT-BEDS.

The most economical way of making hot-beds is to place the manure in pits made in the way described for cold frames, except that they may be made a foot or so deeper, so as to admit at least eighteen inches of manure. The heating material for hot-beds is usually horse manure, but refuse hops, leaves from the woods, or tan-bark, will answer nearly as well when one is more readily attainable than another.

Whatever material is employed, it should be thrown into a heap of sufficient size to generate heat, and be repeatedly turned until the rank heat has been expelled, which will usually be done by turning twice. The mass will be in the proper condition to be put into the pit in eight or ten days from the time of starting with the raw material. In spreading it in the pit, it should be firmly trodden down to the depth of eighteen inches, so that the heat may be longer retained. If the hot-bed is to be used to receive plants in pots, a covering of four to six inches of sawdust, in which to place or plunge the pots, should be put over the heating material. If the bed is to be used for the sowing of annual or other seeds, a covering of six inches of light soil should be put over the manure. Before placing plants, or sowing seeds in the hot-beds, plunge a thermometer in the bed, and when the heat begins to decline from 100 degrees, then operations may be begun with safety. But for whatever purpose a hot-bed is used, in all such latitudes as New York, the beds should never be made before the first week in March ; great risk is run if they are made much sooner, with but little advantage in earliness. Greater caution is necessary in airing than with the cold frame, for with the hot-bed the heat from the manure, together with that of the sun's rays, will often, in an hour, run the temperature so high as to destroy its entire contents, if airing at the proper time has been neglected. Many a merchant, doing business in the city, has gone home in the evening to his country residence to find that his hot-bed, that had been his pride in the morning, had become a scorched brown mass at night for want of attention to the safety-valve of "airing." In such cases, when no competent person is in charge, the safest way is to tilt the sashes a few inches, even before the necessity arises, rather than run the risk of the sun coming out strong, and destroying the whole. In a southern exposure, in a sheltered place, there is rarely danger in admitting air in most days in March or April from nine to four o'clock. But, of course, judgment must be used in extreme cases. The greater heat in the hot-beds necessitates watering freely whenever the surface of the soil appears dry, which, in dry weather, if the heat is strong, will usually be every other day. In the absence of sashes, the " protecting cloth " alluded to in the chapter on cold frames, can be used to cover the hot-bed. Its use is safer than that of glass sashes, for the bed does not heat up as if covered by sashes—in fact, there is no necessity of ventilating at all, if covered by the "cloth sashes," although in mild days they should be taken off altogether to admit the light to the plants, but protecting cloth should not be used on the hot-beds sooner than the middle of March.

CHAPTER XVI.

GREENHOUSE STRUCTURES.

I have a peculiar pleasure in beginning to describe our present modes of constructing greenhouses, well knowing that hundreds of my readers will turn with interest to this page, in the hope that they may be enlightened on a subject on which doubtless many of them have seriously blundered. I have no reason to complain of success in business, but I feel well assured that, for the first ten years of my time, many thousands of dollars were sacrificed in the blunders made in my endeavors to get on the right track.

There was no fixed system ; all was confusion, hardly two of us building alike, and, in my humble opinion, most of us building wrong.

The style of greenhouse to be built must be governed by the purpose for which it is wanted. If for the growing of a general assortment of greenhouse or bedding-plants, many years' experience in working of those on the ridge and furrow system, on the extensive scale in use by us, makes us confident in the belief that this system is all we have previously claimed for it, as being the most economical of space, most economical of heat, and most economical in cost of construction.

For greenhouses to be constructed of movable sashes, figure 16 represents the end section and ground plan of the style of house referred to, which may be used for the purpose of growing Roses, greenhouse or bedding-plants, or anything requiring protection in winter. The greenhouses represented in this plan are 100 feet in length, and each eleven feet wide inside. The heating of the whole (that is, the three measuring from the outside walls thirty-six by one hundred feet) is done by one of Hitch-

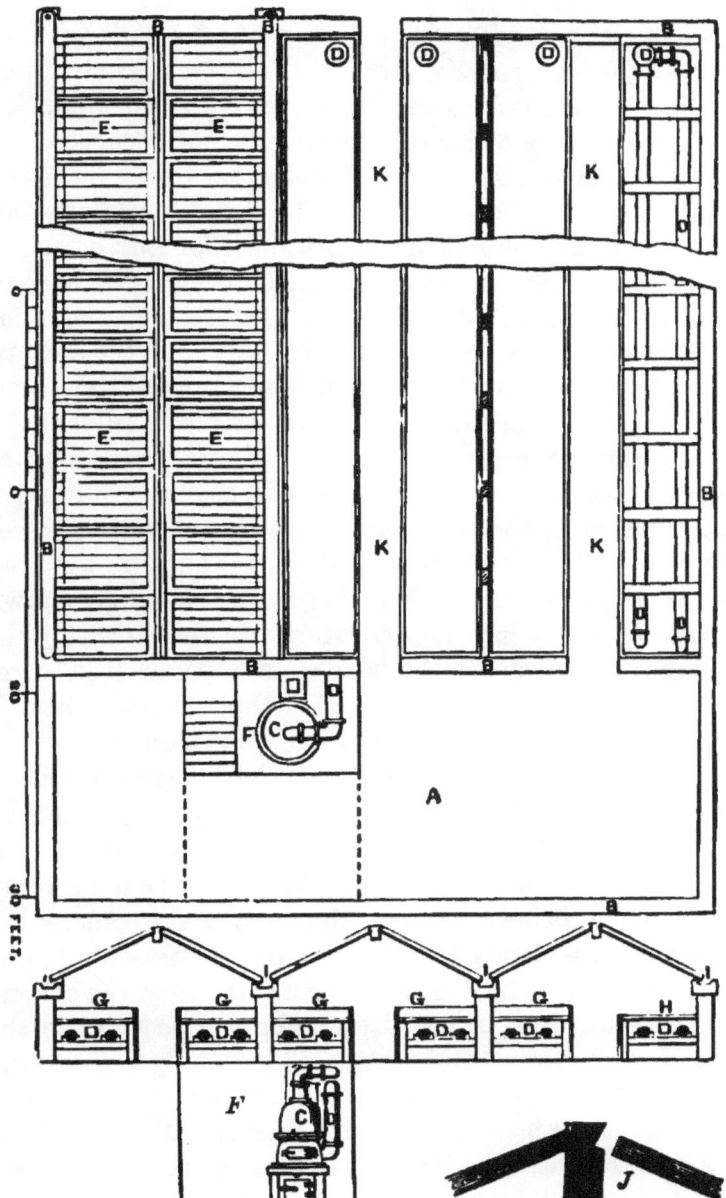

Fig. 16.—GREENHOUSE HEATED BY HOT WATER PIPES.

ing's Combination Boilers (C), heating about 1,200 feet of four-inch pipe (D). The glass roof (E) is formed of portable sashes, each six feet by three feet; each alternate sash is screwed down, the others being movable, so that a full supply of air can be given when necessary.

The movable sash is elevated by an iron bar fifteen inches long, attached to the sash by a staple; in this bar three holes are punched, at distances of three inches apart; by means of these holes the bar can be hooked upon an iron pin placed in the ridge-pole, and thus hold the sash more or less open, to graduate the admission of air. When the sash is shut down, the bar is hooked on to a pin that secures it in place, so that the sash cannot be moved by wind. I am particular to describe this method of airing, as it is, as far as our experience has gone, the best method we have ever seen used. The ridge-poles are cut out exactly as is shown at J, and the sash lays on the shoulder, braced by the angle shown in the cut. The interior arrangements are shown by the end section. G shows the bench, or table, as it is completed. The space beneath the bench, if bottom heat is required for propagating or other purposes, should be boarded up below the bottom of the pipes, the lower board being hinged, so that, on cold nights, additional heat can be given to the atmosphere of the house, if required. But for the general uses of growing plants, the benches must be left open below, so that the heat given out by the pipes will pass freely to all parts of the house. If one house is wanted of a higher temperature than the others, it will be necesary to board up along the posts from the ground to the top of the posts, and by wholly or partially shutting the valves in the pipes of the other houses, throw a greater heat into the one in which the high temperature is wanted. The walks through the house (K) are two feet wide, which leaves four feet and one-half on each side for bench room. These widths we find to be most convenient for the working of the plants ; if narrower, too much space would be lost ; if wider, the further side of the benches could not be reached easily.

The width of the walk, however, must be determined by what the greenhouses are designed for ; if for workmen merely, two feet, or even less room, will do for the walk ; but if visitors are to be accommodated, it should be at least two feet and one-half in width.

A brick shed (*A*) covers the boiler pit (*F*), and is attached to the north end of the houses, the back wall being about twelve feet high, the front eight feet, width sixteen feet ; besides breaking off the north wind from the greenhouses, we find this shed indispensable as a potting and packing room. It will be understood that these greenhouses have their ends north and south ; consequently one side is exposed to the east in the morning, the other to the west in the afternoon, while at noonday the rays of the sun strike directly upon the apex of the roof. There is nothing arbitrary in having the greenhouses end north and south ; a point to the east or west would not make any material difference, but, if circumstances will admit, we prefer them to end direct north and south.

At present prices, built in a plain, substantial manner, with the outer walls of brick or stone, and heated with hot water, they will cost about $8 per running foot, or $2,400 for the three connected—that is, the range of three greenhouses 100 feet long by thirty-three feet wide, together with the shed to cover the boiler-pit ; if put up singly, the cost would be at least ten per cent. more. If walls are formed of wood, which we now prefer, the whole cost might be lessened ten or fifteen per cent.

Another plan in use is shown in figure 17, combining the flue and boiler, from the same furnace. This is the most economical plan in which hot water can be used. As shown in the engraving, there are two houses joined

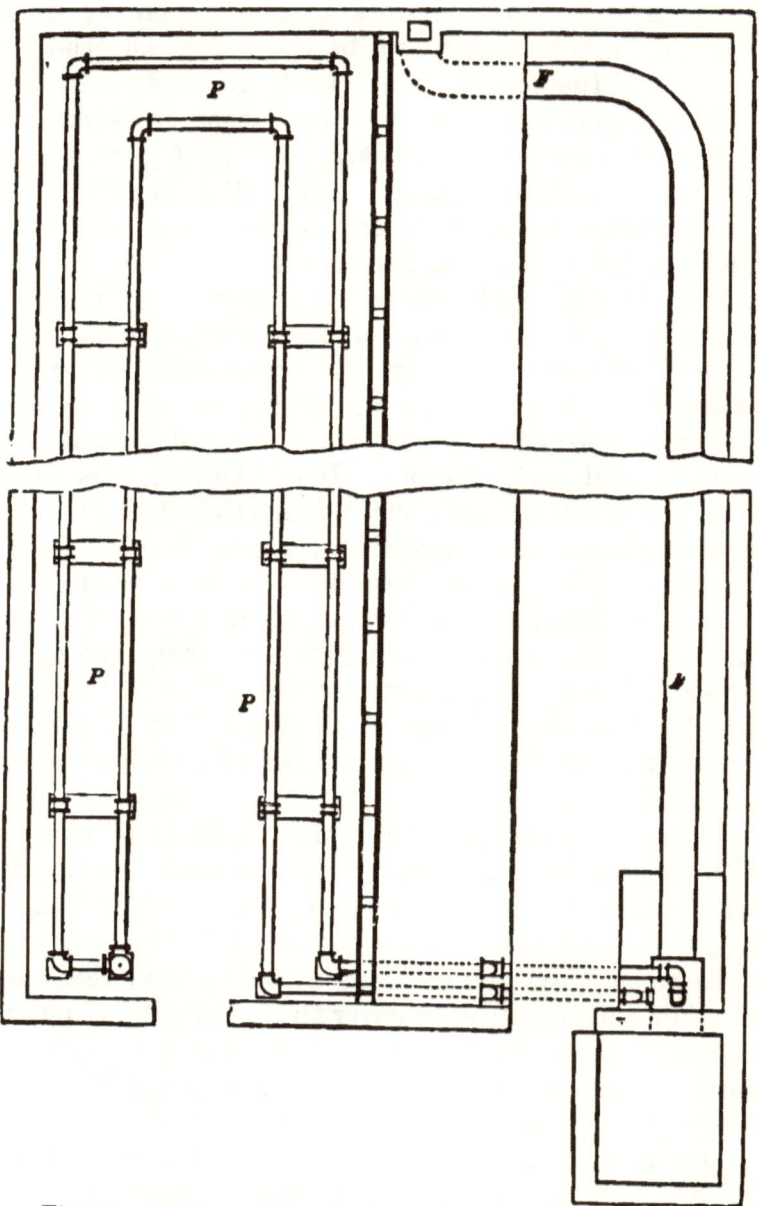

Fig. 17.—PLAN OF HOUSE HEATED BY BOTH FLUE AND PIPES.

together, each eleven feet wide by seventy feet in length. For colder sections of the country than the vicinity of New York, from fifty to sixty feet in length would probably be sufficient, but much depends on exposure, and the manner in which the building is constructed. One of the houses is heated by the flue, *F*; the other by the pipes, *P*. The boiler, *b*, shown in the end view of the same house, figure 18, is what is termed a "saddle" boiler, which answers at the same time the double purpose of an arch for the furnace and a boiler. The fire in this

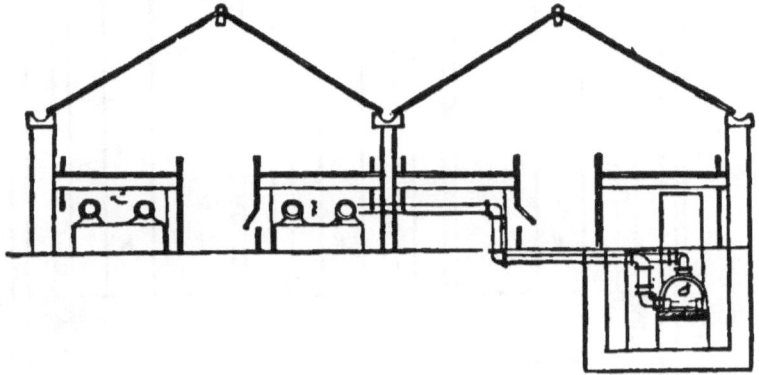

Fig. 18.—END VIEW OF FIGURE 17.

furnace does nearly the same amount of heating as two such fires, if used in heating by flues only. Thus, by this combination of flue and pipes, the construction of the heating arrangements costs about fifty per cent. less than if the house were heated entirely by hot water. The probable cost of two houses of this kind, each seventy by eleven feet, so heated, and otherwise complete, would cost about $1,000. In erecting all houses on the ridge and furrow plan, the site should, whenever practicable, be such as will admit of extension by future buildings, to meet the increase of business. A good plan in beginning is, to erect three houses, as shown in figure 19, fifty feet in length, so situated, that as business increases, and with more means in hand, the south ends can be

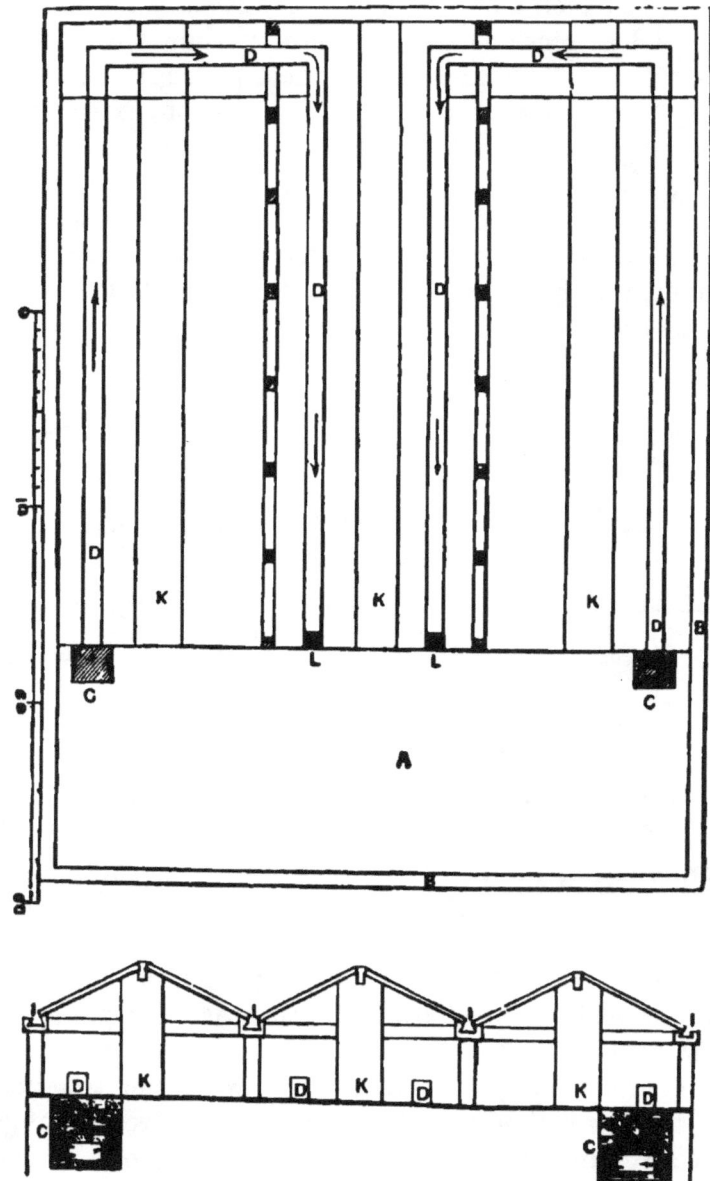

Fig. 19.—GREENHOUSE HEATED BY FLUES.

taken out, the walls extended twenty-five or fifty feet further, the flues thrown out, and the heating done by hot water or steam. For, whenever it can be afforded, the heating by hot water or steam will be found to be much the best; not that there is very much saving in fuel over heating by flues, but it is more durable, more free from danger from fire, or the escaping of gases, so troublesome with flues; besides it is an immense saving of labor, more particularly if the greenhouses are extensive. Although there is less danger from fire when greenhouses are heated by steam or hot-water boilers, yet all care should be used. One of the dangers is in covering the boiler-pit with wooden beams, which, if placed too near the chimney, often ignite. Every season there are many greenhouse fires from this cause. In our own establishment all our pits are covered with railroad iron, over which are built brick arches; even the ladders leading down to the boilers are of iron.

CHEAP GREENHOUSES—HOW TO HEAT THEM.

In the *American Agriculturist* for November, 1874, I described and gave a diagram of a method of heating a greenhouse twenty feet wide by one hundred feet long, by the ordinary smoke-flue and with only one fire. Heretofore it had been believed that it was impossible to heat a structure of that size with but one furnace, and few ever risked a house more than one-third of the size with a single fire. The principle there described, although not a new one (as I afterwards ascertained, as it had been recorded in the Transactions of the London Horticultural Society some fifty years before), had certainly never been generally practised, and its publication in the *American Agriculturist* created a great deal of interest, and also involved me in an extensive correspondence. In that article I showed only its application to that particular structure, which was too large and expensive for the wants of beginners in floriculture. I will here show how other houses of different designs and of smaller dimensions may be heated on the same principle. Figure 20 shows three of the usual ridge and furrow houses, which are sixty feet long and eleven feet wide, each, with a furnace-room or shed, at one end, which is twelve by thirty-three feet. Of course, the length may be increased or diminished as desired, but this width is found to be the most convenient.

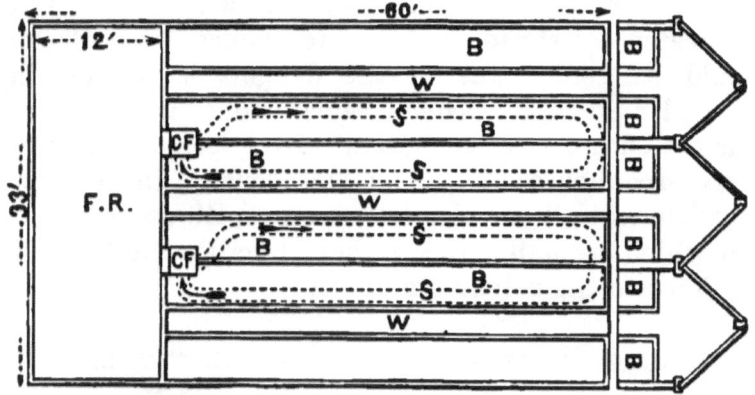

Fig. 20.—PLAN OF THREE HOUSES COMBINED.—Length, 60 ft.; width, 33 ft.

F, R, Furnace Room, 12x33 ft.; B, B, Benches, 4½ ft. wide; W, W, Walks, 2 ft. wide; S, S, Smoke-flue for heating; C, F, Furnace, with Chimney built on top of it.

It will be seen that the three greenhouses are heated by two furnaces, the flue being so disposed under the center benches of the houses as not to cross any of the pathways. This gives, of course, two runs of the flue to the middle house, and only one run each to the outside houses. This would, in coldest weather, give a temperature of forty degrees to the outside houses, and sixty or sixty-five degrees to the middle house, which has two runs of flues. This difference in temperature is indispensable in a general collection of plants, and the neglect of it is, more than anything else, the cause of failure where growers

have but one greenhouse. It will be necessary to have
the flues built as close to the walks as possible, so that
the heat may be evenly distributed in the two outside
houses. The cost of three greenhouses, each eleven by
sixty feet, connected as shown on the plan, heated by
flues, would be about $600 at present prices in this
locality. Figure 21 shows a greenhouse twenty feet wide
by sixty feet long, with furnace-room, or shed, twelve by
twenty feet. Here again the flues are so disposed as to
avoid crossing the walks, being placed under the center
bench, but as near as possible to the walk on each side,

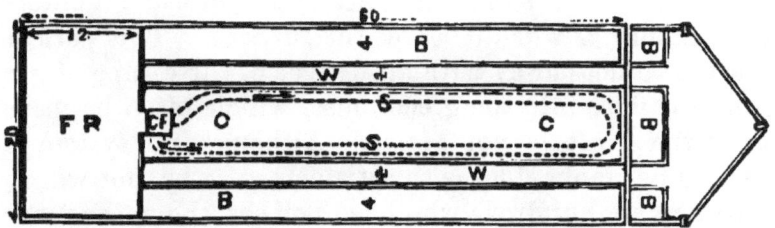

Fig. 21.—PLAN OF A SINGLE HOUSE.—60x20 ft.

*F, R, Furnace Room, 12x20 ft.; B, B, Side Benches, 4 ft. wide; C, C, Cen-
ter Bench, 8 ft. wide; W, W, Walks, 2 ft. wide; S, S, Smoke-
flue; C F, Furnace, with Chimney above.*

so that the heat may be evenly diffused throughout. This
is our favorite style of greenhouse to heat by a flue, and
such as is now mostly used by beginners; it would, in this
locality, at present prices, if built of wood, cost about $400.
If a difference in temperature is required in a house of this
kind, it may be obtained by running a glass partition
across the house, say at twenty-five feet from the furnace
end, which will, of course, make that end the hottest.
It will be seen that the principle set forth in my article of
November, 1874, is carried out in both these plans, and it
would be unsafe to attempt to heat greenhouses of these dimensions without conforming to it. Its peculiarity consists
in running the flue, in each case, back to the furnace
from which it starts and into the chimney, which is built

on the top of the furnace, not in the furnace, as some have supposed. As soon as a fire is lighted in the furnace, the brick-work forming the arch gets heated, and at once starts an upward draft, which puts the smoke-flue into immediate action and maintains it; hence there is never any trouble about the draft, as in ordinary flues having the chimney at the most distant point from the furnace. By this plan we not only get rid of the violent heat given out by the furnace, but at the same time it ensures a complete draft, the heated air from the furnace being rapidly carried through the entire length of the flue, so that it is nearly as hot when it enters the chimney as when it leaves the furnace. This perfect draft, also does away with all danger of the escape of gas from the flues into the greenhouse, which often happens when the draft is not active. Although no system of heating by smoke-flues is so satisfactory as by hot water, yet there are hundreds who have neither the means nor the inclination to go to the greater expense of hot water heating, and to such, this revived method is one that will, to a great extent, simplify and cheapen the erection of greenhouses. Many old-established florists, who have had the old plan of flues in use, have changed them to the one here described, and with great satisfaction. The wonder is that such an important fact has been so long overlooked, for at the time it was discovered, heating greenhouses by flues was almost the only method in use.

In constructing the furnace for flue heating, the size of the furnace doors should be, for a greenhouse twenty by fifty, about fourteen inches square, and the length of the furnace bars thirty inches; the furnace should be arched over, and the top of the inside of the arch should be about twenty inches from the bar. The flue will always draw better if slightly on the ascent throughout its entire length. It should be elevated in all cases from the ground, on flags or bricks, so that its heat may be given out on all sides. The inside measure of the brick flue should not be less than eight by fourteen inches. If tiles can be conveniently procured, they are best to cover with ; but, if not, the top of the flue may be contracted to six inches, and covered with bricks.

After the flue has been built of brick to twenty-five or thirty feet from the furnace, cement or vitrified drain pipes, eight or nine inches in diameter, should be used, as they are not only cheaper, but radiate the heat quicker than the bricks ; they are also much easier constructed and cleaned. Care should be taken that no woodwork is in contact with the flue at any place. It should be taken as a safe rule, that woodwork should in no case be nearer the flue or furnace than eight inches. In constructing, do not be influenced by what the mechanics will tell you, as few of them have any experience in such matters, and are not able to judge of the dangers resulting from wood-work being in close contact with the heated bricks.

On one occasion I had in use two houses heated with flues each about 100 feet in length. The chimneys had been made of wood, and they had been safely used for three winters, but on the occasion of a severe storm in winter, when our fires were going at full blast, both of them took fire within an hour of each other, though fully 100 feet from the furnace. Fortunately the chimneys had been attached to the outside of the house, and were knocked off without material injury being done. On another occasion, a house containing upwards of 10,000 plants took fire by a workman placing kindling wood on the flue near the furnace. The result was great injury to the greenhouse, and total destruction of its contents. I mention these cases, to show the necessity of the utmost caution. Every winter there are are hundreds of fires originating in greenhouses by the woodwork taking fire either from smoke flues, or when the heating is done by hot water. In the case of hot water the dangerous point is from the smoke pipe, which is in many cases placed under the beams that support the flooring that covers the furnace pit. In all such cases the beams should be covered with asbestos, and an air space of at least nine inches left between the beams and the smoke pipe. In our own establishment all our furnace pits are covered over with railroad iron for beams, over which brick arches are sprung; even the ladders used to get down to the boilers are iron, thus using every precaution against fire. This, though somewhat costly, is in the end much cheaper than insurance, for thus protected there is hardly a possibility of damage from fire. Our greenhouse establishment was begun in 1848, nearly forty years ago, and yet in all that time our total loss from fire was confined to the loss of the 10,000 plants above alluded, to which at the season of the year it occurred was replaced at an expense of, perhaps, $200.

The Cost of Construction must necessarily be only approximate, according to the manner in which the work is done, when done, and the ever-changing cost of material and labor. At this date, 1887, greenhouses, as shown in figure 16, when finished and heated by hot water, complete, would cost in this vicinity about $15 per running foot; if by steam, $13 per running foot, or by flues, $9 per running foot, less or more according to the extent—less if joined in blocks of three attached than when built singly.

GREENHOUSES ATTACHED TO DWELLINGS.

One of the most frequent inquiries made to me is: " How can I attach a green-house to my dwelling-house?" Nothing is more simple, so far as the greenhouse is concerned, but the difficulty is to heat a small structure of this kind. Many may not know that even in this latitude, a greenhouse without artificial heat can be made very useful, in fact, even better in inexperienced hands, than one that is heated, if not used before the end of April; after that date, glass protection alone is sufficient for nearly all kinds of bedding plants.

In the diagram of an end section of a simple house, figure 22, the sashes (*B* and *C*) are three feet wide by six long; the top one is so placed that it can be let down over

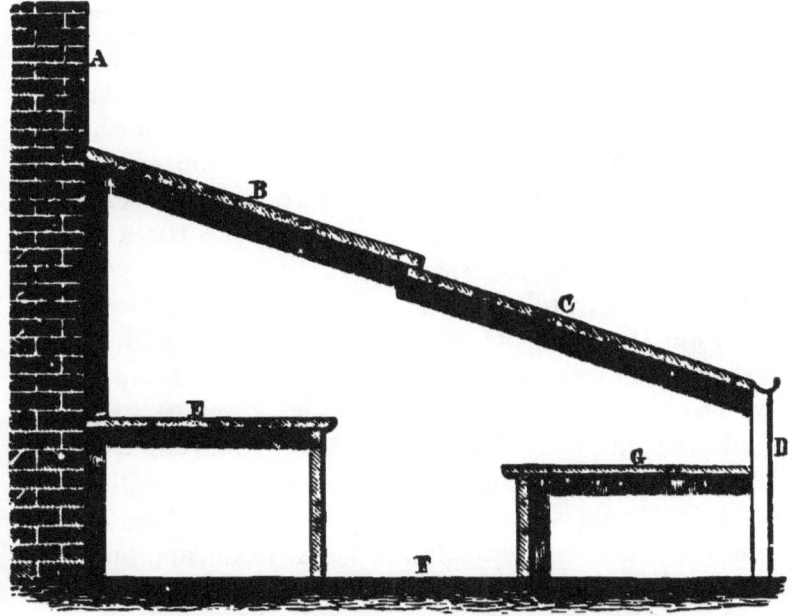

Fig. 22.—SECTION OF A CHEAP GREENHOUSE.

the lower one by weights and pulleys, and thus secure ventilation.

A greenhouse of this kind, twenty-five feet long by eleven feet wide, should not cost more than $100 complete, if plainly built; that is, without heating. Heating is a difficult matter in greenhouses so attached to dwellings, unless in cases where there is a surplus heat at night, from furnaces or stoves in the rooms adjoining. In such cases, the windows or doors, if low enough, could be opened, and enough heat be supplied from the rooms of the dwelling ; or, better yet, if it were so arranged that a register from the furnace opened into the floor of the greenhouse. But when this supply of artificial heat cannot be obtained, the greenhouse as it is, will be sufficient to protect plants against any frost that is likely to occur in this latitude after April 20th, particularly if light wooden shutters are put over the lower tier of sashes. I have recommended this style of greenhouse to many dealers and retail florists in the different States. Those who are simply dealers in plants, experience great difficulty and loss in keeping what they purchase for sale, in stores or dwelling rooms ; for if not sold at once, they quickly get injured. But this cheap and simple style of greenhouse, not only by its appearance advertises their business as dealers in flowers, but it enables them to buy from the wholesale florists at an earlier season. Besides this, they can purchase in March and April, at less than half what the same plants would cost in May, and it gives · them time to repot into larger pots. Placing them in the greenhouse, where they have sufficient space to grow, the plants that are bought for $5 per 100 in March, with but little trouble in potting, airing and watering, will freely retail for twenty-five cents each in May. These greenhouses are also economical and useful to the amateur who purchases for his flower garden in the spring. Bedding-plants, as they are called, cannot be safely planted out in the Northern States until the middle of May, and if the amateur buys from the florist then, he generally pays quite double the price that he could purchase the same plants for in March or April, for the florist always wants room in his greenhouses, and can better afford to sell a dozen Geraniums in March for seventy-five cents than for $1.50 in May. Besides, the plants if purchased in March, and shifted into larger pots, and allowed plenty of room to grow, would be far better than could be purchased at any price from the overcrowded tables of the florists in May. The care of such plants in the greenhouse is very simple. The board benches or tables, *E* and *G*, should be covered with two inches of sand, upon which to stand the pots; place them so far apart that the leaves will not touch; water thoroughly whenever the surface of the soil in the pot appears dry, which will be every day in hot weather. Ventilate by letting down the sashes, more or less, as the day is warm or cold, whenever the thermometer indicates seventy-five or eighty degrees; in other words, keep the temperature in the day-time as near as may be to sixty or sixty-five degrees, as marked by a thermometer in the greenhouse where the sun will not strike it. Burn half a pound of damp tobacco stems on the floor of the greenhouse twice a week, to destroy the aphis. One dealer in Maine informed me, that from a greenhouse so constructed, thirty feet long by eleven feet wide, placed against the south side of a high board fence, he sold in six weeks, sufficient bedding-plants that he had purchased, and vegetable plants that he had raised from seed, to afford him a profit of $200, or nearly double the cost of his greenhouse.

A greenhouse attached to a dwelling, instead of being covered with glass, may be covered by stretching the " protecting cloth " already alluded to over the rafters, which would give light enough and give sufficient protection to any kind of plants by May 1st. A greenhouse twenty-five feet by eleven, so covered, could be built for $50, attached to a wall or dwelling, and plants would do quite as well in it in May or June, as if covered by glass; no ventilation is needed when the protecting cloth is used. There are now hundreds beginning the florist's business, by buying a few plants to sell in spring, that would find their profits doubled by the use of this very cheap style of a greenhouse; the covering by the protecting cloth would cost only about one-tenth that of the glass covering. A glass sash three by six feet costs from $2.50 to $3, while a "sash" of the same size, made of the protecting cloth, would cost from twenty-five to thirty cents. The covering by protecting cloth, however, could not be very well used in winter, as it would not sustain a weight of snow, but it might be used to great advantage in the Southern States.

These greenhouses can also be used for all the purposes of a hot-bed, thus: Soil placed to the thickness of four inches on the benches will grow fine plants of all varieties of vegetables, if the proper time in sowing the different kinds is attended to—presuming that the greenhouse has no artificial heat or other than that produced by the sun's rays which pass through the glass. In this latitude, Cabbage, Cauliflower and Lettuce seed had better be sown about the 15th of March. By attention to ventilating and watering, fine plants may be had in five or six weeks from time of sowing, which will just bring them into the proper season for planting in open ground. Tomatoes, Pepper, and Egg-plant, and the tenderer kinds of flower seeds, should not be sown much sooner than the end of April. True, they would not be so early as if sown a month sooner in a hot-bed, and replanted into the greenhouse bench in May, but if no hot-bed is at hand, the protection of the greenhouse over these tender plants in May will give satisfactory results, if earliness is not particularly desired.

I have so many inquiries about the heating and general construction of cheap greenhouses, that I am compelled to give instructions which are known now to nearly every one in and around our large cities. Yet, simple though the matter may be to us who see so much of it, it is evidently perplexing enough, when they come to construct, for those who have nothing to copy from. Those of us who write on such subjects too often take for granted that those for whom we write know something about the matter, when for the most part they really know nothing.

The cheapest kind of construction is the lean-to just described, that is, where there is anything to lean it against, such as the gable of house or barn. But if the greenhouse has to be constructed entirely new, I think the span-roof is best—see figure 23. The roof can be formed by the ordinary three by six feet sashes, placed as shown on figure 22, "Section of a Cheap Greenhouse," or what is better and which is the plan now in general use, is to make the roof fixed, using bars one by two inches, in which the glass is laid. For ordinary greenhouse work the glass used is eight by ten inches, put in the ten-inch way, but for Rose forcing houses, or for other plants grown for flowers in winter, a larger size glass should be used— say, twelve by sixteen inches, put in the twelve-inch way.

CHAPTER XVII.

WIDE GREENHOUSES FOR BEDDING PLANTS AND ROSE GROWING.

The plans and descriptions of greenhouses given in the preceding pages, have been mainly for narrow greenhouses eleven feet wide, but further experience has led me to believe that the wide greenhouse, twenty feet wide, is for general purposes better than the narrow. The most approved plan of greenhouse for growing bedding plants for commercial purposes is that shown by figure 23, which usually average twenty feet in width, and are of a uniform length of 100 feet. Of course, the length is a matter of convenience, but the width we find is an important point to consider; for if over twenty feet the benches are too wide to reach easily, and if under twenty feet, room is lost by the necessity of having two walks in a narrow space. Figure 24 shows the inside arrangement of this style of greenhouse as we have it in use. One

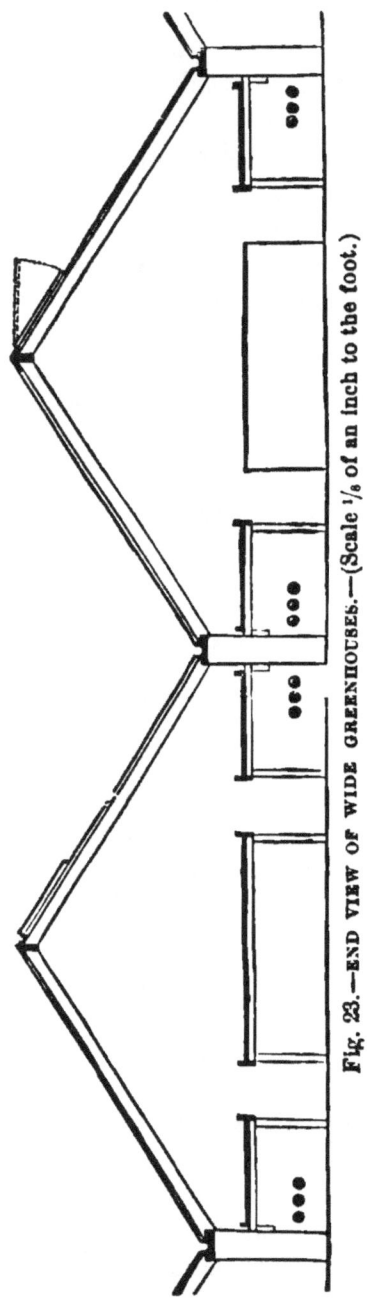

Fig. 23.—END VIEW OF WIDE GREENHOUSES.—(Scale ⅛ of an inch to the foot.)

section shows a bench in the middle, the other either a solid bed of soil or a raised bench, as desired. The scale (one-eighth of an inch to the foot) will give the height of the walls, benches, etc.

These greenhouses are joined together on the ridge and furrow plan, having one slope to the west and the other slope to the east; but if wanted for the purpose of growing rose-buds in winter, or, in short, for almost any kind of plants grown for the flowers during the winter months, this style of greenhouse (that shown by figure 23) is not so well suited, as it is found that, when joined on the ridge and furrow plan, they shade each other in the dull winter months, and that there is not sufficient light for the best development of flowers, so that we now find that for all kinds of flowering plants, Roses particularly, the greenhouse structure should stand alone, leaving an empty space of fifteen or sixteen feet between the houses, and be of the style known as the three-quarter span ; that is, having an angle of about thirty-two degrees to the horizon to the south, and an angle of thirty-six or thirty-eight degrees to the north, as shown by figure 25, which is on the same scale.

For the same reason (the necessity of sunlight in winter), the woodwork should be made as light as possible consistent with strength, and for this purpose I prefer to use well-seasoned yellow pine, as it has more strength, in

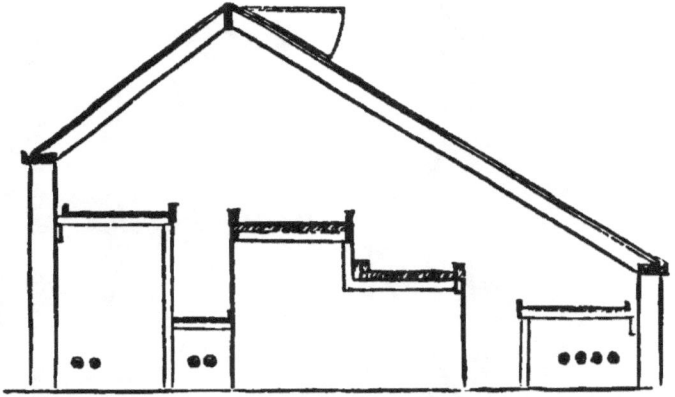

Fig. 24.—ROSE HOUSE, END SECTION.—(Scale ⅛ of an inch to the foot.)

proportion to bulk, than white pine. It is also necessary to use glass not less than ten by twelve inches, put in the twelve-inch way. Many now use twelve by sixteen inches, put in the twelve-inch way. This style of greenhouse is now preferred for forcing Lettuce, Strawberries, and other fruits and vegetables in winter, as well as flowering plants, as they too, require all the light that it is possible to obtain.

Although this style of greenhouse would also shade, if joined together on the ridge and furrow plan, when built on level ground, yet, whenever a convenient location can be had, where the ground slopes to the south at an angle of ten or fifteen degrees, they may be joined together, as

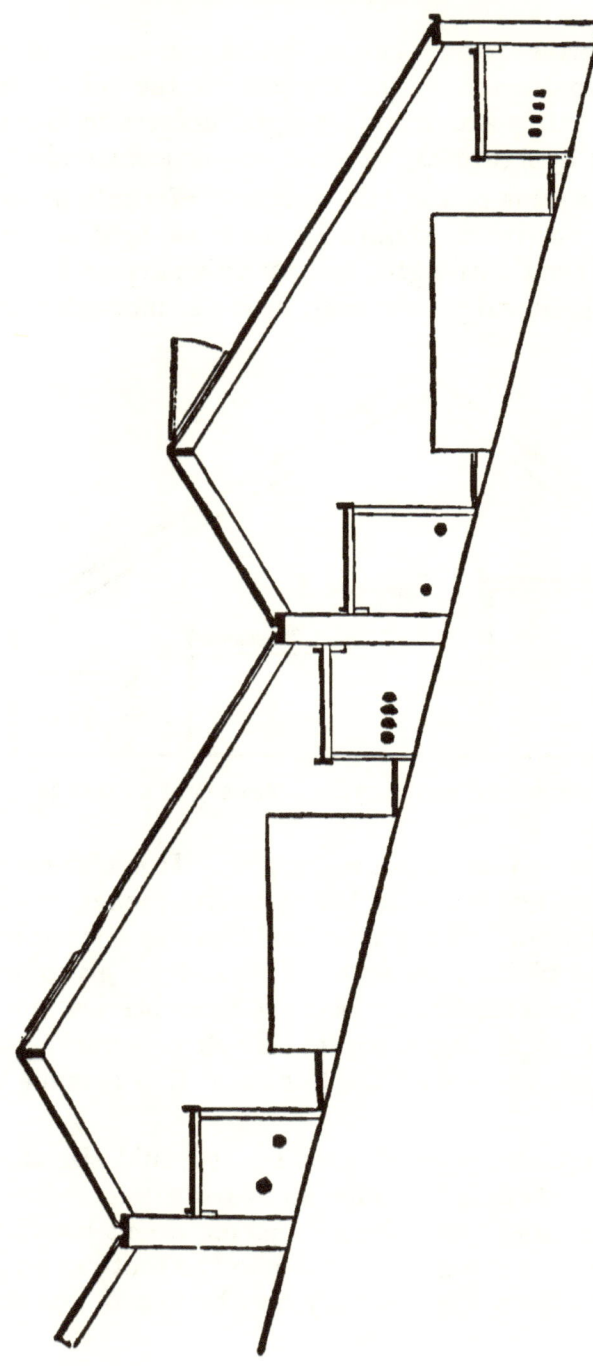

Fig. 45.—GREENHOUSES ON SLOPING GROUND.—(Scale ⅛ of an inch to the foot.)

seen in figure 25 (one-eight of an inch to the foot scale), which shows a slope or angle of fifteen degrees.

It will be noticed in this design (figure 25) that the larger number of pipes are placed under the front bench, there being four there, while there are only two under the back bench. The slope of the ground makes this arrangement necessary in order to secure an equal distribution of heat. It will be observed that there are six "runs" of four-inch pipe for each house; this will give a temperature of fifty degrees at night in the coldest weather. If a higher temperature is wanted, an additional "run" of pipe should be added for every five degrees. For further information see "Modes of Heating," page 98. With the ordinary arrangement of pipes (half under each bench), the back of the house would always be much the warmest, as a moment's reflection will make manifest. The position of the ventilators near the ridge is distinctly marked in this and all the other figures, the dotted lines showing a ventilator raised or open. The position of the benches is also shown. Through the middle there may be either a bench or a solid bed of earth. By use of the scale (one-eighth of an inch to the foot) the proportions of the details of this house may be readily obtained.

The construction of greenhouses when formed of concrete, stone, or brick, is not only more costly, but after the wall has risen to the surface of the ground, it is found that, unless the wall of stone or brick is very thick indeed, the high temperature and moisture inside of a greenhouse soon injures the mason work by warring with the low temperature outside, particularly on the north or northwest side. For this reason it has been found that wooden walls, for ordinary purposes, are equally as good as an eight-inch brick wall for resisting cold, far cheaper, and more durable.

A common error with the inexperienced is to build the

wooden wall of a greenhouse hollow, filling up the space
with sawdust, or some such non-conducting material.
The method found best is to sink locust, cedar, or chestnut posts to the required depth, and at distances of four
or six feet apart; against these (outside) nail common
rough boards; then against these tack asphalt or tarred
paper, and against that nail the ordinary weather boarding. Such a wall will resist cold better than an eight-
inch brick wall, and will last for twenty years, if kept
painted. If a better finish is desired inside, the posts can
be hid by weather boarding; but nothing should be put
in to fill the space. When the walls have been finished
to the required height, the wall plate to secure the rafters
is laid on. Supporting posts should be placed under the
ridge-pole, and also near the middle of the rafters, where
these are very long, as is the case in many of the three-
quarter span houses. At present prices, the cost of a
Rose House, as shown in figure 24, is about $15 per run-
ning foot, heated by hot water or steam, complete, or
$1,500.

CHAPTER XVIII.

GLASS, GLAZING AND SHADING.

If for winter forcing of either fruit or flowers, the
glass should (as we have before said) be not less than ten
by twelve inches in size, and laid in the twelve-inch way.
It should be of what is known as second quality French,
and it is economy always to use the double thick. All
panes should be rejected having flaws or " blebs," as these
will act like lenses, and, forming a focus for the sun's
rays, will burn the leaves of the plants; but even with the
greatest care, some flaws will usually remain, and less or

more burn the leaves after the sun becomes strong; to counteract this, a slight shading had better be used on the glass from April to September. We use naphtha, with just enough white lead mixed in it to give it the appearance of thin milk. This we put on with a syringe, which sufficiently covers up all flaws in the glass to prevent burning, and at the same time tends to cool the house by mitigating the violence of the sun's rays. This is by far the cheapest and best shading we have ever used. It can be gradated to any degree of thickness, and costs only about twenty-five cents per 1,000 square feet of glass, for material and labor.

In glazing, the method now almost universally adopted is to bed the glass in putty, and tack it on top with glazier's points, using no putty on the top. The glazier's points are triangular, one corner of which is turned down, so that when it is driven in, it fits the lower edge of each pane and prevents it from slipping down. A great mistake is often made in giving the glass too much lap; it should only be given just enough to cover the edge of the pane (from one-eighth to one-fourth of an inch). If given too much, the water gets in between the panes, and when it freezes it cracks the glass.

Although no putty is used on the top of the bars, we have found it an excellent plan to fill an ordinary oil-can, such as is used for machinery, with white lead and oil, and by its narrow-pointed funnel run a thin stream of the white lead at the edge where the glass fits against the bar; by shaking dry sand over this, it forms a cement that will hold for many years. We find this, even on old greenhouses, to be an excellent plan for closing up leakage and firming the glass. Had I known of this most excellent method of glazing twenty years ago, I would have saved at least $10,000 that it has cost me in that time for repairs.

CHAPTER XIX.

MODES OF HEATING.

Until the past few years the almost universal plan of heating commercial greenhouses was by hot water, and as that plan has yet many advocates, we herewith give some of the leading points to observe when it is used; further on, we will refer to steam heating as now being adopted in many large establishments.

In heating by hot water, it is important that the work be given to some reputable firm, whose knowledge is such as will enable them not only to judge what is the proper capacity of the boiler for the number of pipes to be used, but also how many pipes are necessary to be used for the surface of glass to be heated. Men who have done a large business in heating greenhouses, have far better opportunities for knowledge in this matter than the average gardener or florist; and if those erecting greenhouses have not had extensive and varied practice, they had better be guided by the men who make a business of heating, as the want of the requisite knowledge of these matters often works serious mischief. Of course, the size of the greenhouse or greenhouses to be heated must determine the capacity of the boiler required; but the boiler being properly apportioned to the length of pipe, the following data, used in our own establishment (which is mostly heated by hot water), may be useful. In our houses, which are twenty feet wide and one hundred feet long, when a night temperature of seventy degrees is required in the coldest weather, ten runs or rows of four-inch pipe, five on each side, are required; when sixty degrees is wanted, eight runs of pipe, four on each side; when fifty degrees is wanted, six runs of pipe will be needed; and when only thirty-five or forty degrees is required, four runs of pipe will meet the requirement. This is for the latitude of New York City, where the temperature rarely falls lower than ten degrees below zero. Latitudes north or south of New York should be graded accordingly. If estimated by glass surface, about one foot in length of four-inch pipe is necessary for every three and a half square feet of glass surface, when the temperature is at ten degrees below zero, to keep a temperature of 50 degrees in the greenhouse. We now place all our pipes under the side benches, as that enables us to use the space under the middle bench for safely stowing away many plants, which otherwise could not be done if the pipes were there. There are scores of kinds of hot water boilers in use, and our opinion is repeatedly asked as to the relative merits of many of them. This can only be determined by a comparative test, which we have never had time or inclination to try. We have used the boilers made by Hitchings & Co. for the past twenty years with the most satisfactory results. There may be better, but we do not know them, and do not care to take the risk of experimenting.

CHAPTER XX.

HEATING BY STEAM.

Two years ago, to satisfy myself of the relative merits of hot water and steam heating for greenhouse purposes, I erected a Rose house twenty feet wide by 350 feet in length. This I heated by steam alongside of another Rose house of exactly the same dimensions, heated by hot water. These have given me an opportunity for a comparative test and we find the result in favor of steam;

first, that it saves twenty-five per cent. in fuel ; second, that our firemen say that the steam boilers require less labor, and, third, that the steam pipes by the use of valves are easier controlled than the hot water pipes. But, above all, is the certainty that, on a large scale at least, heating by steam must be cheaper than by hot water. Leaving out the question of the cost of boilers, which ought to be relatively the same for the amount of work to be done, we find that a one and one-quarter inch pipe, when heated by steam, does almost exactly the same amount of work as a four-inch hot water pipe ; at present prices the one and one-quarter inch steam pipe costs six cents per foot, while the four-inch hot water pipe costs twenty cents. Thus, the piping costs three times more for hot water than for steam, but so far there has been compara-tively little difference in estimates between the two, owing probably to the steam heating of greenhouses being yet in but few hands. From our experience with steam, I believe that whenever greenhouses are erected to the extent of 5,000 square feet of glass surface, steam should be used in preference to hot water ; if for smaller areas, it may be that hot water would be best. As far as the health of plants is concerned, there is nothing to choose, for although a steam pipe at low pressure radiates at from 212 and over, and a hot water pipe at about an average of 170 degrees, yet at six inches from either pipe the tem-perature is almost identical, radiation is so rapid. Any one doubting this can easily test it by the thermometer.

CHAPTER XXI.

BASE-BURNING WATER-HEATER.

For many years a great want has been felt for a better means of heating greenhouses, or rather conservatories, attached to dwellings.   The space to be heated is usually

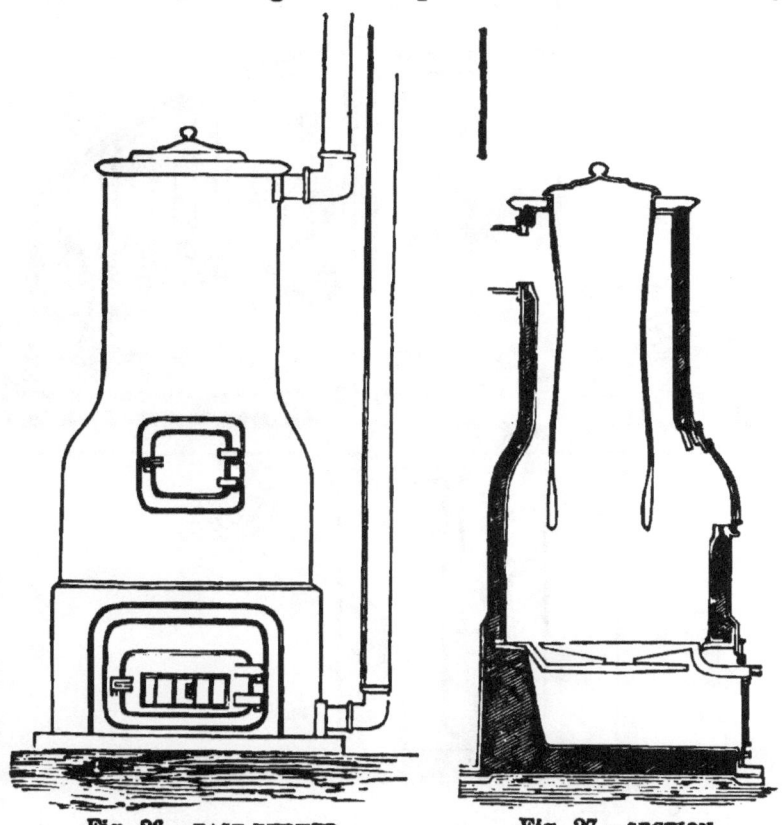

Fig. 26.—BASE-BURNER.   Fig. 27.—SECTION.

so small that the ordinary hot water boilers in use for large greenhouses have been found by amateurs too complicated, and to require too much attention.   Then, when the common smoke-flue was tried, corresponding difficulties arose, it requiring nearly the same attention as the more expensive boiler. Occasionally these conservatories are heated by registers from the furnace heater, just as are the ordinary rooms of the dwelling ; but I have rarely seen any so heated wherein the plants looked well, it being difficult to get the registers so placed as to diffuse the heat evenly. A new base-burning water-heater has been in-

Fig. 28.—SECTION OF HOUSE AND CONSERVATORY.

vented by Hitchings & Co., the well known greenhouse-heating firm. There is nothing new in the principle—nothing to patent, I believe. It is simply making the ordinary base-burning stove to so heat water that it will circulate in iron pipes and warm a small greenhouse or conservatory attached to a dwelling or otherwise, exactly as do our large boilers, which are not usually made on the base-burning principle. The patterns they have thus far made (shown in figure 26 and in section in figure 27) are forty-two inches high and twenty-one inches at base, and are powerful enough to heat a greenhouse ten feet wide by twenty-five feet long, or about 500 square feet of glass surface, taking into account the front and ends. The complete cost of heating, including boiler, pipes and fitting up, will range from $150 to $200. The care necessary in the management of this base-burning water-heater is exactly the same as that required for an ordinary base-burning stove; and it may be safely left for twelve hours without attention, and will keep up a temperature in the house of from fifty to sixty degrees at night, which is about what is required for a general collection of plants. Figure 28 shows the boiler placed alongside the kitchen range, being in a basement and one story lower than the conservatory. It can either be used in this way, or placed in the conservatory itself if so desired. It must be borne in mind, though, in constructing a conservatory, that it must be placed where connection can be made with a chimney, as of course an outlet must be had for smoke exactly as in any ordinary room where a stove of any kind is used. When dwelling-houses are heated by steam it is an easy matter to heat a greenhouse that is attached to a dwelling, as, of course, steam pipes can be run at any level above the boiler. Greenhouses, if need be, can be heated from the steam boiler in the dwelling, even if hundreds of feet distant, always keeping in view the point that, if extra work is to be done by the boiler, it must have sufficient power.

CHAPTER XXII.

PROPAGATION OF PLANTS BY SEEDS.

The most natural way of increasing plants is by seeds, and, whenever practicable, it is preferable to all others. In our own practice we rarely increase a plant in any other way, if we can procure the seed, unless, of course, with particular varieties that we know will not reproduce themselves from seed, and perpetuate the desired color, form, or markings. It is believed that no plant ever produces identically the same individual from seed. The resemblance may be so close that, to casual observation, it may seem identical; but reasoning from analogy, it is fair to presume that no generated organisms of animal or vegetable life, whether from the lowest molecule to the highest type of existence, are ever identical. No two human beings are ever identical in face or form; and even acquired habits, such as handwriting, are never the same.

Some species of animal and vegetable life, when under domestication, become what is technically called "broken." Thus we find the pigeon, when domesticated, running into a great variety of plumage, while its prototypes of the woods seem to be all alike; but it is fair to presume they each possess a distinct individuality, though less apparent than the others. So it is in plant life. When we sow 1,000 seeds of Verbena or Coleus, to the experienced eye no two of the seedlings are ever exactly the same, though the original types from which they sprung will seem to produce varieties identical; but in this case also it is reasonable to presume that a distinct individuality is present, though the distinction is so slight that ordinary observation fails to mark it. The eye requires to be educated to nice distinctions of individuality. Shepherds in charge of five hundred sheep can often individualize every member of the flock, which to the inexperienced observer seem all alike. The reader will excuse this digression; but there is a great deal of misconception on this interesting subject.

In all cases where seed taken from a variety or species will reproduce itself nearly the same, as in special colors of Hollyhocks, or, in cases where a general variety is wanted, as in Verbenas, Petunias or Geraniums, the propagation by seed is largely practised.

Experience only can give the necessary knowledge for the full understanding of the proper temperature and humidity essential for the successful germination of the seeds of different plants. It may be laid down as a safe rule, however, that for the hardier varieties, a low or medium temperature is required, say from forty-five to sixty degrees, and for the tender species, a temperature from seventy-five to ninety degrees.

If Pansy seed is sown in July or August, where the temperature in the shade averages eighty degrees, no matter how moist the soil is kept, if germination takes place at all it will be of so feeble a kind that the seedlings will not continue a healthy existence; but if the same seed were sown in September or October, with an average temperature of, say sixty degrees in the shade, a quick and healthy germination would be the result. The same rule applies to Cinerarias, Calceolarias, Auriculas, Primulas, and all other plants of this half-hardy nature. English, Scotch, and Irish gardeners, before they have had time for experience in this country, are apt to fall into the common error of sowing all these seeds too soon. Though it is proper to sow these seeds in July and August in England, with us, in this section, it must be delayed until September or October, and in warm latitudes still later, or failure is almost certain to follow. In our own practice we prefer to sow all such seeds in March,

April or May, and by cramping the plants in shallow boxes and rather poor soil, we can hold them so that they are none too large for winter work.   On the other hand, if we attempt to germinate Portulacas, Balsams, Amaranths, Zinnias, or other plants of tropical origin, in the medium temperature of fifty degrees, they will either remain dormant until a higher temperature occurs, or perish.   Ignorance of, or inattention to, these conditions is far oftener the cause of failure than want of vitality in seeds.

Whether seeds are sown in the open border, in the window garden of the parlor, in the hot-bed, or greenhouse, the same conditions should be observed, so far as practicable.   In the open border there is not always a choice of soil, but if soil is to be prepared, let it be of a light nature ; leaf-mould from the woods, and well-pulverized muck from the swamps, or, better than either of these, the dust of cocoanut fibre, or of decayed, refuse hops, are excellent to sift on as a covering for seeds.   We have employed these latter materials exclusively, as a covering for seeds of all kinds, for many years, with results which have been vastly superior to those we had when we did not use them.

It must be borne in mind that seeds do not so much need a fertile soil at first, as they do one having the necessary mechanical condition ; this is found exactly in the light, moisture-retaining nature of hop-mould or cocoanut dust.   We can give no better rule than the old one of covering seeds to about their own depth with mould, although something depends on the weight of the material with which they are covered.   One-fourth of an inch in depth of hop-mould, or leaf-mould, would be no more than equivalent to half that depth of ordinary loam ; hence the advantage in using it, as it gives the seed a moist, springy covering, through which the tiny germ can freely push.

We know it is a practice, very common with amateurs and many gardeners, when starting seeds in a hot-bed or greenhouse, to use flower-pots in this operation; they are generally two-thirds filled with potsherds, overlaying which is an inch or two of soil, and on this the seed is sown. Any continuation of dry weather necessitates almost daily watering of the flower-pots; this bakes or hardens the surface, while a day's inattention to them dries the soil while it is in this condition, so as to injure the vitality of the seeds; hence very unsatisfactory results too often follow this practice.

For many years we have entirely discarded the use of earthen flower-pots or pans for the purpose of sowing seeds, and use shallow boxes instead. These we prepare by cutting the common-sized soap-box into three pieces, each one of a depth of about two inches. There boxes are filled with the prepared soil to the depth of one inch and one-half, which is gently and evenly pressed, so as to give an entirely level surface; the seeds are then sown, and a light covering, from one-sixteenth to one-fourth of an inch thick, according to the size or strength of seed, is sifted over them, through a sieve having a mesh only one-tenth of an inch. The covering is gently pressed to prevent the air penetrating the loose soil and drying up the seeds; watering, which it is well to avoid as much as possible, is thus rendered less necessary. Be careful, however, not to let them suffer for moisture, as in the weak condition of seedlings, most plants are quickly injured by neglect of this kind, and, even with all possible care, we experience serious losses. Many varieties will "damp off," as we term it, just as the first rough leaves are being formed; this, however, is not the result of excessive moisture, as it occurs just as quickly in a dry temperature as in a moist one. It is evidently caused by the same insidious spiderweb-like substance that is known among gardeners as the "fungus of the cutting bench," and is probably one of the minute fungi of which we have so many representatives. The best preventive of this disease, as it is sometimes called, is, just as soon as the seedling plants can be handled, to take them from the seed-boxes, and prick them out in boxes of similar mould, from one-half to two inches apart, according to the variety. This is a much better method than that of potting them off in flower-pots, as it not only saves time and room, but they always do better. In the flower-pots they are liable to be dried up, and the tender roots of the seedling plant quickly destroyed.

We use these shallow boxes largely for pricking off cuttings from our propagating benches, instead of potting them off, particularly such plants as are wanted for stock to be planted out in the open ground, as, after being rooted in the cutting bench and planted out in these shallow boxes, they can there remain, occupying less space, and in every respect growing as well as if in pots. Carnations and Roses we work largely in this way.

CHAPTER XXIII.

PROPAGATION BY SEEDS.—WHAT VARIETIES COME TRUE FROM SEEDS?

An intelligent correspondent asks the question given above. He queries still farther and says : " An Apple seed produces an Apple tree, but a Baldwin Apple seed will not produce a Baldwin Apple tree. Wheat of any variety produces the same ; seed of a scarlet variety of Verbena will not always produce its like. Why this anomaly ?" The " why" of the matter cannot be told, but a few general rules may be useful. Seeds of plants

in the wild state, in their native habitats, almost invariably produce a progeny nearly identical with the parent ;
and many species, even after they have been subjected to
long years of cultivation, seemingly never appear to
change in the slightest degree.   Other species under cultivation, quickly develop varieties greatly different from
the original, and become what is technically termed
" broken."   Thus the original species of our well-known
Verbena is indigenous to South America, having a comparatively small scarlet flower.   From this, and probably
some other species hybridized with it, we have the gorgeous and varied coloring of the Verbenas of to-day. But it
took many years to produce these, for we can well remember that in our early gardening days there was no white,
and the furor that took place in the floricultural world
when *Verbena teucrioides,* the first white, appeared. It was
far from being an attractive plant, but the color was novel,
and single plants were sold by the florists of that time at
a price that would now buy a hundred.   The Verbena,
then, is one genus of which the species have given us in-
numerable varieties.   The Chrysanthemum, Dahlia,
Fuchsia, Geranium, Tulip, Hyacinth, Gladiolus, Pansy,
Petunia, the Rose, and many others, are also familiar
examples where the original species has " broken " from
what may be termed its primary condition into everchang-
ing variety. Thus changed, it is probable that their seeds
will never produce two individual plants exactly alike.

It is probable that all species of animals and vegetables, under long years of domestication and cultivation, would ultimately " break " from the original
type, though we know that in some species this tendency
is sooner developed than in others. It is not to be wondered
at that amateur horticulturists, like my inquiring friend,
are puzzled at what looks like inconsistency in nature—
why she refuses to produce always again his Baldwin
Apple, or his Rareripe Peach, his Striped Petunia, or his

Double Carnation, yet gives him back, seemingly identical with the parent, his Corn or his Wheat, his Tomato or his Cabbage, or in flowers his Mignonette or Alyssum. I say "seemingly," for it may be doubted if they are identical, only the variation is so slightly marked that it escapes notice. Many, whose experience in such matters should have taught them better, are always confounding plants raised from cuttings or slips with those raised from seeds, and cannot see why the plant raised from the slip or root of a White Dahlia, or the tree raised from the graft of a Baldwin Apple, should be always identical with the plant or tree from which they are taken, while the seeds taken from either would not produce the same. Any cutting from a root or a branch, whether rooted itself or engrafted on another stock (except in rare cases of sports), will be identical with that of the original form from which it is taken ; in fact, it is only a separated part of the same plant, while the plant raised from seed is a distinct individual.

Very few not engaged in the cultivation of flowers as a business, know that many of the most beautiful ones used for decorating flower beds in summer, and hot-houses in winter, can be raised from seed. The price of seeds, as compared with plants, is very low ; a package of seeds costing twenty-five cents will usually raise as many plants as could be bought from the florists for $25. It is true that care and labor are necessary in starting them, but the pleasure derived from the operation alone well repays that, independently of economic considerations. April is the best month for sowing most of the seeds of tropical plants, and it is best done where there is the convenience of a hot-bed or warm greenhouse. The hot-bed is made in the usual manner (See chapter on Hot-beds). The soil should be, if possible, of a light, sandy nature, mixed with at least one-third of leaf-mould from the woods; if the leaf mould is not procurable, pulverized muck, or

stable manure rotted to the condition of mould, will do
nearly as well.   This is spread over the manure to the
depth of about six inches.   The sashes of the hot-bed
should fit close, and there should be some material ready
for covering the sash at night—either straw mats or shutters.   We ourselves use shutters made out of one-half-
inch stuff, and exactly the size of the sash.   All these prep-
arations being made, insert a thermometer into the soil
covering the hot-bed, and when it indicates a declining
temperature of seventy-five degrees the seeds may be
sown.   Most of the flower seeds may be sown in a hot-
bed just as we sow Egg-plants or Tomatoes, which is best
done for private use by sowing in rows from a quarter of
an inch to an inch in depth, according to the size of the
seed, the distance between the rows being two or three
inches.   Let me here repeat a caution that I have often
given in connection with seed sowing: Be sure that the
soil used for covering the seed is light (See Chapter
XXII on Propagation by Seed for full details).   One-
half of the loss in seeds is in consequence of their being
covered with a heavy, clayey soil.   The power of different
plants to penetrate through the soil varies greatly.   Thus,
while the seeds of the Tomato germinate in almost any soil,
the Egg-plant—a vegetable of the same family—requires
the utmost care.   As soon as the seedling plants have grown
so as to attain the first true leaves—that is, the first leaves
that show after the seed-leaves—they must be replanted
carefully in soft, light soil, at from one to three inches
apart, according to the kind.   This will not only prevent
them from damping off, as many of them are very apt to
do, but they will be much stronger and suffer less when
re-planted in the open ground.   We prefer to re-plant
the seedlings in the shallow boxes already described.
They are more portable thus than if planted again in the
soil of the hot-bed, though, of course, after planting in
the boxes, these are put again into the hot-bed.   After the

seedlings have been planted in these boxes, lightly water them and shade for two or three days. As the season advances attend to ventilation, watering and covering up at night.

Those who have not the convenience of a hot-bed may sow the flower seeds in the shallow boxes above mentioned, and place them in the window of a south or east room, where the thermometer does not average less than seventy degrees. Success would be more complete, however, if panes of glass were placed over the seeds, resting on the edges of the box an inch or so above the soil. This would prevent evaporation and render watering, which has the effect of caking the surface of the soil and preventing germination, less necessary. The protecting cloth, already described, may be used for any purpose for which glass can be used in covering seeds after May 1.

We name in the following list, the varieties of flowers most suitable to grow from seeds :

Canna Indica, or Indian Shot, grown mainly for the beauty of its foliage. Sown in hot-bed in April, and planted out in the open ground in June, will by August attain a height of six or eight feet. In addition to the rich, tropical-looking foliage, the flowers of some sorts are handsome ; colors : yellow, scarlet, orange, etc. A new dwarf variety has just been introduced, growing only a foot and a half in height, with flowers nearly as fine as those of the Gladiolus, and in far greater variety than the taller sorts.

Antirrhinum, or Snap-Dragon.—A beautiful summer flowering plant, presenting a great diversity of coloring, is easily raised from seed in the hot-bed. The Antirrhinums may be planted out in this latitude in May, and flower from middle of June throughout the summer.

Cobæa scandens.—A climbing plant, which will attain, from seed, a growth of twenty or thirty feet in one season.

The flowers are bell-shaped; purple; three inches in length by one inch and one-half in breadth. The seeds are thin and flat, and should be placed on edge when sown.

Coleus.—This famous ornamental-leaved plant is easily raised from seed, and breaks into endless varieties. It is exceedingly tender, however, and had better not be sown before May, nor planted out before June.

Zonal Geraniums are, perhaps, the most valuable of all plants for summer blooming in our climate. They are easily raised from seed, and will well reward the labor by the endless variety produced. A few years ago the only colors of these were scarlet and pink. Now we have them in every shade, from white to crimson, with endless tints of scarlet and rose, double and single. The Zonal Geraniums may be lifted and potted in the fall, and if well pruned in when lifted, will bloom finely in winter.

Lantana is another plant easily raised from seed; the flower resembles the Verbena somewhat, but has, besides many of the colors found in the Verbena, orange and yellow, which are not found in that flower.

Lobelias.—Dwarf plants, well suited for hanging baskets, or for ribbon lining. The flowers range from white to blue. The blue of the Lobelia is often of the richest azure, unsurpassed by that of any other plant.

Pansy.—Of all plants raised from seed by the florist, none is of greater importance than the Pansy; it has now such a diversity of color, and coming at a season in spring when flowers are yet scarce ; it is an ever welcome favorite. The usual plan is to sow the seeds in August or September, so as to get plants large enough to keep over in cold frames through the winter, to bloom in March, April or May ; but many now sow part of their crop in January or February in the greenhouse or hot-bed, and though they come in flower later in spring, yet the younger plants are

much better adapted for blooming through the entire
summer months than those sown in autumn. When
sown in August or September, we find it a good plan to
shade the seed-bed by shutters made of laths or protecting cloth, or some such partial shading, for four or five
hours during the day, while the sun is hot, but they
should never be sown in, or kept in, exclusive shade.
This is true of nearly all kinds of seeds.

Petunias, being of rapid growth, will flower the first
season, even if sown in the open ground, but usually not
before July or August. If sown in the hot-bed or greenhouse in January, February or March, they will bloom
in April, May or June, and make larger and finer plants.
If wanted for summer blooming, and not to sell when in
flower, the seed should not be sown before the middle of
April.

Dianthus.—The Pinks are numerous and varied, many
of them having a rich, clove-like fragrance. They present
an endless variety in color and style of flower.

Salvia splendens, or Scarlet Sage.—Seeds of this sown
in April will flower by July or August, and continue
throughout the season. This, perhaps, is the most gorgeous plant of our gardens; single plants often attain a
height of six feet, and nearly as much in diameter, having a hundred scarlet, plume-like, flower-spikes. The
color is so intense when seen against a green background,
that it is often visible at a distance of half a mile.

Verbena.—This is yet one of the most popular plants
of the day ; it is easily raised from seed, and no other
plant that we know of will so well reward the trouble. The
number of varieties now attained is something wonderful,
even to us in the trade. Every year develops some new
strain. Every color seemingly is obtained but yellow or
orange ; these we never expect to have, as there seems to be
a natural law of the floral kingdom that blue, yellow and

scarlet are never found in varieties of the same species. Thus we have in Dahlias and Roses, yellow and scarlet colors, but no blue ; just as we have in Verbenas blue and scarlet, but no yellow. My readers will do well to remember this, and be saved from investing in "blue" Roses or Dahlias and "yellow" Verbenas, which are occasionally offered, knowing that the seller must either be ignorant of his trade or dishonest.

Delphinium hybridum (Larkspur).—Hardy perennial herbaceous plants of the most dazzling shades of blue, from lightest azure to the deepest mazarine blue. Seeds sown in January or February, in heat, will flower the same season, but the best plan is to sow in September, and winter over in cold frames. They grow from four to ten feet in height. Blue is the rarest color among flowers, and therein Delphiniums are most useful, being hardy and perennial, and once established in the garden they grow without further trouble for years.

Centaureas, Cinerarias and Golden Pyrethrum.— These plants, with foliage which is used for white or yellow lines in ribbon planting, or in massing, are all better if raised from seeds than from cuttings.

Asters are now raised in immense numbers for market. To get the best plants, they should not be sown sooner than the middle of March ; with careful handling at this time they will give fine blooming plants by the middle of June for later flowering. Sow for succession at intervals of twenty to thirty days. They can thus be had through the entire season from June to October. When grown in pots, we find pots of five-inch to be the most convenient size.

Ampelopsis, particularly the species introduced as *A. Veitchii,* but properly *A. tricuspidata,* is best raised from seed ; seeds sown in December or January, potted off into two-inch pots and planted out into the open ground in May, if trained to strings or stakes, will attain a height of six to nine feet before October. There is now an immense demand for this grand climber, and so far the supply has been entirely inadequate.

Balsams should not be sown sooner than May 1st. Sown at that time, they will make fine plants by the middle of June if to be sold in pots; if wanted for cut flowers, they should be sown in the open ground about June 1st.

Carnation.—The monthly kinds of Carnation should be sown in winter or early spring, and if grown either in pots or planted in the open ground, will flower the first season by September or October. But the hardy garden Carnations, so much grown for cut flowers in summer, should not be sown before the middle of May, in the open ground, and should be planted in July, eight or ten inches apart, when they will cover the ground by fall, and will stand the winter in almost any section of the country where the thermometer does not fall below zero ; or in sections such as Canada, where the ground is covered by snow, they will stand a much lower temperature.

Cineraria, Calceolaria and Primula seeds, in our opinion, are best sown in March, April, or May ; we have practised sowing at this time for the past fifteen years, with great success. In England, the practice is to sow in July and August, and it is all right in their cooler climate, but it is a very difficult matter to get seeds of any of these to vegetate freely in hot weather, and we prefer to start the seeds earlier and keep the plants through the summer, pricked off in shallow boxes. The seeds will vegetate freely in September and October, but it is then rather too late to get plants large enough.

Besides the plants thus described in detail, as being suitable to raise from seeds in greenhouse or hot-bed, the

following list (descriptions of which can be found in the
Seed Catalogues), can all be raised from seeds, and make
fine plants for sale by the selling season in May and June,
or to produce earlier cut flowers than when sown in the
open ground:

Abutilon,	Dianthus,	Maurandia,
Ageratum,	Erythrina,	Mignonette,
Alonsoa,	Euphorbia,	Mimosa,
Alyssum,	Everlasting Flowers,	Mimulus,
Amarantus,	Ferns,	Musk,
Anagallis,	Feverfew,	Myosotis,
Antirrhinum,	Forget-Me-Not,	Myrsiphyllum,
Aquilegia,	Fuchsia,	Petunia,
Ardisia,	Gladiolus,	Phlox, perennial,
Aristolochia,	Globe Amaranth,	Phlox Drummondii,
Aster,	Gloxinia,	Poppy,
Auricula,	Gnaphalium,	Portulaca,
Begonia,	Heliotrope,	Primula,
Bellis,	Helianthus,	Pyrethrum,
Browallia,	Helichrysum,	Rhodanthe,
Calceolaria,	Hollyhock,	Ricinus,
Campanula,	Humea,	Senecio speciosus,
Canary Bird Flower,	Ice Plant,	Sensitive Plant,
Canna,	Impatiens Sultana,	Smilax,
Castor Oil Bean,	Indian Shot,	Solanum,
Celosia,	Ipomæa,	Stocks,
Chrysanthemum,	Lantana,	Thunbergia,
Clematis,	Larkspur,	Torenia,
Cockscomb,	Lathyrus,	Tritoma,
Coleus,	Lavandula,	Tropæolum,
Cowslip,	Limnanthes,	Veronica,
Cuphea,	Linum,	Vinca,
Cyclamen,	Lobelia,	Viola,
Dahlia,	Lophospermum,	Wallflower,
Datura,	Lychnis,	Wigandia,
Delphinium,	Marigold,	Zinnia.

CHAPTER XXIV.

PROPAGATION OF PLANTS BY CUTTINGS.

Of all the operations of the florist, the one above all others in importance is the propagation of plants by cuttings. It is the fount from which the supply must come, and becomes inexhaustible in the hands of a careful operator. I say a careful operator, rather than a skilful one, for, in my estimation, a great amount of knowledge is not so necessary to success, as that a never-flagging, careful application of that knowledge should be made. A careful man, who has had the run of a propagating establishment for one year, and who has kept his eyes and ears open, will have acquired a theoretical and practical knowledge of the business, sufficient to enable him to operate with success, provided he is of fair intelligence and studious habits. On the other hand, we find hundreds, who have spent the best part of their lives in the trade, whose careless character renders useless the knowledge possessed, when this branch of horticulture is placed in their charge,

I have long held the opinion that the necessary knowledge to successfully propagate plants by cuttings is very simple, and may be easily imparted by writing, even to one having no acquaintance whatever with the operation.

Propagating by cuttings is the way in which the largest number of plants are multiplied. As now understood, this is a simple matter. Formerly no operation in horticulture was more befogged by ignorant pretenders, who, in writing on, or speaking of the subject, so warped the operation with troublesome conditions as to discourage, not only amateurs in horticulture, but inexperienced professional gardeners as well.

One of the first conditions necessary in the propaga-

tion of plants by cuttings is, that the plant from which
the cutting or slip is taken must be in vigorous health.
If weak or tainted by insects or disease, failure is almost
certain to be the result. If, for example, we wish to root
cuttings of greenhouse or bedding plants, such as Bouvardias, Chrysanthemums, Fuchsias, Geraniums, Heliotropes, Salvias, Verbenas, etc., one of the best guides to
the proper condition is, when the cutting breaks or snaps

Fig. 29.—PROPER AND IMPROPER CONDITIONS OF CUTTING.

clean off instead of bending or "kneeing." If it snaps off
so as to break, then it is in condition to root freely; if it
bends, it is too old, and though it will root, it will root
much slower, and make a weaker plant than the slip that
snaps off on being bent. With very few exceptions, and

those of but little importance, cuttings of all kinds root freely from slips taken from the young wood, that is, the young growth, before it gets hardened, and when in the condition indicated by the "snapping test," as it is called.

I believe I was the first to call attention to this valuable test of the condition of the cutting (snapping), in "Practical Floriculture," first published in 1868. A very general idea is current that cuttings must be cut at or below an eye or joint. The practice of this method is not only rarely necessary, but it leads undoubtedly to many cases of failure; not that the cutting at or below a joint either hinders or assists the formation of roots, but from the fact that, when a slip is cut at a joint, the shoot often has become too hard at that point, while at half an inch higher up, or above the joint, the proper condition will be found. I know that it will root, even when in the too hard condition, but the roots emitted will be hard and slender, and, as a consequence, will not be likely to make a plant

Fig. 30.—DAHLIA CUTTING.

of the same vigor as one made from the cutting in the proper state; besides, as the hard cutting takes a longer time to root, its chances of failing from unfavorable atmospheric conditions are thus increased.

Although we have said that cuttings can be as easily

rooted without being cut at a joint as otherwise, yet there are, in some plants, other considerations that necessitate that they should never be cut except at a joint; for example, a Dahlia cutting will root quite as freely, make as fine a flowering plant in fall, and the tuberous roots increase to the full size; but it will not be able to start again in spring, because the Dahlia pushes only from the crown of the root, and if the crown has not been formed from a cutting made close below a joint, as in figure 30, it is worthless, as the tubers and crown formed without an eye possess no latent or dormant buds; hence the importance of always making Dahlia or Clematis cuttings by cutting immediately below an eye, if the roots are wanted for future use.   Plants, such as some species of Bouvardias, Helianthus, Euphorbias, Gypsophila and Anemone, are best increased by cuttings of the roots, which are cut in pieces of an inch or so in length, placed flat together on the propagating

Fig. 31.—ROOT CUTTING.

bench, pressed down and covered slightly with sand or light soil.   Figure 31 shows a root cutting of *Anemone Japonica.*

With these instructions for the proper state of the cutting, I now proceed to describe the medium wherein it is to be placed, and the conditions of temperature, moisture, etc. If these are strictly followed, failure is an impossibility;

for the laws governing the rooting of a slip are as certain as those governing the germination of a seed. In our own practice, when these conditions are strictly followed, failure is unknown, when the cutting or slip is in the proper condition of health.

The best degree of temperature to root cuttings of the great majority of greenhouse and bedding plants is sixty-five degrees of bottom heat, indicated by a thermometer plunged in the sand of the bench, and an atmospheric temperature of fifteen degrees less. A range of ten degrees may be allowed, that is, five degrees lower or five degrees higher; but the nearer the heat of the sar.d can be kept to sixty-five degrees, and that of the rest of the house to fifty degrees, the more perfect the success will be. If a much higher temperature be maintained, it will be at the expense of the ultimate health of the plants. These temperatures refer to propagation under glass from November to April. Of course, when the outside temperature is higher these temperatures cannot be maintained.

Sand is the best medium in which to place cuttings ; color or texture is of no special importance. What we use is the ordinary sand used by builders; this is laid on the hot-bed or bench of the greenhouse, to the depth of about three inches and firmly packed down. When "bottom heat" is wanted, the flue or pipes under the bench of the greenhouse are boarded in, so that the heat strikes the bottom of the bench, thus raising the temperature of the sand. We prefer the bottom of the bench to be of slate, as it is a better conductor than boards; but in the absence of slate, boards will answer.

From the time the cuttings are inserted in the sand until they are rooted, they should never be allowed to get dry; in fact, our practice is, to keep the sand soaked with water until the cutting is just on the point of emitting roots, the cutting bench being watered copiously every

morning, and often, when the atmosphere is dry, again
in the evening, (when the greenhouse is artificially
heated). Kept thus saturated, there is less chance of the
cutting getting wilted, either by heat from the sun or
from fire heat; for if a cutting once gets wilted, its juices
are expended, and it becomes in the condition of a hard
cutting, the condition in which, when bent, it will not snap
nor break, which has already been described. To avoid
this wilting or flagging of the cutting, every means that
will suggest itself to the propagator is to be used. Our
practice is to shade and ventilate in the propagating
house or hot-bed just as soon in the forenoon as the action
of the sun's rays on the glass raises the temperature of
the house to sixty-five or seventy degrees. Of course,
in hot weather the temperature cannot be thus lowered,
and for this reason the propagation of plants is a difficult
matter during the months of June, July and August,
except with such plants as Coleus and others of tropical
origin. In addition to the shading and watering, we
always use in the late spring or summer months, a layer
of paper over the cuttings (kept sprinkled four or five
times a day), until within a few days of their rooting;
this paper is used only on bright days, from ten to four
o'clock. The same plan is followed after the cuttings
are potted off, for four or five days, or until they begin to
strike root into the soil.

This practice of ventilating the propagating house or
hot-bed is, I am aware, not in very common use, many
contending that the place where the propagating is done
should at all times be kept close. I have tried both
methods long enough, and extensively enough, to satisfy
myself beyond all question, that ventilating and propagating at a low temperature, are capable of producing a
larger number of plants during the season than a high
temperature and a close atmosphere. There need be no
failures; and it has the important advantage of produc-

ing a healthy stock, which the close or high temperature system would fail to do in the case of many plants. I have often heard propagators boasting of rooting cuttings in five days. I am well aware that this may be done, but I am also aware that it is often done in damp and cloudy weather at the risk of the whole crop, and it must be done at a high temperature, which at all times causes the plants to draw up slender, and thus impairs their vitality.

FUNGUS OF THE CUTTING BENCH.

Permitting a moderate circulation of air in the propagating house, tends to prevent the germination of that spider-web-like substance, which, for want of a better term, is known among gardeners as the "fungus of the cutting bench." Every one who has had any experience in propagating knows the baneful effects of this ; how that, in one night, it will often sweep off thousands of cuttings that a few hours before were in heathful vigor. But this dangerous enemy of the propagator requires, like vegetation of higher grades, conditions suitable to its development, which are a calm atmosphere, and a temperature above sixty degrees at night, or seventy degrees in day-time. Hence, to avoid this pest, we make every effort, by shading, airing and regulation of fire heat, to keep the atmosphere of the house so that it shall not exceed fifty-five degrees at night, with ten degrees higher in day-time. This, of course, is not practicable when the outside temperature in the shade is above sixty degrees, but the temperature can be reduced considerably by dashing water on the pathways and other parts of the house. It is rarely, however, that the outside temperature ever exceeds sixty degrees at night for any length of time in the vicinity of New York before the middle of May, and all propagating had better be finished previous to that time, unless of tropical plants. In the fall months, about the middle of September, operations in propagating may

again begin. As an additional preventive against the
ravages of the "fungus of the cutting bench," we take
the precaution to scrape off an inch of the sand, after
taking out each batch of cuttings, and replace it with
fresh sand, and, at least twice each season, we remove the
sand that has been in use, wash the benches with hot
lime wash and replace with fresh sand, thus, as far as
possible, destroying the spores or germs of the fungus.

The temperature is prevented from rising in the house
in various ways, some using canvas, or bast matting, or
syringing the glass with a mixture of naphtha and white
lead, made about the color and consistency of thin skim
milk.   We find, however, the best and most convenient
shading to be that formed by flexible screens made of
common lath, planed and attached together like Venetian blinds, the laths being an inch or so apart.   These
can be quickly rolled or unrolled, and give an ever varying modified shade, sufficiently cooling to the house, yet
not darkening the cutting enough to impair its vigor.
These are not unrolled in the morning until the temperature inside indicates it to be necessary (usually about
nine o'clock), and are rolled up in the afternoon as soon
as the sun ceases to shine on the glass, for it is of the
utmost importance that the cuttings receive as much
light as they will bear without becoming wilted. An ob-
jection to these screens, however, is their expense, as they
cost about ten cents per square foot.

The time required by cuttings to root varies from eight
to twenty days, according to the variety, condition of the
cutting and the temperature.   Verbenas, Fuchsias or
Heliotropes, when in proper condition, and kept without
ever being allowed to wilt, will root, in an average bottom
heat of sixty-five degrees, in eight days, while Roses,
Pelargoniums or Petunias will take at least double that
time under the same conditions.

It is best to pot off the cuttings, when rooted, at once,

no matter how small the roots may be; half an inch is a much better length for them to be when potted than two inches, and the operation is much quicker performed when the roots are short, than when long. But the main evils of delaying the potting off of cuttings are, that when left too long, the cuttings grow up weak and spindling, the roots become hard, and do not take as quickly to the pot. Nearly the same care is required in shading and watering the cuttings after potting, as when they are in the cutting bench; for no matter how carefully taken up, in the operation of potting, the delicate roots get more or less injured, and until the cuttings begin to emit new roots, they are nearly as liable to wilt as the unrooted cuttings.

Cuttings should always be placed in small pots, the best size being from two to two and a half inches wide and deep; if placed in larger pots, the soil dries out too slowly and the tender root, imbedded too long in a mass of wet soil, rots, and the plant dies. Though we generally prefer soil to be unsifted in potting large plants, yet for newly-potted cuttings it is better to be sifted fine, not only because it is more congenial thus to the young roots, but also that the operation of potting is quicker done with finely-sifted than with coarse soil.

After potting, the cuttings are placed on benches covered with an inch or so of sand, watered freely with a fine rose watering pot, and shaded for four or five days; by that time they will have begun to root, when no further shading is necessary.

CHAPTER XXV.

"SAUCER SYSTEM" OF PROPAGATION.

The above methods of propagating by cuttings are such as are now practised by commercial florists who have all the needed appliances, but for florists beginning in a small way, or gardeners who have charge of private green-houses, there is usually no necessity for a propagating house, unless the requirements for plants are unusually large, as the "Saucer System" of propagation will answer every purpose, and it is the safest of all methods in inexperienced hands. I was, I believe, the first to introduce this system some twenty years ago, and here repeat the directions first given in one of the horticultural journals at that time :   Common saucers or plates are used to hold the sand in which the cuttings are placed. The sand is put in to the depth of an inch or so, and the cuttings inserted in it close enough to touch each other. The sand is then watered until it becomes of the condition of mud, and placed on the shelf of the greenhouse, or on the window-sill of the sitting room or parlor, fully exposed to the sun, and never shaded. But one condition is essential to success : until the cuttings become rooted the sand must be continually saturated, and kept in the condition of mud ; if once allowed to dry up, exposed to the sun as they are, the cuttings will quickly wilt, and the whole operation will be defeated.

The rules previously laid down for the proper condition of the cuttings are the same in this case, and those for the temperature nearly so ; although, by the saucer system, a high temperature can be maintained without injury, as the cuttings are in reality placed in water, and will not droop at the same temperature as if the sand were kept in the regular condition of moisture maintained in the propagating bench. Still, the detached slip, until rooted, will not endure a continuation of excessive heat, so that we advise, as we do in the regular method of propagating, that the attempt should not be made to root cuttings in this way, in this latitude, in the months of June, July and August, unless with plants of a tropical nature. When the cuttings are rooted, they should be potted in small pots, and treated carefully by shading and watering for a few days, as previously directed. All kinds of plants may be rooted by this method when the young green wood is used, whether of soft wooded plants, such as Fuchsias, Carnations, Geraniums, Heliotropes, etc., or of hard-wooded plants, such as Roses or Azaleas, provided that the same condition of cutting is adhered to as advised for the other methods.

In many of the operations in floriculture, as in vegetable gardening, success or failure depends upon their being done at the proper time, and though it may seem like a needless repetition, I cannot too strongly enforce upon the novice the importance of observing the dates that the experience of our best cultivators has shown to be best under our peculiar climate. Whoever in this matter follows the directions of an English work upon horticulture, will be sure to fall into difficulties, although its teachings may be exactly suited to the English climate. I would here refer to the evils arising from the too common practice of many of our agricultural and horticultural journals, of selecting from English papers articles that often seriously mislead. For example, a Boston magazine a year or two ago copied a long article from the English "Journal of Horticulture," telling us in a very patronizing way how to propagate the Golden Tricolor-leaved Geraniums. The writer laid great stress on having a sharp knife and cutting the slip in a particular manner, then to insert it in silver sand, and a lot of other nonsense that any boy of six months' practice here would have known was absurd ; but, above all, the operation was to be performed in July ! He might have got the sharpest knife that was ever made, and the purest silver sand that ever lay on the seashore, but he would have most likely failed in our climate, if he attempted the work in July. This is only one of scores of such absurd selections as we see yearly in some of our horticultural journals. If the conductors of such have not original matter to fill up with, better far that they leave their pages blank than to show their utter ignorance of what is suitable to our climate.

CHAPTER XXVI.

PROPAGATING SOFT-WOODED PLANTS IN SUMMER.

Every one who has attempted the propagation of plants by cuttings during the high temperature we have in the months of July and August, is aware of the great difficulty experienced in doing so, no matter what system or process is resorted to. In those months, plants of a succulent nature, such as Carnations, Geraniums, Petunias, etc., etc., grow rapidly, and the shoots formed are in consequence watery and soft, so that, when detached from the plant and used for propagation at that hot season of the year, when the thermometer will average seventy-five or eighty degrees in the shade, the chances are that few will root, but will, as gardeners term it, "damp off" in a few days after being put in as cuttings. In ordinary cases, with those having the means of propagating plants, this difficulty of rooting cuttings during the summer months is not of much importance, as florists usually reserve stock enough to enable them to produce all the cuttings they require at the proper season for propagating-namely : September, October and November. But with amateurs, who have but a plant or two of some favorite variety, and who wish to safely increase it, or to the florist wishing to make the most of some valuable importation, this practice, as yet little used, is likely to prove of some benefit, particularly with such plants as the Variegated-leaved Geraniums, like " Mrs. Pollock," " Happy Thought," " Mountain of Snow," etc.   Layering in the usual way, by bending them down to the ground, is, of course, in plants of that habit of growth, all but impracticable.   To take off cuttings would not only enfeeble the plants, but the prospect of rooting these cuttings in hot weather would be nearly hopeless ; so a compromise is made by a method which, for want of a better term, we call " layering in the air." The shoot is "tongued" in the manner of an ordinary layer.   This has the effect to arrest the upward flow of the sap at the incision, which, of course, acting to some extent as if the shoot had been taken off, induces a branching out below the " layer," providing shoots for further operations.   But the effect on the vigor of the plant is much better than if the layer or shoot had been detached ; for, by the time it takes to become hard and form a callus, the shoots branching out below the cut are fit to supply the loss of foliage sustained when the layer or cutting is detached.   The cutting or " layer " is in condition to be cut off in five or six days from the time it has been tongued, and will be found to be not only healed up, or callused, and in such a condition that it will quickly emit roots, but the whole cutting presents a well-ripened, firm condition, not easily described, but readily detected by the practical propagator. When detached, these should be treated in all respects as ordinary cuttings, duly watered and shaded for a few days until they strike out roots, when they are potted off in small pots in the usual manner.   In wet summers we find that many of the plants of the Variegated Zonal Geraniums and Variegated Rose Geraniums, operated on in this manner, produce roots half an inch in length as they hang in the air ; but this is of no special advantage, as we find that those layers that merely heal up and callus make just as fine plants as those that have formed roots before being cut off.

Plants thus formed, make much finer plants than reg-

Fig. 32.—CUTTINGS PARTLY SEVERED.

ular layers, as they are to all intents and purpose cuttings, and consequently, unlike layers, are not long dependent on the parent plant for support, being indebted little or nothing to the old plant during their development.   By this system of propagation, we have often had the satisfaction of doubling our stock of many rare and valuable plants, which it would have been perfectly impracticable to do in the usual manner during the hot months.

Another method of propagating plants in the hot months, which in principle is somewhat similar to that of the plan of "layering in the air," is as follows :

Instead of tonguing the shoot to be used for a cutting, as before, it was merely snapped short off, at a point where the condition of the shoot or slip would make it hang on to the plant by the merest shred of bark, as shown in figure 32. Slight as this strip of bark appears to be, it is sufficient to sustain the cutting, without any material injury from wilting, until it forms the "callus," or granulated condition, which usually preceeds the formation of roots.   The cutting or slip may be detached in from eight to twelve days, after it has been broken in the manner described ; and then potted in two or three inch pots.   If watered and shaded rather less than required by ordinary cuttings, it will form roots in eight or twelve days more, and not one in a hundred will fail, even of plants of the Tricolor Geraniums, which we all know are difficult to root under the ordinary modes of propagation, particularly in hot weather.   We recently propagated in this way nearly 10,000 plants of the Tricolor class, with a loss of but one per cent.; had we adopted the ordinary method, even with the plants in good condition, our experience has shown that a loss of at least ninety per cent. might have been expected.

This plan is applicable to many other plants besides Geraniums. The following may be propagated with great certainty by this method, using the young unripened shoots : Abutilons, Begonias, Carnations, Heliotropes, Crotons, Cactus of all kinds, Lantanas, Oleanders, Petunias (double), Pelargoniums, or Geraniums of all sorts, Poinsettias, together with nearly all kinds of plants of a woody or succulent character.   Besides the absolute certainty of having the cuttings root by this method, it has another most important advantage :   All propagators know that many kinds of plants when cut back for cuttings, become weakened so much that, if not carefully handled, they may die ; also if two or three crops of cuttings are taken off as they grow, the cuttings are weakened and the "stock plant" becomes permanently injured. By this method of breaking the slip, so that it hangs by a shred to the parent plant, the roots have to use their functions for its support nearly the same as if it remained entirely attached to the plant.   This results, exactly as we wish, in causing the parent plant to strike out shoots below the broken slip, and these again, in their turn, can be so treated.   I may say that, in certain conditions of the shoot, instead of snapping, it will "knee" or bend only ; in such cases, it will be necessary to slip it two-thirds through with a knife, but in most instances it will snap and hang by the shred of bark, which is the best condition.

CHAPTER XXVII.

PROPAGATION OF ROSES BY CUTTINGS.

As the propagation of Roses by cuttings is a matter of very wide-spread interest, I will give a special description of our method.   The rule that applies to the proper condition of soft-wooded plants, such as Fuchsias, Heliotropes or Verbenas (that is, that the young shoot should be in a state to snap or break off instead of bending), does not apply to the proper condition of Rose cuttings.   The young shoot of the Rose is also what is to be used, but it must be hard and woody.   For example, when a Rosebud is developed enough to be cut, the shoot on which it grows is in about the right condition for cuttings, each leaf of the shoot, with its bud at the axil, and two or three

inches of stem, making a cutting ; that is what is called
a single eye cutting. They are simply made by making one rather slanting cut between the joints, or about
half an inch above the eye. About one-third of the leaf
is cut off, mainly for the purpose of allowing more cuttings to be put in the cutting bench. If by any accident the leaf is taken off, the Rose cutting in this condition will never root to make a good plant ; or if, from any
cause, the leaves drop off while the cuttings are in process of rooting, not one in ten will ever make a satisfactory plant. Besides the method of using cuttings made
from one eye or bud, the " blind wood," so called (that
is, the shoots that do not produce flower buds), is also
used, and generally makes the safest and best kind of cuttings, as these blind shoots are hard and slender, and
root rather quicker than cuttings made from single eyes.
These shoots are usually too short-jointed to be made into
single eye cuttings, and have often two or more eyes to
the cutting ; but the foliage should be shortened off about
one-third, as in the single eye cuttings. A good length
for a Rose cutting is three inches, though in some short-
jointed kinds no more than one inch in length of cutting
can be obtained.

There is no difficulty in propagating Roses from cuttings of young wood, if it is grown under glass, any time
from September to May (provided the plants are entirely
vigorous and healthy; if affected with red spider, mildew
or other disease, failure to root cuttings satisfactorily will
be certain); during the months of June, July and August,
it is a process requiring great care and attention. We,
however, grow hundreds of thousands in this way by the
following method : About the middle of May we plant
out our "stock plants," so called, though they are young
plants from three-inch pots (that have been rooted in the
January previous) on the greenhouse benches, in three
or four inches of rather poor soil, containing not a par-

ticle of manure, the object being to produce a hard and slender woody growth of cuttings, instead of a soft and pithy one. Obtaining cuttings of this kind, there is no difficulty in rooting them, if the proper attention to shading and watering, already described, has been given. I will state, however, that after they are potted off, carefully shading from the hot sun is necessary until the root strikes through to the side of the pot. I have found it to be a great help in propagating in summer, to sift a thin layer of fine moss, sawdust, or cocoanut fibre, over the Rose cuttings after potting. This keeps them moist, acting as a mulch, and also, after they have rooted, it keeps them cool in hot weather, both materials being excellent non-conductors.

It is a curious fact that, no matter how healthy Rose cuttings may be when growing in the open ground, they can rarely be got in condition, during the summer months, to root. I have tried them at all seasons and in all conditions, but do not think I ever made a success during the months of June, July, or August. They invariably drop their leaves, and this means failure every time. Why they should do so more than those grown inside, I have never yet been able to discover, but that such are the facts, any one trying it will very quickly find out. My experience in this matter has been confined to the latitude of New York. I believe that in some sections of the country, when the shoots become better ripened, they may be successfully propagated from outdoor wood in the summer.

Hybrid Perpetual, and even Monthly Roses, however, can be propagated from cuttings of well-ripened hard wood grown in the open ground, put in in October or November in any place (a cold greenhouse or a cold frame), where they can be kept just above the freezing point at night—say from thirty-two to forty degrees, with ten to fifteen degrees more during the day. They must not get much

frost, though a few degrees would do no harm, except to
retard them; but artificial heat above forty degrees for
any length of time to hard-wood cuttings is almost certain to destroy them.   I remember, some years ago, my
foreman insisted that we should put in a lot of prunings
of several new Hybrid Perpetual Roses that we had received in December from Europe, in our regular propagating house.   I told him it was useless, but he insisted
on being allowed to try.   I gave him the privilege, provided he did the work in his own time at night.   He worked
most diligently, and got three or four of the hands to help
him for a week at nights.   He had some 20,000 cuttings
in the propagating bench, where the temperature of the
sand marked sixty-five degrees.   The cuttings threw out
shoots an inch in length, callused beautifully, and up to
that point, any one who had not gone through the thing
before, would have said that the operation was a success.
One morning, about ten days after putting them in, he
called me to witness his victory ; but I astounded him by
saying, that for every plant he made from the 20,000 cuttings I would give him twenty-five cents.   He watched
and redoubled his care ; but it was no use.   In less than
a month every cutting had blackened and rotted.

Had the temperature of the sand never exceeded forty
degrees, a large proportion would have rooted ; but it
would have taken three or four months to do so; and then
the results are never so satisfactory as when cuttings are
made from the green wood, taken from plants growing
under glass.   When, however, there is no greenhouse at
hand, but only cold frames, such as are used for Cabbage,
Lettuce, Pansy, or Daisy plants, the hard-wood cuttings
of Roses placed in such in October, if not too much
frozen, will be rooted by April.   One of our market gardeners here has followed the plan for twenty years.   His
cold frames, where he keeps his Cabbage plants, are well
sheltered, and he roots thousands of Hybrid Perpetual

Rose cuttings by simply sticking them between the rows of Cabbage plants.   He thus gets four or five hundred in a three by six sash without serious detriment to the Cabbage plants, as the cuttings are leafless, and look like dried sticks until the Cabbage plants are taken out in spring.   The cuttings then begin to leaf out, and are rooted sufficiently to pot by the 1st of May.

PROPAGATING ROSES IN THE SOUTHERN STATES.

The method of propagating Roses at the South is very simple, particularly in the vicinity of Charleston, S. C., Savanna, Ga., or in almost any part of Florida.   There, the long, heated summers raise the temperature of the sandy soil as high as that of the atmosphere at night in the winter months, if not higher, forming, in fact, a sort of natural hot-bed.   All that is necessary to do in such a case is to make cuttings of Roses, either Monthly or Hybrid Perpetual, in lengths of five or six inches, and make a trench deep enough to plant them, leaving only one or two eyes or buds above ground.   Care must be taken to firm the cuttings well in with the foot, so as to exclude the air.   The cuttings may be set in the trenches four to six inches apart, and two or three feet between the lines. Cuttings of Roses planted in this way, in these or similar localities, in November and December, will form roots by February or March ; and if left to grow where they were placed, without being disturbed, will have made growths of from one to five feet by the following September, according to the variety or class.   The cuttings of Roses grown South are best got from the North.

PROPAGATION BY LAYERING.

Propagation by layering in the usual way, in the soil, is but little practised now-a-days, since the ways of rooting plants by cuttings have been so greatly simplified ; but occasionally some one may want a few plants of a

Rose or other shrub growing in the open ground who has not other ways of propagation at command, when this method may be safely adopted.

Although layering may be done with the ripened wood of vines or shrubs of the growth of the previous season, yet it is preferable to use the shoot of the present year in its half-green state ; for example, a Rose or flowering shrub is pruned in the usual way in spring ; by June or July it will have made strong shoots, one, two or three feet in length from or near the base of the plant. Take the shoot then in the left hand (after having stripped it of its leaves for a few inches on each side of where it is to be cut), keep the fingers under the shoot, and make a clean cut on the upper part, an inch or so in length, and to about half the thickness of the shoot, then slightly twist the " tongue " or cut part to one side. Having opened a shallow trench, fasten the branch down with a hooked peg, and cover with earth. It is a good plan to place a flat stone over the buried part of the layer, to prevent the soil from drying out.

This plan of cutting the shoot on the upper side, I have never seen in illustrations showing the manner of layering, it being usually made either on the side or below ; but I have found in practice, that it is much the safest plan, as the " tongue," when cut on the top part of the shoot, has far less chance of being broken off.

PROPAGATION BY LAYERING IN POTS.

This is the process of layering shoots or runners of plants in pots, so that, when the root forms in the pot, the plant can be detached without injury to it, as the roots are confined exclusively to the soil in the pot. Layering plants in pots can be done with Roses, vines or shrubs of any kind, with always more certainty of making a plant quicker than by the ordinary way of layering the shoot in the soil, because when lifted there is no disturbance of the roots. This method of propagating Strawberries has been largely practised during the past ten years in the United States, and is now a favorite method.

CHAPTER XXVIII.

PROPAGATING ROSES BY GRAFTING AND BUDDING.

This is the system almost entirely used in Europe, and although it has the disadvantage of necessitating watchfulness in removing the suckers that come from the stock, it is no doubt the quickest way that new varieties can be increased ; besides, in many weak-growing kinds, it imparts greater vigor to the plant. We have found it to be the only method of renewing the weakened vitality of kinds that have been injured by over propagation from cuttings, or by continuous forcing for winter flowers, which is well known has so weakened many of the kinds used for that purpose, that failures the past few years have increased largely. The main reason why the grafted plant imparts greater vigor is, that the operation, as usually performed, compels the stock to be rested for several months ; it is well known that, in the way Roses are usually propagated from cuttings, they are taken from plants that have had no rest. If we would attain the greatest vigor in a Rose plant, a proper amount of rest is imperatively demanded. The "Manetti" is the stock most generally preferred for grafting or budding roses. They are usually imported from England, costing $6 to $7 per 1,000. When received in November, they are potted in three inch pots, kept free from fire heat, in cold houses or frames, or covered by leaves in the open ground, until January, February, or March. The operation of grafting is very simple, and is done by the method shown in the engravings, figure 33; it is the simple "splice graft," or "whip graft." In our opinion, it makes no difference what form is used, provided that care is taken that a complete junction is made on at least one side; if on both sides, all the better. After the graft has been placed on the stock, it is carefully tied up with Raffia, so as to exclude the air and keep the graft in place. Some prefer to cover the tie with grafting-wax, but that is not indispensable.

The temperature of the greenhouse or frame, in which the operation of grafting Roses is done, may run from

Fig. 33.—GRAFTING THE ROSE.

sixty to seventy degrees at night, with ten degrees higher during the day, but it is absolutely indispensable to success that the pots should be so plunged that a bottom heat of at least five degrees higher than the air of the house can be given. This must be done, or there will not be complete success. This bottom heat can be secured either by the hot water pipes, or by the ordinary hot-bed, or by using a foot or so of hot manure placed on the benches in the greenhouse; we ourselves use the latter plan, enclosing the manure by sashes, so as to exclude the air until the grafts have "taken." That plants can be quicker made by grafting than by cuttings, there is no question. When the American Beauty Rose was first sent out in 1885, our propagations from cuttings made in August of that year, grown with all possible care, did not attain half the size or vigor at a year old that grafts put on Manetti stocks in March, 1886, made in five months. In other words, the cutting plants required only an eight-inch pot in August, while the grafted plants required a ten-inch pot, being nearly twice the height and twice the breadth.

Budding Roses is usually performed on stocks planted out in the open ground in July and August, or as late as the buds will take ; the bud is usually placed low enough on the stock, so that it can be earthed up to protect it in winter. Generally only the hardy or Hybrid Perpetual Roses are thus budded. It is practised to only a slight extent by some of our florists and nurserymen in the United States, as our climate is not so suitable for the work as that of England or France; besides, the low rates at which Roses are now sold in Europe, make the operation of budding Roses in the open ground no longer profitable here, on account of our higher rates of labor.

CHAPTER XXIX

PLANTS MOST IN DEMAND IN MARKET IN SPRING.

GROWN IN GREENHOUSES.

These plants are grown in pots in greenhouses, and I will arrange them, as nearly as possible, in the order of their importance in the New York markets, which is perhaps, as good a criterion as can be fixed upon for the whole country.

Roses.—These, comprising both Monthly and Hybrid Perpetual sorts, are usually sold in four, five or six inch pots, and when sold in open market must be in bud or bloom, as few market buyers know anything of Roses by name, hence the color must be shown. There are two methods of growing Roses for market purposes ; that yet most used by florists is, to plant the young Roses that have been propagated in spring, in the open ground in May, lifting when they have attained their growth in October or November, and placed in four, five or six inch pots, according to the size of the plants. The plants are then placed in cold pits, or cold greenhouses, where the temperature at night runs from thirty-five to forty-five degrees, with ten degrees higher in day-time, as for the best development of strong root-growth the temperature must be kept low. After the pots are filled with healthy white roots, which will be about the end of February or March, they may be given a temperature of ten degrees higher, but great care must be taken to avoid too high a temperature until they have formed roots, or the chances are if they do not die outright they will be so enfeebled as to be worthless. The Tea or Monthly Roses require a higher temperature than the Hybrid Perpetuals.

The best monthly kinds for market are : Hermosa, Agrippina, Perle des Jardins, Sunset, Bennett, American Beauty, The Bride, Chas. Rivoli, Duchess de Brabant, Marie Guilott, Souvenir d'un Ami, and La Phœnix. These comprise all shades of color, are all free blooming, of easy growth. For full descriptions, see florists' catalogues.

Of the hardy Hybrid Perpetual class, the following are found to be the freest blooming, and having the greatest variety of color that can be had in a dozen sorts. Baroness Rothschild, Merveille de Lyon, Anna de Diesbach, Magna Charta, Ball of Snow, Jacqueminot, Paul Neron, Auguste Mie, Marie Bauman, Madam Gabriel Luizet, Louis Van Houtte and Pæonia. For descriptions, see catalogues.

Of Climbing Roses there are only some few desirable

'ones that are hardy in this latitude, among which are the Blush and Crimson Boursalt, Russell's Cottage, Prairie Queen and Baltimore Belle.

Of the monthly varieties of Climbing Roses there is a greater variety of color, but none of these are sufficiently hardy to stand our winters north of Richmond, Va. Among the best of the Climbing Monthly Roses are : The New Waltham, Gloire de Dijon, James Sprunt, Mareschal Niel, Setina, Lamarque, Madam Berrard and Cloth of Gold; these represent all colors. Descriptions will be found in the catalogues. Next in importance as a market plant, is the

Zonal Geranium (*Pelargonium zonale*).—Properly called, if we followed strict botanical correctness, " Pelargonium." The true genus Geranium, being herbaceous perennial plants, natives of nearly all parts of this country ; but common usage has dubbed the *Zonale Pelargonium* "Geranium," both here and in England, and it would only lead to confusion to use the true botanical name now. Of this, the grandest of all our summer flowering plants, or, for that matter, of winter flowering, there are now hundreds of varieties under name, both double, semi-double and single, running through all shades from pure white to pink, to scarlet, to crimson, in every gradation of shade. It is useless here to name varieties ; the catalogues teem with new and improved kinds each year, and we again refer the reader to these. In our own business, we find the sale for Geraniums increasing more rapidly than that of any other plant we grow, particularly for the semi-double kinds, which flower, many of them, quite as freely as the single kinds, and have the merit of not dropping their petals when cut or when dashed with rain. From the cuttings made during winter, we repot and harden off our "stock" plants in cold frames, so that we can with safety plant them

out in the open ground here the first week in May; this
can be done in this latitude with perfect safety, provided
the plants have been well hardened, as when thus hardened, even if the thermometer falls to the freezing point,
which it sometimes does with us in the first week in
May, they will not be injured.   We generally plant them
in beds, eighteen inches apart each way, so that they can
be easily worked by the wheel hoe, and also to give them
room enough to develop the shoots from which the cuttings are to be taken in the fall.   I find it best to take off
the cuttings at different times, two or three weeks apart,
to guard against accident.   While the Geranium roots
freely at certain seasons, when the conditions are all
right, yet I have seen a batch of 10,000 cuttings nearly
all fail.   They were put in in September, when the
plants were growing vigorously, and the shoots full of
sap.   The time to put in the cuttings should be chosen
after a spell of dry weather, such as would harden
and to some extent ripen the growth.   Cuttings in this
condition, put in in the usual way the first week in October, will root freely in ten or twelve days, although cuttings taken from the plant the first week in November
will be still safer.   There is an advantage in having
them early, however, as each plant can be doubled or
quadrupled by taking the tops from the plants as they
grow.   Geraniums are sold usually in four and five inch
pots; it is a great saving in weight to use as small a pot
as it is possible in which to flower the plants, but
such plants as Geraniums must have plenty of food, else
they will not develop flowers freely.   A good plan, when
the pot is full of roots, and it is wished to dispense with
a further shift into a larger pot, is to "top dress" the
pot with a compost of six parts soil, six parts rotted
manure and one part bone; "top dressing" is the removal of an inch or so of the exhausted soil from the top
of the pot and replacing with this mixture.   We use this

plan with Roses and many other plants with excellent results.

The Fancy Pelargoniums (*Pelargonium grandiflorum*), or "Lady Washington Geraniums," as they are called in most of the Eastern States, require in all respects nearly the same culture as the Zonal, except that they are best kept in pots during summer when wanted for stock.

Fuchsias, Heliotropes, Lantanas and Petunias require a little higher temperature than Geraniums, but their general culture is very similar when grown during the winter for market ; but Astilbe (incorrectly *Spiræa*), Carnations, Dicentra, Feverfew, Hollyhocks, Pinks, and all other half-hardy plants, should be treated like Roses— that is, kept in a low temperature, thirty-five or forty-five degrees at night in winter, until they have formed new roots.   The use of Hollyhocks as market plants may be known to few of our readers, but the new Dwarf Holly-hock, "Crimson Pyramid," has proved excellent for that purpose in the New York markets, and if, as is likely to be the case, it comes to " break " into all the colors of the Hollyhock, we will here have a grand and showy feature in our market flowers.   The seed of the Hollyhock, " Crimson Pyramid," if sown in August, will give plants strong enough to be suitable for five or six inch pots by November, when they should be kept in a cool green-house or frame until March, when, if started in heat of sixty degrees at night, they will flower abundantly by the middle or end of May.   This Hollyhock grows to a height of twelve to fifteen inches, forming a well-defined pyramid, clothed from base to summit with rich, crim-son semi-double flowers.   Although it can be propagated from cuttings, it is best grown from seeds, which it produces freely in July and August.

CHAPTER XXX.

THE CULTIVATION OF THE VERBENA.

This would seem to require a special chapter. Comparatively few florists have success in growing it, and as I have grown it successfully for upwards of thirty years, I have confidence, if the instructions here given are strictly followed, that it can be successfully grown anywhere and by any one. The principal trouble in growing the Verbena is, to prevent it from being attacked by the insect which produces the black rust, or Verbena disease, as it is sometimes called. I will make the starting point the first of April. At that date take cuttings from healthy plants ; see that they are taken in the condition described in the chapter on Propagation—that is, that they are in such a state that they will break on being bent. They will root fit to be potted off in eight or ten days, and will be fine, healthy plants to put in the open ground in thirty days after. Verbenas are not at all particular about soil, provided it is not water-soaked ; we have planted them on soils varying from almost pure sand to heavy clay, and, provided it was enriched by manure, there was but little difference in the growth or bloom. Planted out in May, by August they will have spread to an extent of three feet, the plants profusely covered with flowers and seed-pods. Now at this time, say the middle of August, this profuse flowering and seeding of course lessens the vitality of the plant and puts it in the condition to invite the attack of the insect which causes the rust. To sustain the vitality of the plant and recuperate its exhausted forces, we cut back the extremities of the shoots some six inches, in all plants from which we design to propagate, free the plants of decayed leaves, and thin out where too thick at the center. Then we fork up the soil around each plant, adding a compost of equal parts of fresh soil and rotted manure to the depth of two or three inches. Young shoots, as they develop, root into this with avidity, producing a soft and healthy growth, which, by the first or middle of October, gives us just the style of cutting we require. Now the process of propagation begins, which may be carried on either in the propagating house in the usual way, or by the saucer system, as before described; but by whichever method the propagation is effected, let me again mention the importance of taking the cutting in that succulent condition in which it will snap on being bent.

Do not attempt to pot the old plant, or the layers of the Verbena, or even to take a shoot for a cutting which has formed a root in the ground; for in most cases the roots so formed are so low down that the shoot is hard and woody at that point, and will not be likely to produce such roots as will give a healthy growth. It is by starting wrong in the fall, and impairing the vitality of the plant and placing it in an enfeebled state, that disease is invited.

In the directions given in the chapter on Propagation great importance is attached to the necessity of potting off cuttings immediately after being rooted. If this is necessary with any plant, it is especially so with the Verbena, as no plant is more susceptible of injury from allowing the roots to become elongated and hardened in the cutting bench. Cuttings thus neglected make hard, slim plants, which, even if they do escape the insect pest, are not likely to make thrifty plants. On potting the cuttings, they are placed in a greenhouse or frame, and shaded in the usual way for two or three days, or as long as the condition of the weather may require. As soon as they have struck root in the soil of the pots, they should be kept cool, and abundantly supplied with air.

Fire heat need only be given sufficient to keep them

above forty-five degrees, and if a temperature can be sustained throughout the entire winter months averaging fifty degrees, at night, and not to exceed fifteen degrees higher during the day until the middle of March, there is no doubt whatever of having a healthy and vigorous stock, providing proper attention has been given to watering and to fumigation by tobacco.

Continued fumigation is of the utmost importance in the culture of all plants under glass, but it is perfectly indispensable to the welfare of the Verbena. In all our Verbena houses we fumigate, on an average, two or three times each week ; we do not wait to see the *aphis* or Green-fly, but apply the antidote solely as a preventive. No omission is so inexcusable as that of permitting plants to be injured by this insect.

Although I have elsewhere stated (see chapter on Insects) that the very minute one which produces the troublesome " black rust" on the Verbena seems invulnerable to the fumes of tobacco smoke, yet I have a belief that our unremitting practice of fumigating may be, after all, the true reason of our comparative exemption from its attack ; for although this insect may have the faculty of imbedding itself in the leaf on the approach of danger, its eggs, being stationary and exposed, may be destroyed by the action of the smoke ; at all events, we have repeatedly brought varieties of Verbena severely affected by the rust into our collection, which in a few weeks appeared entirely free from the disease, showing that our treatment, in some way or other, destroyed the enemy.

There is no question that this insect, so fatal to the health of the Verbena, is most active and destructive in a high temperature ; hence we find that whenever Verbenas are kept in a mixed greenhouse collection, where Fuchsias, Pelargoniums, Heliotrope, etc., are grown (usually in night temperature of fifty-five or sixty degrees), the Verbena becomes affected by black rust, showing that its minute enemy is at work sapping its life current.

Verbenas, whether grown for sale or for private use, if we would have plants in fine health and vigor in May, should not be propagated sooner than January. To be sure, the "stock" plants, to produce the cuttings, must be raised previous, in October or November, but such plants become exhausted by spring and are inferior to later propagations. The "stock" plants, from which we propagate, are usually thrown away by March 1st.

In our own practice the necessities of our business require us to put in an almost uniform number of cuttings every two weeks from November to April ; the last lot, which we pot off at the end of April, usually making the finest plants. For the raising of Verbenas from seed, see chapter on Propagation by Seeds.

CHAPTER XXXI.

THE PLANTS MOST SOLD IN MARKET IN SPRING.

GROWN IN COLD FRAMES.

Pansies are the most important of the millions of plants raised in cold frames now sold each spring. For our manner of raising, see " Pansies " in chapter entitled " Propagation by Seeds." Also, for manner of constructing " cold frames," see chapter under that head.

Daisies are usually raised by setting out the stock plants in spring in some cool and partially shaded place. If they grow freely, each single plant set out in spring will divide to a dozen or more, ready to be set out in the cold frames in September or October. Very good varieties can also be raised from seed, particularly the double white, by sowing seed in August and transplanting to cold frames in October. We ourselves raise tens of thousands in this way, as we have not suitable soil to keep the established kinds, that are propagated by division, alive through the hot summer.

Cowslips, Primroses and Auriculas are beautiful spring plants, when kept over as are Pansies in cold frames. They are also increased by division, like the Daisy, but the process is slow and they are often, like the Daisy, difficult to keep through our hot and dry summers, but they can all be easily raised from seed, which should be sown about the same time in spring as we sow the Chinese Primula. See Chapter 22 on Propagation by Seeds.

Myosotis (Forget-Me-Nots).—When wintered over in cold frames, the Forget-me-nots bloom freely in early spring. They can easily be kept over the summer by planting in some cool, partially shaded place, and increased by dividing in fall, or they may be grown from seed, exactly as recommended for Cowslip or Primrose.

In addition to the plants just named as being grown in cold frames, to bloom in early spring, the following half hardy plants that bloom later in the season can all best be raised from seed and grown in cold frames during winter: Aquilegia, Delphinium, Digitalis and Hollyhocks. Although these are all hardy in this latitude, we find that better plants can be had the first season from seed by protecting them in cold frames. The distance apart at which plants are set in cold frames must be governed by the size and kinds; we ourselves plant from 100 to 200 in a three by six foot sash.

CHAPTER XXXII.

PLANTS MOST IN DEMAND FOR WINDOW DECORATION IN WINTER.

For this purpose most kinds of plants should be grown in pots during the summer ; it is more troublesome to obtain good results by lifting plants in the fall that have been planted in the open ground, although such plants as Bouvardias, Carnations and Chrysanthemums, if lifted carefully and placed in pots in September or October, and shaded until they have taken root, will do quite as well as if they had been grown in pots during the summer, but Abutilons, Azaleas, Begonias, Cinerarias, Calceolarias, Chinese Primulas, Callas, Crotons, Camellias, Daphnes, Dracenas, Fuchsias, Ferns, Geraniums, Genistas, Heliotropes, Impatiens, Jessamines, Libonias, Palms, Salvias, Solanums, Tropæolums, and Roses, all of which are suitable as decorative plants for greenhouse, parlor, or sitting-room, in winter, had all better be grown in pots during the summer, shifted, of course, as their necessities require, into larger pots.   On an average, six-inch pots would be sufficiently large to flower them in during winter, though strong growing species may be grown to a size requiring eight or nine inch pots.   All the plants named above, with the exception of Bouvardias, Begonias, Crotons, Dracenas, Ferns, Palms and Salvias, will do well in a temperature of fifty degrees at night, with ten to fifteen degrees higher in the day-time; these last named will require about ten degrees higher. Nearly all plants grown inside in winter, require great care in watering.   Very little injury can be done to plants by being freely watered when growing vigorously in bright weather from May to October, but in the dull, dark days from November to March, it is better to adopt the safe old rule never to water a plant unless the surface

of the soil of the pot or bench indicates that it is dry by
becoming lighter in color; then water may be given
freely, provided that there is sufficient drainage to allow
it to pass off readily.   Avoid manure water and all stimu-
lants to plants in winter, until the days begin to lengthen
and the sun gets to be brighter in February.

The insects that attack plants used for winter decoration are, principally, the *aphis*, or Green-fly, the
Red-spider, and the Mealy-bug.   The first is easily
killed or warded off by the use of tobacco, either as
smoke, dust, or steeped so as to form a liquid of the
color of strong tea.   The Red-spider is not so easily dis-
lodged, and can only be kept under by continued sponging of the leaves, mainly on the under side, or by heavy
syringing.   The Mealy-bug is the most difficult of all
insects to get rid of, but the use of Fir tree oil, diluted
in the proportion of one pint of the oil to five gallons of
water, if syringed on the plants once a week, will entirely
suppress the Mealy-bug; for small lots, dipping the plants
into the mixture is the best way.   We have found the
use of Fir tree oil, diluted as above, an excellent means
of keeping down the ravages of all insect life by steadily
syringing with it at least once each week.   For further
instructions, see chapter on Insects.

CHAPTER XXXIII.

CULTURE OF WINTER FLOWERING PLANTS FOR CU . FLOWERS.

Since the first edition of "Practical Floriculture" was
written, in 1868, the varieties of plants used for cut
flowers in winter, as well as the methods of culture, have
so changed that the instructions then given would be of
but little use now.   Camellia flowers that were then the
most valued, are now almost entirely discarded.   Tube-

roses that averaged $8 per 100 from November to June, are now hardly salable at any price in the vicinity of New York, Boston or Philadelphia. Rose buds have for the past ten years nearly supplanted all else in the way of cut flowers, and still continue to do so, many hundreds of acres of greenhouses now being used for their culture. As Roses, then, are the most important of all flowers for this purpose, I will begin with their culture, following with the other plants used for cut flowers in winter, in the order of their present importance.

CHAPTER XXXIV.

ROSE GROWING IN WINTER.

To propagate the plants to produce Roses in winter, strong, healthy cuttings are put in to root at any time from September to February. We keep the sand in our cutting benches about sixty-five or seventy degrees Fahr., with the temperature of the house ten degrees less. Rose cuttings, under these conditions (if the cuttings have been taken from plants in vigorous growth, and are free from mildew and insects), will root in from twenty to twenty-five days, and are then potted in any good soil, in two and a half inch pots, and placed in a greenhouse having a night temperature of about fifty-five degrees, with ten to fifteen degrees more in the day-time. (See chapter on Propagation of Plants.)

The young Roses are regularly shifted into larger pots as soon as the "ball" gets filled with roots, great care being taken that the plants at no time get pot-bound. Syringing is done once a day to keep down red spider, and fumigating by burning tobacco stems to kill the *aphis* or Green-fly must be done twice a week. With such attention, plants which were put in as cuttings at the seasons named above, by the middle of June will be from one to one foot and a half in height, with roots enough to fill a six-inch pot. I may state that when shifted from a four-inch to a six-inch pot, two inches of drainage is used, so that when the roses are planted in the shallow benches, the "ball" of roots taken from the six-inch pot will be but four inches deep, or about the depth of the soil of the bench. They should at this date, or before, be placed out-of-doors, and stood on rough gravel or cinders, so as to make certain of free drainage. It is not the universal practice to put Roses out in the open air ; in some sections, particularly in the vicinity of salt water, it is almost impossible to keep them clear of mildew when placed out of doors in summer, so that now some of our largest and most successful growers keep them all the time under glass, giving as much ventilation as possible.

If intended to be grown in pots, the shifting into larger pots should be repeated whenever the ball gets filled with roots (which is usually in about four or five weeks after every shift), until the 1st of October, when they will have reached a size requiring a pot of eight or nine inches in diameter. These pots should be amply drained with broken pots or charcoal, using soil composed of three parts decomposed sod from a good loamy soil to one of well-rotted cow manure, or the soil hereafter advised for benches will do equally well. They are then in condition for winter forcing, no further shifting being required. But if they are to be planted out on benches, or in solid beds of soil, the planting should be made from the pots from the 1st of June to the 15th of August, but the sooner the better.

SOLID BEDS AND RAISED BENCHES.

There is quite a difference of opinion as to whether Roses can be best grown in solid beds or on raised benches. We believe that it really makes but little difference, as we find them grown with nearly equal success by both methods where drainage is perfect, although the method mainly in use in the vicinity of New York (where Roses are at present better grown than in any other section of the country), is the raised bench system. There is no doubt, however, that the raised bench plan is much more expensive, as it is found (to have the best results), that the plants must be renewed each year ; that is, that the young plants that have been propagated in January and grown on in pots and planted out in June or July, to produce flowers during the fall, winter, and spring months, must be thrown away in May or June and new beds formed with fresh soil, replanted again as before with young plants, and so on each season ; occasionally crops are carried over for two or three years on the raised benches, but rarely with as good results. The small quantity of soil gets exhausted, and, besides, there is a greater chance for injury from the rose bug the second season on raised benches, which, however, is not so much the case when planted in solid benches, as in that case the roots get stronger and deeper. It is my impression that even Tea Roses will yet be mainly grown in solid benches. There are many instances of marked success by this plan. One of my near neighbors has had a fixed roof greenhouse eighteen by seventy feet, heated by a flue, planted over twenty years ago with Tea Roses, that is yet in the highest condition of health and vigor, giving abundance of grand buds throughout the entire season. They were planted originally one foot apart, but have been cut out so that they stand three feet apart and are now bushes six feet high. No pruning is done except to shorten the shoots when they get against the glass, and to thin out the weak shoots. The most approved greenhouses used for Rose growing in winter are about twenty feet wide, and are what is known as three-quarter span (see

Fig. 34.—PERSPECTIVE VIEW OF ROSE HOUSE. 350 FEET LONG BY 20 FEET WIDE.

Greenhouse Structures); that is, three-quarters of the glass roof slopes to the south at an angle of about thirty degrees, while the other quarter slopes north at an angle of twenty degrees, giving a base space for the benches on which the Roses are to be planted (taking out the walks), of about fifteen feet. The benches may be either a level platform, or divided into four or five platforms about three feet wide, or so as to be at about equal distances from the glass (see end section, Greenhouse Structures); the bottom of the benches may be from three, four, or five to six feet from the glass, as desired.

Fig. 34 shows a perspective view of a Rose house put up for us on Jersey City Heights, N.J., in 1884, by

Fig. 35.—CROSS-SECTION OF ROSE HOUSE.

Lord & Burnham. The length is 350 feet by 20 feet in width. It is believed to be as near what the best model of a Rose house should be as has been constructed. The frame is of iron throughout; the glass used is double-thick, second quality French, size twenty by twelve, put in the twelve way. The heating is done by steam, the eleven dots indicating the number of one and a quarter inch steam pipes (see cross-section figure 35). Although eleven pipes are put in, not more than eight or nine of these are used, unless in extraordinarily severe weather, the others being shut off by valves. The two boilers used are Lord & Burnham's No. 5. The cost of a Rose house of this style, complete in everything, at present prices, is about twenty dollars per running foot, or $7,000 for the 350 feet; if the frame had been constructed of wood it would cost ten to fifteen per cent. less.

There is no necessity for bottom heat for Roses, so that it is best to have the pipes for heating run under the front and back benches of the rose house, with none under the middle benches, as in this way the space under the middle benches may be utilized for other purposes.

VENTILATION

is an important matter. In a rose house twenty feet wide, sufficient ventilation will be obtained by having lifting sashes, to the width of thirty inches, placed along the whole of the roof on the south side, hinging them so that they will open at the ridge pole. For this purpose the patent ventilating apparatus should be used, which costs from fifty to sixty cents per running foot.

SOIL AND BENCHES.

The soil in which the Roses are to be grown should not exceed five inches in depth, the boards being so arranged as to allow free drainage for the water. Perhaps the best way to make the bottom of the bench is to use wall strips or other boards, not to exceed four inches wide, leaving a space of at least half an inch between the boards or strips, so as to make certain of perfect drainage. The bottom is first covered with thin sods, grass side down, or what in our opinion is better, the new packing material called "Excelsior," and then the soil is placed on to the depth of four inches. This soil is made from sods cut three or four inches thick from any good, loamy pasture land, well chopped up, and mixed with one-fourth of well-rotted cow dung to three-fourths of sods. In our own practice we use, in addition to the cow manure, one-thirtieth part of pure bone dust. It is perhaps best to let the sod be well rotted before it is used, although, if this be not convenient, it will do fresh, if well chopped up. Of late years we have used the Acme harrow to break and mix up with the manure all soil used for Roses, at a saving of three-fourths of the labor.

DISTANCE TO PLANT.

The distance for Roses such as I describe (those that have been grown in six-inch pots, and averaging one foot high), should be one foot each way, so as to get the full benefit of a crop by January. It is true that, if planted twice that distance, they would be thick enough before spring; but they will not fill up sufficiently until the middle of January, if planted much wider than one foot, and it is always before that date that Roses are highest in price. The temperature at which Roses are grown in winter is an average of fifty-five degrees at night, with ten to fifteen degrees higher during the day. Consequently, if heated by hot water, in this latitude, a house twenty feet wide will require eight runs of four-inch pipe to maintain that heat; if sixteen feet wide, about six runs; and if twelve feet wide, about four runs. If heated by steam, a one-and-a-half-inch pipe will be about equal to a four-inch hot-water pipe.

WATERING AND MULCHING.

Watering is a matter of the first importance, and requires some experience to know what is the proper condition. It is not often that Roses require to be watered. The heavy syringing necessary each forenoon in clear weather to keep down Red-spider is generally sufficient to keep them in the proper condition of moisture; of course, good judgment must be used to syringe heavier in warm, bright weather, when the plants are in vigorous growth, than in dull weather, or when the plants are not so vigor-

ous. Better to err on the side of dryness, particularly
from October to March. Whenever there are indications
of the soil being too wet, stop syringing, but keep the
air of the house moist by watering the paths. The best
growers now use very little mulching until the days begin
to lengthen in February or March, the "food" given
being usually a top dressing every three or four weeks,
from October to February, of half an inch of compost,
consisting of two parts of well-rooted cow dung, to one
part fresh soil, to which is added about one-tenth part of
pure bone dust. Frequent light stirring of the soil is of
advantage to admit air to the roots and assist the evaporation of moisture from the soil.

There is some difference of opinion as to the value of
liquid manure in Rose forcing in winter. In our experience, we have found that it had better not be used on
Roses growing on the benches until about February 1st,
when the days begin to lengthen and the sun becomes
brighter. In the case of Hybrid Perpetual Roses growing in pots, that have been started from dried off or rested
plants about October 1st, which should come into bloom
during December and January, it is well to water such
plants once a week with liquid manure, so as to get the
best development in color and size of buds. We prefer
liquid manure from cow dung to all else. It is perfectly
safe, no matter how strong it is made, and we think it is
more lasting in its effects than liquid made from guano
or similar fertilizers. Fumigating with tobacco smoke
for the suppression of the *aphis* (Green-fly), should be
done twice a week ; or, what will answer equally well, a
mulch of two or three inches of tobacco stems spread on
the walks or under the benches, will keep off the green
fly by renewing it every five or six weeks. Rose growers
practice this method now almost entirely, as it is quite as
effective and safer than fumigating, as that less or more
discolors the buds.

PRUNING.

But little pruning is done to Tea Roses until they begin to get too thick, towards spring ; the "blind wood" should then be gradually and judiciously thinned out, care being taken not to cut too much off at once, as that would be certain to less or more check the vitality of the plants by gorging the rootlets with water, if too many shoots had been taken ; hence, after pruning, for a few days water sparingly.

VARIETIES TO FORCE.

The varieties grown are changing every season, and no list we can give to-day is likely to remain as the best, ten years hence. The favorite Tea Roses now grown for winter are Perle des Jardins (yellow), Sunset (orange), Papa Gontier (carmine), Niphetos (white), Catherine Mermet (rosy pink), Souvenir d'un Ami (delicate peach color), Cornelia Cook (white), Marshal Robert (pale yellow), Madame Cusin (pink), Bon Silene (carmine), Bride (white), William Francis Bennett (crimson), and American Beauty (light crimson), The Puritan (white)— these three last named are "Hybrid" Teas, but they are usually grown as Teas.

Of climbing Roses, which are grown on the rafters of the greenhouse, Mareschal Niel (yellow), Lamarque (white), Gloire de Dijon (salmon rose), Red Gloire de Dijon (carmine), and the new Waltham Climber (deep crimson), are the best. This last has not yet been largely tested, but in all probability it will supply a want long felt. It is a double Rose of fine form and of exquisite crimson color, equal in nearly all respects to our finest Hybrid Perpetuals—all dark Roses that we have hitherto had in climbers being shy bloomers with inferior flowers.

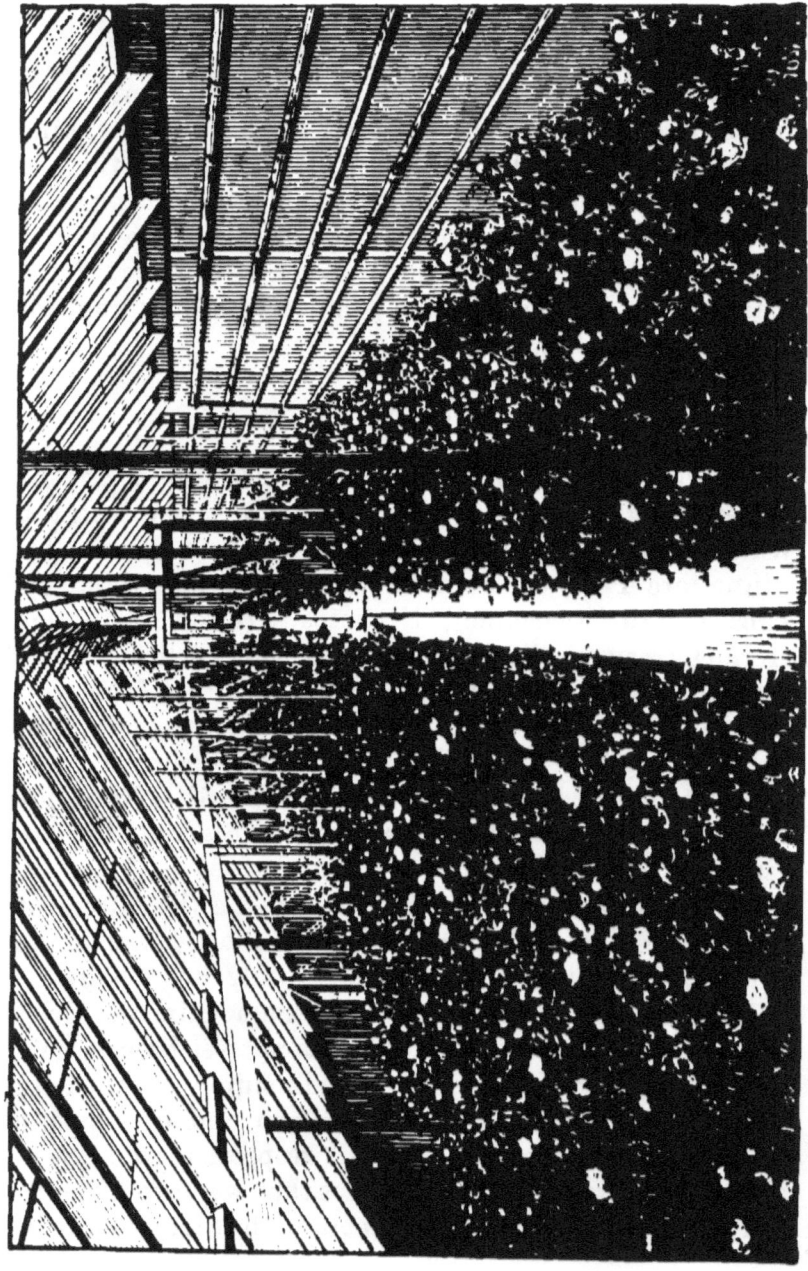

HYBRID PERPETUAL ROSES.

To get the Hybrid Perpetual class early (say during December and January), requires special skill and care, but it well repays the trouble, as this class of Roses now bring an average of $50 per hundred buds at wholesale from the 15th of December to January 15th. The method found to be necessary is, to grow these Roses in pots, exactly as is recommended for the evergreen or Tea Roses, except that, as they have a tendency to grow tall, the center should be pinched out of the leading shoots before they get a foot high, so that from five to six shoots run up, and thus not only make the plant bushy, but, what is of more importance, these slimmer shoots are less pithy and ripen off harder, thus insuring with more certainty a greater production of buds. The varieties of Hybrid Perpetuals best adapted for early forcing are : Anna de Diesbach (rich pink), Countess of Oxford (very large, soft, rosy carmine), Magna Charta (splendid bright pink), La France (rich peach color), Mad. Gabriel Luizet (light pink, splendid), Paul Neron (immense size, dark pink), Baroness Rothschild (rich shade of rose), Rosy Morn (cherry rose, large and full), Merveille de Lyon (pure white, other characteristics same as Baroness Rothschild), Anna Alexis (dark pink), General Jacqueminot (crimson), Princess C. de Rohan (crimson, almost black), Dinsmore (crimson, scarlet), Marquis de Castellaine (brilliant, pinkish carmine), Pride of Waltham (peach color).

The plants, if started from cuttings any time from September to January, the season in which we prefer to root them, will, if properly grown, by August 1st (or at less than one year old), have filled a seven or eight-inch pot with roots. Now is the critical point. The plants must be ripened off and rested, if a crop of buds is wanted by December, January or February; so, to do this, at a season as early as the 1st of August, the plants must be gradually dried off sufficiently to make them drop their leaves, though not to wilt them so violently as to shrivel the shoots. A rest of two months is necessary, so that the plants, which we commenced to dry off by the 1st of August, may be started slowly by the 1st of October, and those begun to be dried off by the 1st of September may be started, also at as low a temperature as possible, by the 1st of November. On first starting, give the dry balls a thorough soaking of water. If placed in sunken pits or greenhouses, where there is no fire heat, the one good watering will usually be enough until the buds swell, though the wood should be kept moist by syringing twice or thrice each day. These, like the Monthly Roses, are best ripened off by placing them in the open air ; though, if continued wet weather occur when they are thus placed to dry and ripen their wood, the pots must be placed on their sides, or some arrangement contrived to keep them from getting wet, otherwise the rest absolutely necessary for early forcing cannot be obtained. In our own practice we cover up the Roses every night while drying them off, either with sashes or sheeting, as one drenching rain during the period of drying off would defeat the whole work. The best kinds for early work are : *Magna Charta, Anna de Diesbach, and Gen. Jacqueminot.*

When the forcing of Hybrid Perpetual Roses is success-ful, it is very profitable. And it is profitable because of the unusual care and skill that are required to have the plants in the proper condition. We may here state, that many failures have resulted from the attempt to grow the Hybrid Tea Roses without resting, notably the Duchess of Edin-burgh, which was sent out from England some five or six years ago as a "Crimson Tea." The misleading name of "Tea," induced hundreds of florists to attempt its growth under the same conditions as the Perle des Jardins or Bon

Silene class, and the consequence was in every case, almost complete failure. This type evidently partakes more of the Hybrid Perpetual than of the Tea class, and as they are hardy and deciduous, refuse to blossom in midwinter, unless given the rest that their nature demands. So far, however, the new Roses, William Francis Bennett and American Beauty, seem to prove an exception to this rule, as they do well under the same treatment as the old Teas. The past season we have found American Beauty to do excellently well, if dried off like the regular Hybrid, showing it to do well under both conditions.

HYBRID PERPETUAL ROSES IN SOLID BEDS.

Immense quantities of Roses of this class are now grown in solid beds. These beds require no special preparation where the soil is naturally good, and the natural drainage perfect, but where this is not the case, the same compost recommended for Tea Roses will answer, only using a greater depth, from nine to twelve inches, over a well-drained bottom. Hybrid Perpetual Roses, planted out in solid beds, cannot be had so early as when grown in pots, as, when thus grown, they cannot well be given the rest necessary for early forcing; as a rule, in this district, they are rarely in market before February, and from then they are brought in, in succession crops, until the Roses from out doors in June come in. The distance at which they are planted is usually from fifteen to eighteen inches each way.

MILDEW.

Roses, when grown under glass, with proper attention to temperature and moisture, are not usually attacked by Mildew; but as a preventive it is well to paint the hot-water pipes once every two or three weeks with a mixture of sulphur and lime or sulphur and guano, made of the consistency of whitewash (the guano or lime is merely to make the sulphur stick better to the pipes). We also use this mixture of sulphur on our steam pipes, but only on about one-sixth of the diameter ; if the whole pipe was covered as in the hot water pipe, the fumes would hurt the plants. The fumes of sulphur, as diffused by the heated pipes, is a never-failing means of destroying the germs of Mildew or any other fungoid growth, and also holds in check, to some extent, the Red-spider, an insect often so troublesome to the Rose. In the summer, or at such seasons of the year when no fire is used, it is well to dust the foliage lightly with sulphur once a week as a preventive of Mildew.

THE ROSE-BUG OF THE GREENHOUSE.

For the Rose-bug (*Aramigus Fullerii*), so detrimental to success in Rose growing under glass, there seems no sure remedy except the slow one of catching and killing the insect as soon as it is seen on the leaves. It is not easily observed, as it gets under the leaves and close to the shoots of the plants. Its presence is known by the bitten leaves showing where it is feeding. It will be understood that it is not the Rose-bug in its perfect state that does the injury. The bug deposits its eggs close to the root of the plant ; these quickly hatch into larvæ or maggots, which at once begin to feed on the roots of the Rose, destroying it completely. Many years ago we adopted the plan of paying our boys one cent apiece for the bugs which they caught at their dinner-hour, and by this method have completely kept them under, so that to see one now is a rarity.

The only safety, when the Rose-bug is known to be present in sufficient numbers to injure, is to throw out the plants and start with young ones. I know, of course, that there are many rose houses that are even nine to ten years old, that never fail to produce abundant crops, particularly such as Mareschal Niel and other climbers;

but in such cases it seems to be that the Roses planted
either had escaped the visitation of the Rose-bug altogether, or had got so deeply and strongly rooted before
being attacked, that the grub could not injure the plants.

Professor C. V. Riley, the Government Entomologist,
who has given the habits of this insect careful study,
says : "This habit of simulating death upon disturbance
is common to many insects of this family. They feed

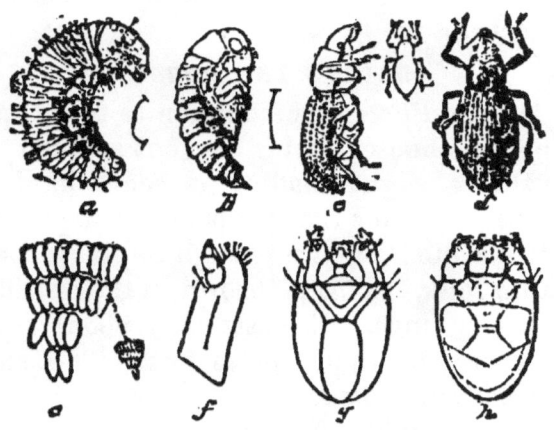

Fig. 37.—ARAMIGUS FULLERI.

a, larvæ ; *b*, pupa : *c*, beetle, side view ; *d*, same, dorsal view, the outline between showing natural size ; *e*, eggs, enlarged and natural size ;
f, left maxilla of larva, with palpus ; *g*, under side of head ; *h*, upper
side of same, enlarged (after Riley).

upon the leaves, but do more injury by severing them
than by the amount of foliage consumed. The eggs are
laid in flattened batches, consisting of several contiguous
rows, and each batch containing from ten to sixty. The
individual egg is smooth, yellow, ovoid, and about one mm.
in length. The female shows a confirmed habit of secret-
ing her eggs, which are thrust between the loose bark and
the stem, especially at the base just above the ground." *

---

* This is a different insect from the Rose-bug, so destructive to Roses
and other plants in the open grounds, which is *Macrodactylus subspinosus.*

The larva of the May beetle, a large white grub, with a dark-brown head, must not be confounded with the larva of the Rose-bug. This, too, is often destructive to Roses, but usually only on newly-planted beds. It acts by cutting the roots clean off, killing the plant outright. However, it is rarely so destructive as the Rose-bug, and not so much to be feared, as it is not propagated inside the house, the grubs being simply carried in with the soil. Care should therefore be taken to avoid all soil in which these large grubs are seen.

SHADING THE HOUSE.

There is some difference of opinion as to the propriety of shading rose houses during the hot summer months. I believe that a slight shading is beneficial from May to September, and for that purpose use naphtha, mixed with a little white lead, just enough to give it the appearance of thin milk. This is thrown on the outside of the glass with a syringe. It costs only about twenty-five cents for every thousand square feet. This shading is the best I have ever used. It is just enough to take the glare of the sunlight off, without much lessening the light ; and though it will hold on tenaciously during the summer, it is easily rubbed off in the fall after the first frost, when it has been lightly put on, but if thickly put on it is quite troublesome to get off. Another method is, to use common whitening mixed with water, put on with a brush on the glass inside the house. This plan has the advantage of the shading being much easier washed off than the other, although it is a little slower to put on. Of course it could be syringed on quickly, which would, however, spatter the foliage, making it look unsightly for a few days, but doing no injury.

GARDEN CULTURE OF THE ROSE.

But little need be said on this branch of the subject, all that is wanted being a deep, rich soil, enriched with cow manure or bone dust, in an unshaded position. For the dry climate of the United States, a class of Roses should be grown very different from those grown in England. There the "Remontants," or "Hybrid Perpetuals," in the humid atmosphere that prevails, with few exceptions, flower nearly as freely as the "Monthly" Roses do here; but with us, experience has shown that, after the first bloom in June, no full crop of flowers is again obtained, unless with the comparatively new class known as the Hybrid Teas, of which La France (rose color), Duchess of Edinburgh (crimson), The Puritan (white), American Beauty (carmine), and the new variety introduced in 1887 known as Dinsmore (scarlet crimson), are types; so that, when a continued bloom of Roses of all colors is desired during the entire summer and fall months, the class known as monthly (embracing Tea, Bourbon, Bengal, Noisette, and Hybrid Tea), are the best. True, these varieties, except the Hybrid Teas, are not usually hardy, unless in that portion of the country where the thermometer never gets twenty degrees below the freezing point; but they can be saved through the winter in almost any section, if pegged down and covered up with five or six inches of leaves or rough litter. This covering, however, should not be done until quite hard frost comes; in the locality of New York, about the first week in December. If done sooner, there is danger, if the season is mild (as it usually is here until December 1st), that the shoots may be smothered and rotted by a too early covering. This same rule we adopt in covering Grape-vines, Clematis, Raspberries, Strawberries, or, in fact, any other plant or shrub that is believed to be benefited by winter protection, as I have never yet seen injury done to half-hardy plants by frost previous to that date. In this matter of covering, the inexperienced in gardening often errs; first, from his anxiety to protect his plants before there is danger in

the fall ; and next, in his enthusiasm in the spring, he
is deceived by some warm day in March to uncover plants
which cannot be safely exposed until April.

ROSEBUDS IN SUMMER.

A good plan to obtain Rosebuds during the summer
months is as follows : In August strong plants are set
out in cold frames (such as are used for keeping Cabbages,
Pansies, or other half-hardy plants), at a distance of one
foot each way. On the approach of cold weather in
November they are mulched with two or three inches of
dry leaves, and by the time the thermometer begins to
fall to ten or fifteen degrees below the freezing point, the
sashes are put on, care being taken to give ventilation, so
as to keep them cool. They thus become hardened
enough to go safely through the winter, when covered
with straw mats, so that they will be protected from
severe freezing. In sections of the country where the
thermometer does not fall lower than ten above zero,
there would be no need of the straw mats. By the
middle of April, the sashes may be left entirely off, provided care has been taken to keep them cool throughout
the winter. Roses being thus " rested " (which is the
great necessity for the best results in Rose culture), an
abundant crop of buds may be expected from June to
October, provided that proper attention has been given
to watering and mulching with well-rotted stable manure,
or moss and bone dust, in summer. This mulching
should take the place of the dry leaves (which were
placed on in the fall), about the latter end of May or first
of June.

The Roses to be used for summer buds must be all full,
double flowers, else they will quickly fall to pieces in hot
weather. Such kinds as Safrano, Bon Silene, Bennett,
and Douglas, are of no use for this purpose. The kinds
best suited are as follows : Perle des Jardins (yellow),

Cornelia Cook (white), La France (light rose), Coquette des Alpes (pure white), Madame Welch (blush), Duchess of Edinburgh (crimson), Malmaison (deep blush), Catherine Mermet (rosy pink), Letty Coles (carmine and blush), Devoniensis (deep blush), Sunset (the new orange saffron variety), Dinsmore (scarlet crimson), The Puritan (white), American Beauty (deep crimson), and Bride (pure white), all of which, under proper conditions, will give perfect flowers in the hottest weather.

THE DISEASES AND INSECT PESTS AFFECTING ROSES

Have been in part referred to in the Cultural Directions. Mildew, the most common, quickly succumbs to sulphur, if applied as directed in chapter on Insects and Diseases Affecting Plants. The *aphis*, or Green-fly, should never appear, if preventive measures have been taken with tobacco, as directed in the same Chapter.

But there are other pests encountered in Rose growing not so easily got rid of. The Red-spider, the insect so small as hardly to be seen by the naked eye, that works on the under side of the leaves, giving them a dry and reddish appearance, luxuriates in a dry, hot atmosphere, but persistent forcible syringing in the forenoon, when the sun is shining, will generally keep it down; care should be taken, however, to thin out all weak, useless wood, so that the syringing can take effect on the leaves affected by the spider.

For the remedy for the Rose-bug, see Chapter on Insects, etc.

The Black Spot, so called for want of a better name, is a disease most injurious in its effects on roses, particularly the Hybrid Perpetual and Hybrid Tea classes. There is quite a difference of opinion about this disease of the Rose, some contending that it is altogether atmospheric, others that it is solely caused by the destruction of the working roots. Certain it is, that it is first caused by a sudden lowering of temperature, accompanied by a damp atmosphere, so that the injury to roots and leaves may be simultaneous in this case. But we also know that it occurs in hot and dry weather, where there has been no sudden change of temperature, which would indicate, in this case, that it was caused solely by the injury to the tender roots by long continued drouth. In any case, whatever be the cause, it is the only safe plan to avoid, as far as possible, extremes of temperature and moisture. In the summer of 1886 we had about a thousand very fine plants of American Beauty Rose (one of the most liable to be attacked with Black Spot), growing in the open air in eight-inch pots—splendid plants, without speck or blemish. About the middle of July, half of the plants were taken into the rose house, where they kept in splendid condition all fall and winter, while the other half was left outside ; both lots looked equally well until near the end of August, when the lot left outside began to show indications of the Black Spot, and although they were removed under cover of the green-house at once, they never recovered, and were almost a total loss. A lot of the Bennett Roses left out at the same time were also so affected by the Spot as to destroy them. The conclusion arrived at was that the lot left out in the open air had undergone some quick lowering of temperature sufficient to chill the leaves and roots of the plants. The remedy, then, is to get them under cover, where they can be controlled, in time to prevent such contingencies.

There is still another disease, which, however, is less common than the Black Spot or Mildew, that affects Roses when grown under glass ; it is called Club Root, Knot Root, or Wart Root. The indications that this trouble is at the roots are given by the young shoots of the Roses getting light in color, and occasionally, if the roots are badly affected, the leaves assume an appearance of being burned or rusted, together with an unusual tendency in the plant to drop its leaves. There is, I think, no remedy for this root trouble. It is, I think, a consequence rather than a cause of disease—a consequence of lessened vitality in the plant, brought about by over propagation, or other debilitating causes.

CHAPTER XXXV.

BULBS FOR WINTER FLOWERS.

Next in importance to Roses, come the various kinds of bulbs that are now forced during the winter and spring months for early flowers. Immense quantities are imported annually for this purpose, quite a number of florists about New York, Boston, and Philadelphia, use upwards of a hundred thousand bulbs annually, two or three in New York growing now upwards of half a million each year. With few exceptions, all these bulbs are imported ; they are of little use after being forced, and we find by experience, that (with the exception of Lilies), it is more profitable to import each year than to attempt to grow bulbs, that have been used for forcing, into good condition again.

The bulbs used for forcing are : Roman Hyacinths, Paper White Narcissus, Early Roman Narcissus, Single Tulips, Lily of the Valley, Lilies and Daffodils, Freesia (*Freesia refracta alba*), Tuberoses and Callas. A few illustrations are given of the flowers of the different bulbs, to give our readers who are not familiar with them, some idea what they are.

Roman Hyacinths, Narcissus, Daffodils and Tulips, are usually received by the middle or end of August, and they should at once be placed in the pots or boxes in which

they are to be grown; if to be grown in pots, six
inches is a convenient size, in which place four to five,
according to the size of the bulb.   If to be grown in
boxes, use such as are about three inches deep, the
ordinary soap box is a convenient size.   Use any good
rich soil, such as is used for general potting, press down

Fig. 38.—NARCISSUS, TRUMPET MAJOR.

the bulbs (two or three inches apart) into the soil, so as
to leave about one-fourth of their depth uncovered, or
deep enough to steady them nicely in the soil, as of
course the roots are only emitted from the bottom of the
bulb.   Now prepare a nice level spot in the open ground,
taking care that you choose it where the water will pass
freely from, then place the potted or boxed bulbs on this
close together in beds four or five feet wide (for conven-
iance), then cover them up at once with four or five inches

of rough manure, spent hops, well rotted leaves, or anything that will act best as a non-conductor, the object
being to prevent them from drying up by the sun, and
at the same time as cool as possible.   As the season
advances, this covering will not be enough to keep out the
frost, so cover up further with manure or leaves, so as to

Fig. 39.—POLYANTHUS NARCISSUS—PAPER WHITE.

prevent them from freezing hard.   On first placing the
boxes or pots containing the bulbs give them a good watering, which will be all they will require, as the covering will
keep them sufficiently moist afterwards.   The bulbs put
in by September 1st will, most of them, be well rooted
by October 15th, at which time, some of the earliest,
such as Paper White and Early Roman Narcissus, may

be placed in the forcing house, but they must be forwarded slowly; the temperature at night should not exceed sixty degrees; this will bring in the crop of Narcissus early in December.

Roman Hyacinths had better not be started until a month later, as it is found, if we attempt to flower them too early, the crop is always inferior.   In most places the demand for cut flowers continues through the

Fig. 40.--DOUBLE NARCISSUS INCOMPARABLE.

winter and into spring, hence the bulbs are brought in from out-doors and forced as wanted.   The temperature at night should range from sixty to sixty-five.

It is imperative for the success of either Hyacinths, Tulips, or Narcissus, that they be well rooted in the boxes or pots before being brought into heat, if they are insufficiently rooted, failure will result; to be in proper condition to force, the pots or boxes should be matted around with the roots.

The best single varieties of Narcissus for forcing are : Paper White, Trumpet Major, Minor and N. poeticus. Of double : Incomparable, Roman, Von Sion (all yellow).   Of double whites, Alba Plena Odorata is the best.

The single kinds of Tulips, mostly, are used for forcing. The following varieties may be recommended : Duc Van Thol (red and yellow, scarlet, white, yellow, rose, purple, and crimson), which are about all the colors needed for the earliest forcing—that is in December.   Below is a good selection for January forcing, after which time nearly all Holland Tulips may be forced with success :— For scarlet or red : Rembrandt, Artus, Vermillion Brilliant, Roi Cramoise, and Fire-flame.   For white : Pottebakker, Princess Mary Ann, Queen Victoria, Snowball, White Swan, and Grand-master of Malta.   For yellow : Canary-bird, Yellow Prince, Duke of Orange, Duchess of Austria and Lucretia.   For rose or pink : Cottage Maid, Rosamundi, Rose Adeline, Proserpine, Bride of Haarlem and Everwyn.   For red and yellow striped : Duchess de Parma, Kaiserkroon, Queen Emma, Samson, Ma plus Aimable.

Daffodils require the same treatment as the above named Tulips, and should not be put in to force before the middle of January.   Those kinds named below are the best :—Double : Incomparabilis (yellow and orange), Orange Phœnix (white and orange), Silver Phœnix (white, very double), Von Sion (yellow).   Single : Trumpet Major (fine yellow), Trumpet Minor (yellow trumpet and white perianth), Princeps (creamy yellow, and large trumpet), Bulbocodium (yellow), Bulbocodium (white), Single Incomparable (yellow and white).

Of Roman Hyacinths there are four kinds :—The Early White is that in general use, and the best.   Next the Rose, or Red-skinned ; the color is a rich blush, and is now getting popular among florists.   The Blue Roman is not desirable, unless as a variety ; and the

Nantes White Spring Hyacinth, classed as a Roman, and used for late work, completes the list of varieties.

Lily-of-the-Valley roots are not received until much later than the Holland bulbs, usually about the middle of October. They are generally imported in separate pips, in bunches of twenty-five or fifty. When received the bunches should be placed close together in boxes, with a little fine

soil sifted over them, placed like the bulbs, in the open air, and covered up in the same manner. Unlike Hyacinths, or Tulips, Lily-of-the-Valley will make no roots outside. The object of placing them outside, is to rest them before forcing into flower, and the longer this rest, and the nearer it comes to its natural time of flowering, the better is the crop. It is found that if attempted to be had as early as Christmas the results are often hardly half a crop. If wanted for Christmas, they should be placed in heat about December 1st, as it takes, on an average, at that season, about three weeks to get

Fig. 41.—HYACINTH
WHITE ROMAN.

them into flower. In placing the Lily-of-the-Valley to force, the best place is a greenhouse facing north ; or if that is not at hand, the ordinary greenhouse must be shaded in the part they are placed. They should be planted in benches or boxes of sand, deep enough to let the pips be one inch or so above the sand ; these are placed almost touching. Planting is best done by cutting trenches in the sand, deep enough to receive the roots, making the lines only an inch or so apart. Water the sand freely twice a day with tepid water, and keep the temperature of the sand at not less than ninety degrees at night.

To get this high "bottom heat" in the sand of the bench, it will require, if heated by hot water, three four-inch pipes under a bench three or four feet wide, "boxed in" so as to confine the heat; if by steam, an

Fig. 42.—LILY OF THE VALLEY.

equivalent of steam pipes—say, three one and a half-inch pipes.

When the flowers begin to develop, withhold water overhead, as otherwise it will injure the flowers. Like all other plants used for winter forcing, Lily-of-the-Valley should be brought into the house in lots for succession. It requires, when taken from the open ground to the forcing house from two to three weeks for a full development of the flowers, but by first bringing them into a cool shed or cellar, and sprinkling them enough to keep them moist, and keeping in this position for a week, then placing them in heat, a saving of nearly half the time in bringing them into bloom will be made. This plan is but little known; one of our best growers having found it out by accident a few years ago. He now practices it entirely, with the best results—saving five or six days in time in getting forward each batch. Lily-of-the-Valley flowers are now obtained every month in the year, by placing the roots, when they arrive, in "cold-storage" warehouses. Where the temperature is being kept just above the freezing point, the roots can be kept dormant for twelve months, if desired. In this dormant condition they are taken out of the cold storage, placed in the necessary heat, and forced into flower at pleasure. Many other kinds of Bulbs could be retarded in this way, only that in all other cases except the Lily-of-the-Valley, Bulbs so retarded would require to be placed outside to form young roots, in the manner already described, before they could be forced into flower, but in the case of the Lily-of-the-Valley roots, this is not necessary.

Lilium Harrisi, or Bermuda Easter Lily, was introduced into general cultivation about 1878 ; there is some question whether it is a "sport" from the old *Lilium longiflorum* or Trumpet Lily, or whether long years of cultivation in the congenial climate of Bermuda has so changed the nature of the plant as to give it the wonderful free flowering properties it possesses. I am inclined to think the variety is distinct from *L. longiflorum*, for it is not only much more prolific in flowering, but the flowers are wider and the whole plant more robust, a result not to be expected from any temporary cultivation in a climate, no matter how congenial. The rules for the cultivation of the Bermuda Easter Lily are almost iden-

Fig. 43.—BERMUDA EASTER LILY.

tical with those in use for Roman Hyacinths and Tulips
already described, except that, after the boxes or pots are
filled with roots, the time for the development of the
flower is longer. The dry bulbs, however, usually can be
procured as early as first week in August, and if potted
or boxed up at that time and placed outside, will form
roots, sufficient to allow them to be brought into the

Fig. 44.—FREESIA REFRACTA ALBA.

greenhouse by the 1st of October, and if kept in a temperature of sixty degrees at night, with ten or fifteen
degrees higher during the daytime, will give a crop of
flowers by Christmas ; like all other bulbs, succession
crops should be brought in to force. The Bermuda Easter
Lily is largely used for decoration at Easter, and for that
season, beginning to force in January will be soon enough.

Lilium longiflorum and *Lilium candidum* require exactly the same treatment, except that neither of these can be made to flower so early as the Bermuda Lily.

Freesia refracta alba is a more tender bulb and cannot be submitted to the open air treatment to form roots like the hardier bulbs. As the bulbs are small, they can be placed in shallow boxes (three inches deep), two or three inches apart, or in pots, using any good mellow soil. Place them in a cool greenhouse; under the benches will do until they start to grow; then place them in the light and treat exactly as advised for Hyacinths, etc. The flowers are pure white, and produced in great abundance.

Calla (*Richardia Ethiopica*), or Lily of the Nile, is not usually grown or classed as a winter flowering bulb, but we have found that by using the dry, well-ripened roots, as grown in California, it is one of the most profitable plants to force. These dry, well-ripened bulbs produce an abundance of fine flowers and make but very few leaves, consequently by using such bulbs a great many more flowers can be had on the same space than when the foliage is kept on the plants as is usually done.

TUBEROSES.

Forcing the Tuberose, so as to have the flowers from January to March, is an exceedingly difficult operation, and is now but little attempted here, as present prices will not justify it. The plant being of tropical origin, to have it at all times in a growing state requires a high temperature—not less than an average of eighty degrees; consequently, few ordinarily-heated greenhouses or private sitting-rooms are at a temperature high enough to insure the continued and uninterrupted growth necessary to the production of flowers in the dark winter months. It is, however, comparatively easy to force so as to produce flowers during April, May, and June, and again, by retarding the bulbs, during November and December.

By the first method, the bulbs are, about the 1st of January, placed closely together in boxes three inches deep, having two inches or so of damp moss in the bottom. These boxes are placed in some warm spot, where the temperature will average seventy-five degrees.   If for greenhouse culture, the best place is under the benches on the hot-water pipes.   In about four or five weeks the Tuberoses will have rooted all through the moss, and they should then be potted in four or five-inch pots, or planted in a bench of soil four or five inches deep, and kept in a temperature at no time less than seventy-five degrees, and flowers will be had in abundance in April. For succession crops, place the dry bulbs in moss, at intervals of three or four weeks.   The last crops will usually be the best, as by May and June the natural temperature will have increased, and less artificial heat will be required.

If flowers are wanted during November and December, the retarding process alluded to is resorted to.   This is done by selecting such bulbs as are wanted (care being taken to use only such as are sound and firm), and placing them in some cool, dry place until the middle of August, when the first crop may be planted, either in pots or in a bench of the greenhouse, as described above for the spring crop.   This planting will produce a crop by November.   For the succession crop of December, planting must be delayed until the middle of September, this being as late as the bulbs can be kept sound in the usual way ; but they may be retarded in refrigerators or . in the cities in cold-storage vaults, as is done with Lily of the Valley, and in that way may be had all through the winter months, provided a high enough temperature, with plenty of light, can be given.   The same high temperature is indispensable as in the spring crop, namely, an average of seventy-five degrees.   The variety best for forcing is the Pearl, which grows only about half the height, and has flowers nearly twice the diameter of the old sort; but for planting in the open ground in the ordinary way, when the flowers are only wanted for fall, the common double variety is the best ; as, being less double, the flowers open better under the often unfavorably dry atmosphere that we have in October.   The Pearl Tuberose originated in this country in

Fig. 45.—TUBEROSE BULB WITH SETS.

1865, in the grounds of John Henderson, Flushing, L. I. I purchased the entire stock of Mr. Henderson in 1866, paying him $500 for a barrel of the roots.   I sold it for the first time in 1867.   It is now the favorite variety for forcing, both in this country and in Europe.

Tuberoses are often forwarded, so as to be had in flower in the earlier fall months, in sections of the country where the season is too short. This is done exactly in the way recommended for the spring forcing, by starting the bulbs in damp moss; but for this purpose the

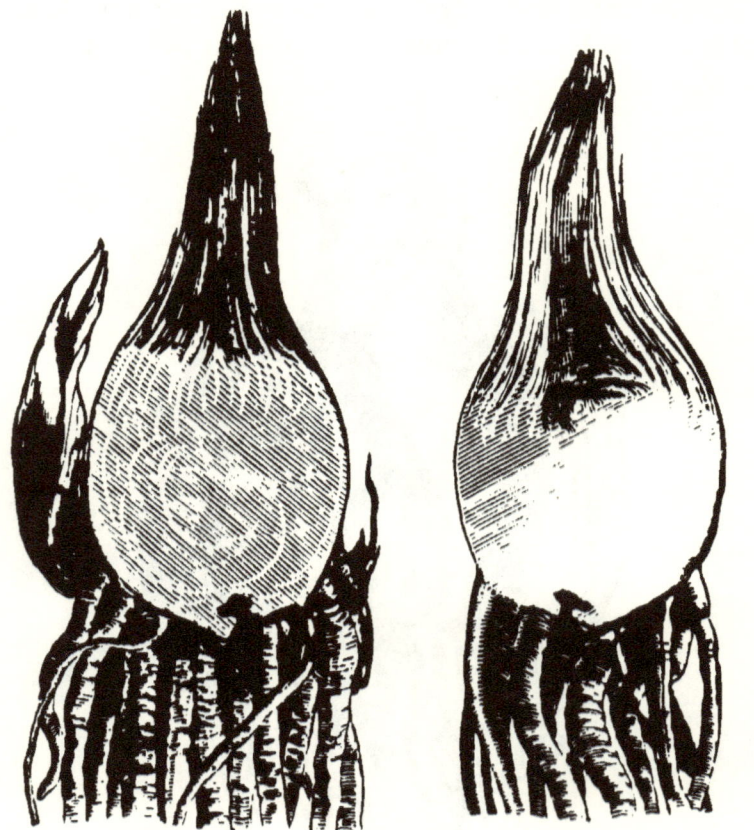

Fig. 46.—SOUND BULB.   Fig. 47.—BULB DECAYED AT CENTER.

dry bulbs should not be placed in the moss until the middle of May. By the middle of June, when the weather has become warm, and they are set out, they will start to grow at once, and will in this way flower from three to four weeks earlier than if the dry bulb had been put in the open ground, cold as it is in the most of the Northern

States in May. Of course, it will be understood, that when the dry bulbs are placed in the moss to start, it must be in a greenhouse or in some place where the thermometer will average seventy-five or eighty degrees, or they will not start at all, or, at least, very feebly. It will thus be seen, from the foregoing remarks, that it will be utterly useless to attempt to grow Tuberoses at all seasons, unless in a tropical temperature, which at no time should be less than seventy-five degrees, and if it averages eighty degrees, all the better.

One of the most important points in Tuberose culture is to have sound bulbs of sufficient size. Figure 45 shows what size a good sound Tuberose should be. Figure 46 shows how it should be when cut through. Figure 47 shows the heart or center rotted, in which condition it is worthless to flower.

CHAPTER XXXVI.

VIOLETS, CHRYSANTHEMUMS, CARNATIONS AND MIGNONETTE.

Violets are yet, and are likely to continue to be, one of the important winter flowers. The price for the past two years averaged higher than it has done in twenty years previous, owing to the fact that in nearly all sections of the country the Violet has been subject to a disease, a spotting and yellowing of the leaves, which has been completely destructive in a great majority of cases. The cause of this disease I believe to be from the same source as that affecting the Rose, Carnation, and many other kinds of plants used for forcing in winter, namely, that the continued high temperature necessary to produce flowers is contrary to what the nature of these plants demands, a season of rest in winter; this being in part denied them, the plants are weakened in vitality and consequently become more or less a prey to disease. To avert that as much as possible, cuttings should be taken from the runners of the Violets in October, rooted and kept in cold frames over winter, which gives them the necessary season of rest, and planted out at one foot apart each way as soon as the ground is dry enough to work in spring, by midsummer they will have started to grow freely; from that time until the middle of September be careful that all runners are pinched off, so that the whole force of the root can be used to form the crowns for flowering, exactly as Strawberry runners are pinched off to produce fruit. The plants thus prepared for flowering about the end of September are dug up with balls and potted in seven or eight-inch pots, or planted in five or six inches of soil in the benches of the greenhouse at a foot apart. Shade and water for a few days until they have made young roots, after which give all the ventilation possible until November. By this time fire heat may be required, but be careful never to let the temperature get over fifty degrees at night. As the plants start to grow, all yellow leaves and weeds should be removed.

The greenhouses used for forcing Violets have usually been the narrow eleven foot houses, but I am convinced that the rose house structure (page 158) would answer better, as the greatest amount of light in winter is indispensable for all flowering plants. Care, however, must be taken that the heating apparatus is so arranged as to secure the necessary low night temperature. Thus, when eight runs of four-inch hot-water pipes are necessary for the rose-house twenty feet wide, six runs will be ample for such plants as Violets, Carnations, Primulas, Stevias, Azaleas. Camellias, or Mignonette; when a ten or eleven-foot greenhouse is used, three runs of pipes will usually be found sufficient in the latitude of New York, to give a night temperature of forty-five or fifty degrees in cold weather. The varieties used of the double kinds of Violets are : Neapolitan (light blue), Maria Louise (dark blue), and Swanley White (white); of the single blues the Schön-brunn is the best. A new Double Red or Carmine-colored Violet has been introduced this season (1887), known as Madam Millet. It will no doubt be greatly prized, as it is an entirely new and unexpected color. It has all the characteristics of the Maria Louise variety, in fragrance, vigor of growth, and profusion of flowering.

CHRYSANTHEMUMS.

Chrysanthemums until recently were not regarded as winter flowering plants, they being only used to fill in the months of October and November, a season at which flowers are usually scarce. Now, by using the late flowering kinds, and pinching them back as late as it is safe to do so, say September 1st, there is no difficulty in having them in bloom until the 1st of January, though they hardly can be had much later. Another value of chrysanthemums, not generally known, is that the flowers can be kept in water in a cool place for three weeks after being cut, which is longer by one-half than they will keep on the growing plants after they are fully developed.

Two methods are used to grow chrysanthemums for flowers ; one is by growing them on during the summer, beginning to shift from small pots in May or June, until seven or eight inch pots become necessary by October. The other is to plant young plants in June at twelve or fifteen inches apart, each way, inside a greenhouse, or somewhere where they can be covered with glass by middle of October ; in both cases the plants must be grown without check, being watered freely, and supplied with liquid manure if the soil is not rich enough, and regularly " topped," so as to make them bushy, the early kinds, however, must not be " topped " later than

1st of August, though the late kinds may be pinched back a month latter. When extra large flowers are desired, all buds, but one, as soon as they can be seen, should be removed from each shoot, this will produce flowers such as are seen at Exhibitions, the large kinds often measuring six, seven and eight inches in diameter. There has been quite a run on these large flowers in New York lately, single flowers of Mrs. Wheeler, Count of Germany, and Cullingfordi, selling for fifty cents each ; ordinary flowers average, perhaps, $2 per hundred.

As it is of the utmost importance in growing chrysanthemums to be used as cut flowers, to choose the earliest and the latest kinds, I append a list of each class, which has been most carefully chosen, and is the very best that can be selected at this date.

EARLY FLOWERING CHRYSANTHEMUMS : Bouquet Nationale, fine large double flowers, pure white, with lemon centre ; Bouquet Fait, delicate rosy lilac, shaded silvery white ; Elaine, beautiful waxy white, perfect form, extra fine ; Early Red Dragon, dark yellow, streaked bronze and crimson ; Gloriosum, bright sulphur yellow, very free flowering ; Geo. Glenny, a fine old early yellow, incurved ; J. Collins, salmon maroon, shaded bronze ; Mrs. Brett, round, sulphur yellow ; M. Lemoine, dark yellow, streaked bronze and crimson ; Md. Grame, pure white, fine incurved flower ; Mrs. S. Lyon, large single white, golden centre ; Souce d'Or, intense yellow, shaded "old gold."

LATE CHRYSANTHEMUMS, "CHRISTMAS" COLLECTION. —Comprising such kinds as perfect their flowers in the house about the holiday season : Bend d'Or, pure golden yellow, as the flowers mature, the petals lap over, forming ribbon-like belts; Cullingfordi, scarlet and crimson; Count of Germany, vermillion and gold ; Christmas Eve, pure white ; Fantasie, pink, shading to white ; Fair Maid of Guernsey, clear dazzling white, immense ball-like flowers ;

Golden Dragon, very large, color dark golden yellow, broad heavy petals ; Jupiter, brilliant reddish crimson ; Jas. Salter, clear light yellow, beautifully incurved, as the flower opens ; Lord Byron, dark rich crimson, shaded old gold ; Lady Slade, delicate purple pink, beautifully incurved ; Mrs. C. L. Allen, carmine, yellow centre ; Moonlight, immense size, beautiful lemon white ; Mrs. C. H. Wheeler, vermillion and old gold ; Maid of Athens, very large, pure snow white ; Talford Salter, dwarf compact grower, color rich crimson, streaked golden bronze ; Yellow Eagle, very large, dark golden yellow, ribbon-like petals ; Thorpe Jr., rich yellow, Anemone-formed center ; one of the best.

CARNATIONS.

The cultivation of the Carnation is very simple. It is rooted from cuttings at any time from October to April, and as the plant is almost hardy, it may be planted out with safety in the open ground in early spring, as soon as cabbage, lettuce, or any other plant of that nature. Many, for want of this knowledge, keep Carnations, in the greenhouse or pits until the time for setting out tender plants in May, thereby not only having the useless trouble of taking care of them, but depriving them of six weeks of a season well adapted to their growth.

They are best planted out in beds of six rows, nine inches apart, and the same distance between the plants, with eighteen inch alleys between the beds. The Carnation is very impatient of a wet soil, and care should be taken that the land be dry naturally, or it must be drained. As the Carnations grow they throw up flower shoots, which must be cut off all through the season, until about the 1st of September. If the plants are wanted for winter flowering, this pinching back of the flower shoots induces a dwarf and stocky growth, which is very desirable in the Carnation. If they are grown in large quantities for winter flowering, by far the best way is to plant them on the benches of the greenhouse, at about the same distance as they were growing outside, any time in October ; but if only a few are required, to mix in with a general collection of plants, it is more convenient to grow them in pots, so that they may be moved about as may be necessary.

In nearly every section of the country for the past ten years, there has been great loss, from an insidious disease attacking Carnations, causing them to die off rapidly, both in the field and in the green-house. There is apparently no remedy.for this, but prevention. As in the case of Violets, Roses, and other plants grown for winter flowers, there is but little doubt that the continued forcing, without rest, debilitates the plants to such a degree as to invite the attack of fungi and other parasites. The remedy then is to rest the plants, bringing them as nearly as possible to their natural condition. To attain this in my own practice, we have for many years rooted the cuttings of Carnations, Violets, and all such nearly hardy plants, before January, planting the rooted cuttings into boxes, or potting them in small pots, and when sufficiently rooted in the boxes or pots, stowing them away in cold greenhouses, or cold pits; until the time of planting out in spring. By this method it is rare that we have any symptom of disease.

Although we have some hundreds of varieties, as in the case of Roses, we have only a few suited for winter flowering. The best of which are : Hintzs (white), Sunrise (orange yellow), Century (deep carmine), Garfield (scarlet), Grace Wilder (light rose), Pride of Penhurst (clear yellow), Royal Purple (crimson), and Crimson King (crimson), Quaker City (white) very late, La Purité (carmine).

The flowers of La Purité and other colored sorts sell in New York at $2 per hundred, the whites usually at $3 per hundred, when cut with long stems ; for short stems, about half the price.   Even at these low prices they are a fairly profitable crop, as the bulk of the flowers is given previous to the middle of February, when the forced plants, being of but little use, are usually thrown out to make room for other plants.   Although the Carnation is nearly a hardy plant and may be kept anywhere in winter in a cold greenhouse, or pit even if occasionally slightly frozen, yet it is also susceptible of being forced freely.   We usually keep our houses, when we are forcing for flowers, at from fifty to sixty degrees at night, with ten degrees higher in day-time.

CHAPTER XXXVII.

BOUVARDIAS, STEVIAS, EUPATORIUMS, HELIO-TROPES, POINSETTIA, AND OTHER WINTER-FLOWERING PLANTS.

BOUVARDIAS

Are propagated by pieces of the roots, in April, or by cuttings, during the summer months (see Propagation), and when these, from the root cuttings, have thrown up a growth of two or three inches they are potted in two-inch pots and planted out in the open ground at a distance of nine or ten inches apart, in the latter part of May.

The plants that have been put out in the open ground in May will have grown to a fine, bushy form by September 1st, if due attention has been given to nipping off the tops every two weeks during summer.   By this date they should be taken up and potted, not later, as the Bouvardia requires warm weather to form roots ; if possible, they should be lifted with balls of earth adher-

ing to the roots, as they wilt very easily, and the plants
require great care in lifting. In any case, it is necessary
to shade and freely water for six or seven days before
exposing them to full sun. They had better be stood in the
open ground or in a cold frame, after being potted, rather
than put in a greenhouse, as it is very necessary that they
be fully exposed to light and air for as long a time as possible, before placing them in their winter quarters in the
greenhouse; but this outside exposure must not be
risked too late, not later than October 1st, in this latitude, unless they can be covered up before there is danger
to be apprehended from frost, as the Bouvardia is a very
tender plant, and will be injured by a very slight degree
of frost. They may either be grown in pots, or planted
out from the pots to the benches, as we do with Carnations and many other things. Our own practice, as we
have before said, is to set all such plants out in the
benches, as the flowers produced are much finer, owing to
their having a more regular condition of moisture at the
roots; besides, this gives a greater area for the roots to
run in. We have said the Bouvardia is a hot-house
plant; therefore if flowers are wanted in the early part
of winter, the temperature at night should range from
fifty-five to sixty-five degrees. The leading varieties of
Bouvardia are: Double Pink; Double White; Elegans,
single, bright carmine; Vulcan, single, scarlet; Priory
Beauty, single, rose color; Dazzler, single, deep scarlet;
Vreelandi, single, white; Humboldti is a beautiful, Jessa-
mine-scented variety, with large, waxy-white flowers, but
it is only useful in early fall and in spring, as it will not
flower freely in midwinter. Bouvardia flowers sell at
about $2 per hundred trusses.

STEVIAS AND EUPATORIUMS.

Stevias and Eupatoriums are yet much used for winter;
they are white-flowering plants, of no particular beauty

in themselves, but admirably adapted from their feathery-like sprays, for mixing in with bright-colored flowers. They are of easy propagation, and being of rampant growth, had better always be grown in pots throughout the summer—plunging the pots to the rim in the usual way, to save watering.   They can all be grown to flower in a low greenhouse temperature, and as many of them bloom rather early in the winter, every expedient is used to keep them as cold as possible, without freezing.

Stevia compacta and *Stevia compacta nana*, very dwarf, flower during November; *Stevia serrata* and *Stevia serrata folia variegata* flowers rather denser than the green-leaved variety and beautiful when grown as a specimen greenhouse plant; both flower in December. We have just obtained a dwarf kind of this variegated variety, which will prove valuable for white ribbon-line planting.

Eupatorium arboreum flowers from November to January, by retarding portions in cold frames; *Eupatorium salicifolium* flowers throughout January; *Eupatorium elegans* from February to March.   The flowers rate at about the same price as Bouvardias.

HELIOTROPES.

The manner of growing the Heliotrope for winter flowers is nearly identical with that for the Stevia or Eupatorium, during the summer months; only, like the Bouvardia, it requires heat to bring the flowers out in profusion in winter.   The varieties best adapted for forcing are : White Lady, nearly white ; The Queen, violet white eye ; Negro, blackish purple ; Birnie, lavender, richly fragrant.

The Heliotrope flowers without intermission during the entire season, if kept growing.   Flowers average about $1 per hundred.

POINSETTIA PULCHERRIMA.

The *Poinsettia pulcherrima* is grown from cuttings of the green, or of the ripened wood in April or May, and shifted as required during the summer, plunging the pots in beds in the open ground.   In my own practice, I find that boxes eighteen by thirty inches and six inches deep, are more convenient than growing them in pots.   Six plants are set out in each box, and when placed on the benches where they are to flower, the sides are knocked from the boxes, and the space between the squares of earth filled in with rich compost.   Place it in winter quarters before the weather has become cold enough to chill it, not later than October 1st, as it is a tender tropical plant, and requires a hot-house temperature of not less than sixty-five degrees at night for its full development.

Grown in this heat, it is a plant of the most gorgeous beauty, the bracts or leaves surrounding the flower-clusters averaging, on well-grown plants, one foot in diameter ; grown as a hot-house plant, it is in full perfection at the holidays, and is now largely used for decoration. Many thousand heads are sold in New York annually, at an average of $25 per 100.

Euphorbia jacquiniflora and *E. splendens* are plants of the same family as Poinsettia, and require similar treatment in all respects.   The former, from its style of growth, is much used for wreathing, but neither of them are as yet extensively grown.

BEGONIAS—OF SORTS.

The Begonias cultivated for winter blooming have drooping Fuchsia-like flowers of different shades from white to scarlet, and are used to a considerable extent as a "fringe flower" for sides of baskets and vases. *Sandersonii, metallica* and *fuchsioides* are fine, having bright scarlet flowers produced in great abundance; *car-*

nea, a rich pink, and *marmorata,* a flesh-colored sort, are also desirable.   *B. rubra,* a most gorgeous carmine scarlet, has panicles one foot in length on well grown plants. The price for the same size is about the same as for Bouvardias.

FUCHSIAS.

There are but few kinds of Fuchsias adapted for continuous blooming in winter, but these are very desirable, and whether grown as ornamental specimens for the conservatory or for cutting for flowers, they are much valued.

The best in our experience are *F. speciosa, F. aurora,* Earl of Beaconsfield, Beacon, Mrs. Geo. Rundle, Beauty of Swanley, all of which have long drooping flowers of light colors; few of the dark kinds flower in winter. Two-year-old plants bloom in the greatest profusion, plants one foot in diameter giving upwards of 100 flowers, which are much esteemed for their rare color and graceful drooping habit.

JASMINUM GRANDIFLORUM.

This is grown to the best advantage by permanent planting out in the greenhouse, and training to a rafter or trellis.   Its pure white flowers and delicious fragrance make it much prized at all seasons.   The flowers do not carry well, as they drop off easily, but it is valuable for home use.

DOUBLE BALSAMS.

Beginners with limited means, when short of stock for winter flowering, may very cheaply procure flowers of the Double Balsams, particularly for the late fall months.

If sown in August and potted into six or seven-inch pots, in light, warm hot-houses, they will flower until the holidays.

BIGNONIA VENUSTA AND JASMINOIDES.

These are greenhouse climbers, which only do well as permanent rafter plants, usually not flowering until they are two or three years old ; by that time, however, they usually cover the rafters to a length of twenty or thirty feet. *B. venusta* is bright orange ; *B. jasminoides* is purple and white. The flowers are formed in immense clusters and are extensively used during winter. The colors of both, although entirely different, are novel additions to our usual colors of flowers.

SWEET ALYSSUM.

· Sow in August in a cold frame, thin out so that the plants will stand six or eight inches apart, and leave without the covering of the sash until frost is expected in September or October ; these plants will flower abundantly until January, if covered up by sash and mats so as to exclude the frost ; or they may be sown in August or September, and grown in pots and flowered in a cold greenhouse during the winter months.

MIGNONETTE.

The following article on Mignonette is copied from the "American Florist" of November, 1886, written by Mr. Charles Bird, Arlington, N. J., who has for years been one of the most successful growers of Mignonette in winter for the New York market :

" I will first describe what I consider the proper kind of a house to grow this plant in ; afterwards the treatment. The house should be a low one, without benches, as experience has demonstrated to me that sufficient soil cannot be accommodated upon a bench to allow the roots of this plant the freedom and depth necessary to properly develop itself. I would prefer to have the house running from north to south ; that is, having one side facing east, the other west, and of eleven feet in width. Dig out a walk in the centre about eighteen inches deep, brick up the sides with one course of brick laid flatwise, giving them a slight coating of cement to strengthen them.

"Now we are ready to prepare our border, and this is an operation in the cultivation of mignonette about which a great deal might be said. I once read an article written by a practical florist in a weekly paper about the cultivation of flowers, in which he stated that 'most flowers liked deep, rich soil; there were some, however, that thrived equally well in any soil;' and mignonette was one of the plants he enumerated as among the latter class. I have seen mignonette grown, and offered for sale, under the latter conditions, but it was a very different article from that grown in a well-prepared border. I have seen roots that extended down by actual measurement seventeen inches, and have no doubt that under very favorable conditions they would root much deeper. My advice, therefore, to those who would have fine mignonette is to spare no pains in the preparation of the bed. Enrich it thoroughly with plenty of well-rotted cow manure—one part in four is none too much—to a depth of not less than eighteen inches; mix thoroughly and pulverize well. Of course the bed must be drained artificially, if the subsoil is such that the water will not pass through freely.

"Sow your seed directly in the bed, or put out your plants from seed sown in pots, any time after August 15. Be careful not to allow them to crowd each other too much. I have at this writing, October 1, two houses, each one hundred feet long and eleven feet wide, beds made as before described, sown in mignonette, plants all thinned out eight inches apart each way, and by mid-winter very little of the soil in the border will be visible by reason of the foliage of the plants. This distance, of course, only applies to the large strong-growing varieties. The plants of the common old variety might be left four by eight inches, the latter being the distance between the rows.

The plants will thrive much better if the surface of the soil is gone over frequently and kept loose, and great care should be taken that no chickweed is left after the plants have become too large to continue this operation, as this pest luxuriates in the cool, rich border, and will give you endless trouble later on, by making a complete tangle of your bed. I find, in watering mignonette, that if kept moderately moist it is tougher, and will keep better, than if kept too wet. When planted out in a bed like the one I have previously described, during the winter months, one watering each month will be found sufficient (if thoroughly watered), which is my plan under all circumstances. A great many failures in the cultivation of flowers and plants arise from the habit of half watering. My plan is to soak thoroughly, and then withhold water entirely until the appearance of the soil or plant indicates need of more moisture.

"I have adopted a system of 'brushing'—using branches such as are used for supporting peas; only, of course, of a size suitable to height of the mignonette—between the rows to keep the plants perpendicular, for unless they have some support they will fall in every direction, and the result is crooked stems and altogether too many shoots. By keeping the plants as near upright as possible and breaking the shoots well back in picking, the number of shoots needed can be calculated very easily; and the last spikes gathered in June will be nearly as fine as those picked in November and December, for the roots are down feeding in the cool, rich soil at the bottom of the border.

"The temperature must be low, about forty degrees at night; no matter if it touches freezing point; give plenty of air whenever the weather will permit. It will not mature as fast as if kept warmer, but your spikes will be all the finer, and you will find a steady demand and ready sale. I don't know any plant that 'mixes' as easily as this. The greatest care must be taken in saving seed if you would preserve pure any particular strain, and I find, instead of improving by mixing and promiscuous gathering of seed, that the reverse is the case. A neighbor of mine has a number of hives of bees, and in the early spring the odor of my mignonette attracts them, and they literally swarm among the blooms; of course if there are any plants of inferior quality in the beds the other plants are thoroughly fertilized from them by the bees, and my crop of seed is badly mixed; hence the importance of weeding out any plants of inferior quality before any blossoms have developed from which you intend saving seed. A notion prevails that home-grown seed is not as good as imported seed. This is sheer nonsense; it may apply to some varieties of plants, but certainly not to mignonette. When home-grown seed has failed to give satisfaction it is because of lack of pains in harvesting, or poor cultivation." This is true of nearly all seeds; it is not *where* it is grown, but *what* is grown, that determines its value.

AZALEAS.

These are grown to a considerable extent as specimen greenhouse plants; propagated from the young wood in March; potted and planted out in the open ground in May they make fine plants by fall, but most of the varieties do not bloom freely until the second year; as they can be grown cheaper in Europe, we of late years import nearly all we sell. The Azalea is a plant having very fine roots, and consequently requires a soil composed largely of leaf mould or peat to grow to the best advantage. There are now several hundred sorts, many of them of great beauty. They are used to a considerable extent in cut-flower pieces, particularly the white varieties, double whites being preferred, as the flowers of the double keep much longer than the single. The plants, particularly the whites, are largely used for church decoration. In growing the plants in winter the temperature should not exceed fifty degrees at night.

HEATHS.

Heaths are at present little grown here for winter flowers, our hot summers making their culture troublesome, except with a few of the freer growing sorts, such as *Erica gracilis* (carmine), *E. persoluta* (deep rose), *E. persoluta alba*, *E. vernalis* and *E. Actea*, all white. They are best grown from cuttings of the young wood in March, in soil similar to that used for Azaleas; if planted out in the open ground in May in light rich soil, they will in one season make plants large enough to flower the first season; but, like Azaleas, they are cheaper to import than to grow. Winter culture very similar to Azaleas.

CHAPTER XXXVIII.

ORCHIDS.

ORCHIDS MOST SUITABLE FOR FLORISTS' WORK.

Having no experience in Orchid culture, I addressed the following queries to Mr. William Gray, of Albany, N. Y., whose knowledge of Orchid culture is second to none in this country and probably not to any in Europe. The replies to the questions are in every instance from the pen of Mr. Gray :

1st—What are the best twelve or twenty-four kinds of Orchids most suitable for florists' work ? The best twelve for florists are *Cattleya triamnæ, Dendrobium nobile,*

*Dendrobium Wardianum, Lælia anceps, Cælogyne cris-
tata, Lycaste Skinnerii, Odontoglossum Alexandræ,
Odontoglossum Pescatorei, Cypripedium insigne, Phajus
Wallichii, Calanthe Veitchii, Calanthe vestita.* The next
twelve are *Cattleya Mossiæ, Cælogyne ocellata, Cypripe-
dium Spicerianum, Cypripedium villosum, Dendrobium
crassinode, Phajus grandifolius, Phalænopsis amabilis,
Phalænopsis Schilleriana, Phalænopsis Stuartiana,
Vanda cærulea, Vanda Sanderiana, Zygopetalum
Mackayi.*

2d—What kinds of these are best suited for growing in
pots, and what is the soil used ? *Cattleyas, Dendrobiums*
and *Odontoglossums* do well in coarse chopped peat, pots
nearly filled with crocks ; *Cælogyne* and *Lycaste,* coarse,
sandy peat, with chopped, half decayed leaves ; *Cypripediums, Phajus* and *Zygopetalums* in peat and loam, and a
little rotten manure ; *Phalænopsis, Vandas* and *Laelias*
do well in baskets, pots or small pans, in chopped sphagnum ; the drainage must be perfect. *Calanthes,* chopped
sods of sandy loam, with not over fine leaf mould ; the
plants must be made steady with stakes and copper wire.

3d—What kinds are suited to grow on bark or cork, or
other such material, and what compost or other substance
is used ? *Cattleyas, Laelias, Phalænopsis, Vandas* and
Dendrobiums do well on blocks of cork, rafts, cylinders,
etc., with sphagnum or other moss; but take more care, as
they dry so quickly. A plant on a block will take water
twice a day, the same in a basket only once in two
days ; blocks can be hung overhead, but the expense of
dipping the blocks twice a day in water would, for a
florist, not be remunerative.

4th—At about what night and day temperature should
such varieties as you have named be grown ? *Phalænopsis, Vandas, Dendrobiums* and *Cypripediums* in winter—thermometer, sixty to sixty-five degrees at night, to

206   PRACTICAL FLORICULTURE.

seventy-five degrees by day, with air ; in summer, seventy
degrees night, ninety or more degrees by day, with plenty
of air and ventilation at night. *Cattleya, Lælia, Phajus,
Calanthe, Cœlogyne* and *Zygopetalum*—in winter, fifty-
five or sixty degrees at night, seventy degrees with sun
by day ; in summer, sixty-five degrees at night, eighty-five
degrees by day, with plenty of air. *Odontoglossums*—in
winter, fifty-five degrees at night, sixty-five degrees by
day ; in summer, as cool as they can be kept. All want
abundance of atmospheric moisture night and day.

5th—What period of the year is the growing season ?
Phalænopsis and *Vandas* grow at all seasons ; *Cypripediums, Cattleyas* and *Lælias* in spring ; *Calanthe, Cœlogyne, Phajus* and *Zygopetalums* in summer ; when any
plant grows in winter (except *Odontoglossums*) it should
be placed in a warm house ; *Odontoglossums* do best at a
temperature of fifty-five to seventy degrees, never hotter,
if possible.

6th—What period of the year is the resting season ?
Orchids are at rest when the growth is mature. *Cattleya
trianæ, Lælia anceps* and *Cypripedium insigne* bloom
during the resting period, which is from December to
January. *Phalænopsis* and *Vandas* grow all the year ;
during the short dark days of fall and winter less food is
given by withholding water. *Calanthe, Cœlogyne* and
Phajus bloom with the maturity of the growth, then
lay dormant until spring.

7th—What is the best shading for an Orchid house
when ground glass is not used ? The *Phalænopsis* and
Odontoglossums I shade with canvas raised eighteen
inches above the roof ; all other houses I shade with thin
paint, made of turpentine and whiting or white lead ;
lay it on the middle of March and brush it off the middle of
October ; the plants do well. Ground glass is too dark
from October to March for plants ; nothing does well with

me under it. I use first quality glass. The glass is shaded with canvas from March to October, from nine o'clock in the morning to four o'clock in the afternoon, except on cloudy days.

8th—Any further information that you think would be useful, please add.

Orchids grown to pay a florist would have to be grown in quantity, each species with a house to itself. The most of the twenty-four species named could be had in flower from November to April in a house 150 by 20 feet; all plants with a tendency to early maturity should be placed at the warm end of the house, or in the fall partition off fifty feet at the warmer end for the most forward. The plants would have to be imported from the woods at first cost (established plants at present prices would be too expensive), and the flowers sold cheap to become popular. Orchid growing to-day is where Rose growing was thirty-five years ago. To sum up: In the cultivation of Orchids all plants when newly potted should be made firm, otherwise if the plants move by syringing, or other cause, the rootlets will be destroyed. The atmosphere of an orchid house should always be moist, winter and summer, in winter allowing the pottery material to become more dry. Light and air are essential to vigorous growth, deluging with water when in active growth, but never closing top ventilation; never having a stagnant atmosphere, gradually withholding water as the growth approaches maturity, and then only enough to keep from shriveling. As to time for re-potting the cultivator is guided by the commencement of growth; plants should always be under-potted as long as the plant is not top-heavy, such as *Cattleyas, Lælias, Dendrobiums*, etc.; a top dressing is all that is needful. *Calanthe, Phajus*, etc., are re-potted annually.

Insects, such as thrips and aphis, are kept under by filling the evaporating pans, or other vessels, with chopped tobacco stems covered with water. Slugs are kept down by placing lettuce leaves, sliced potatoes or carrots on pots, which examine daily and destroy; roaches and water bugs, by mixing roach poison and molasses, placed on oyster shells at convenient points in the greenhouse. These same remedies will be found effective against insects attacking any kind of green-house plant.

CHAPTER XXXIX.

CHINESE PRIMROSE, GERANIUM, CAMELLIA AND EUCHARIS.

CHINESE PRIMROSE.

Chinese Primroses, particularly the double white, were eighteen years ago, when I first wrote "Practical Flori-culture," among the most valued of winter flowers; but since then the fashion of using flowers mainly with long stems, such as Roses, Carnations and similar flowers, has thrown the modest Primrose nearly out of cultivation for the purpose of cut flowers. The Chinese Primrose should be grown in rather a low temperature, say not more than fifty degrees at night. The double varieties are propagated by divisions or cuttings in March or April, and require a shaded, cool house for summer growth. Single Primroses, of which there are now some very grand varieties, both in size of flower and truss, and in brilliancy of colors range from richest crimson, through all intervening shades, to purest white. These are all raised from seed; we have found the best time to sow is in February, in shallow boxes (see Propagation of Plants from Seed), picking out into similar boxes as soon as the seedlings are strong enough, at an inch or so apart; they can remain in these boxes until May, when they should be potted into thumb pots and kept outside, covered by lathed shutters, which give them the necessary shade, at the same time allowing an abundance of air. In case of long continued rain storms, they must be covered with sashes, but not otherwise, until they are taken into the greenhouse in October. If wanted of a large size for winter-flowering, those plants of which the seeds were sown in February will be big enough to be put in seven or eight-inch pots by November, they will be at least one foot in diameter, and produce abundance of flowers during the entire winter. No plant is so satisfactory as a decorative plant as the single Chinese Primrose for winter, and large numbers are now grown by florists to sell in fall and winter.

GERANIUM.

The semi-double varieties of the Geranium make a most brilliant addition to our winter flowering plants. They are of all shades of scarlet, crimson, carmine and violet, together with the purest white; the flowers can either be used singly or in full trusses. To get the most abundant crop of winter flowers from the Geranium, the stock should be started from young plants in spring, and shifted on in summer, until large enough to fill a seven or eight-inch pot with roots, when it should not be further shifted, as too much pot room induces too great a growth of leaves; the flowers should be rubbed off of the plants during the summer. Plants thus treated will give abundance of flowers from November to May.

CAMELLIAS.

Twenty years ago Camellias were the most important flowers used in the construction of flower work; now dame Fashion has put her veto on the Camellia, and the price in twenty years has gone from fifty dollars per hundred to five dollars per hundred flowers, with little demand even at that low price ; still, it seems a capricious and invidious "boycott" against this grand flower, and the day may yet come when it will be appreciated as it deserves. The Camellia requires winter treatment and temperature similar to the Azalea—cool, partial shade and low temperature for the best results. To such as desire full particulars of propagation and general management of the Camellia I would refer them to the excellent work on the "Culture of the Camellia and Azalea," by Robert J. Halliday, Baltimore, Md.

EUCHARIS.

When the Eucharis, or Lily of the Amazon, is grown successfully, it is greatly valued, being much used in the best funeral work. The point is to get clean, healthy plants, free from mealy bug (which is a great pest to this plant). Keep potting it on as required until October. When the ball is well matted with white roots it may be grown in a partially shaded greenhouse, both during summer and winter, with a night temperature in winter of sixty or sixty-five degrees. Water should be sparingly given after the pots have become filled with roots, only enough to keep the plants from wilting, from September to October, until the plant begins to throw up flower shoots in November, when it may be watered freely. There are several species now, but the best for winter appear to be *E. candidus* and *E. grandiflorus*.

TROPÆOLUMS.

The single and double scarlet Tropæolums, when trained on rafters, which can be often done without much interfering with the growth of other plants in the greenhouse, are very useful, particularly for country florists having a local demand for cut flowers, as few

things flower so freely, and the scarlet coloring is unex-
celled in brilliancy by anything else grown in winter for
cut flowers.

CHAPTER XL.

PLANTS USED FOR FOLIAGE—SMILAX, ASPARAGUS, FERNS, ETC.

In the formation of cut flowers into bouquets, etc., the
leaves form an indispensable part.   In trimming the
edges of baskets, Camellia leaves are yet much used,
also *Cissus discolor,* a climbing hot-house plant, with
brownish-crimson leaves splashed with white ; it requires
a temperature of at least sixty degrees in winter, and
never develops its rich coloring unless at a high temperature.   *Myrsiphyllum asparagoides* (Smilax) is yet unsurpassed for all kinds of floral decorations, whether for
the person, or in adding grace to floral ornaments for the
table or room.   Its leaves, or what passes for leaves, are
small and glossy, are attached to very delicate wavy
stems, and have the quality of retaining their firmness
for a long time without wilting.   The plant is raised from
the seed, or the roots may be purchased from dealers.
The root consists of a cluster of fleshy tubers that throw
out several slender stems, which, if furnished with sup-
ports, will climb to the height of twenty feet.   In the
vicinity of all our large cities greenhouses are devoted exclusively to the cultivation of Smilax—the roots being
planted in boxes, or in beds upon the ground, and the
stems trained by strings up to the rafters.   The plants
are usually set at four inches apart each way, and the
stem quickly attaches itself to the strings, which should
be at least eight or ten feet long.   The best plants of

Smilax to plant are such as have been grown the year previous from seed ; these, if set out in August, will give a full crop by November.   The stems being cut the roots will produce another crop by March, and yet another by May, if well handled ; the night temperature, after November, should be from fifty-five to sixty.   As Smilax does not require a specially light house, if such a house is used for it in the summer months it had better be shaded.   Any good rich, loamy soil will grow Smilax.

Since Smilax was introduced we have had two rivals useful for festooning purposes—namely, the Climbing Fern (*Lygodium scandens*) and Climbing Asparagus (*Asparagus tenuissimus*), but neither have taken well, and I believe that a few years longer will put them out of cultivation for the purposes for which Smilax is used. The cultivation of these is almost identical with that of Smilax, except that the Asparagus does not seed and is raised from cuttings.

ROSE, LEMON AND APPLE-SCENTED GERANIUMS.

The leaves of various scented geraniums are also used for mixing with flowers.   When used in the summer months the plants are usually planted out, but when required for winter the treatment should be the same as for winter-flowering geraniums.

FERNS.

Ferns are much used for winter decoration, both as plants and to mix with cut-flower work.   The species used are comparatively few and are mainly the *Adiantums*, or Maiden Hair Ferns.   Small plants of *Adiantum* are now used to mix in with baskets of cut flowers, instead of using the cut fronds.   Among the best are : *Adiantum cuneatum, A. amabilis, A. Roenbeckii, A. Williamsii, A. decorum,* and *A. Farleyense.*   Of other genera are ; *Davallia Mooriana, Pteris tremula,*

Pteris cretica alba lineata, Nephrolepsis exaltata and *Onychium Japonicum.*   As the culture of Ferns is a special part of floriculture, requiring conditions of structure not usually found in ordinary florists establishment, I advise the purchase of plants from those who make a special business of growing ferns, of which there are now some in the vicinity of all large cities.

CHAPTER XLI.

PLANTS USED FOR DECORATION OF ROOMS.

In many cities of Europe, but particularly in London, an immense business is done in loaning plants for the decoration of public halls, churches and private dwellings.   For the past dozen years a good deal has been done in it in our own large cities; but our climate in winter is often such that it is a very hazardous matter to transport tropical plants, even for a short distance, when the thermometer stands at zero, with a high wind, unless tight covered wagons are used, with some means of heating them inside; even a distance of a half a mile may be fatal to the plants.   Such risks taken into consideration, together with the injury often done to plants by gas, getting dry, or other accidents, at least twenty-five per cent. of the value of the plant should be received per night for the loan; that is, for each plant the selling value of which is $10 the nightly rent should be $2.50 if for one night only; of course, if for a longer time the price might be reduced accordingly.   Again, the distance and the time of the year should enter into the question; if the distance is great and the weather severe, the risk to the owner of the plants is increased, and he should charge accordingly.

The kinds of plants used are comparatively few, and are such as are valued for grace of form and foliage more than for flower. The place where the plants are to be used must determine their size and their kind ; if for very large halls, then large palms, often six feet in height and diameter are used ; but if for church decoration, to be simply used on the platform, plants from one to three feet are best ; and here, flowering plants, particularly at Easter, are used in preference. Among the palms best suited for decoration are : *Latania Borbonica, Seaforthia elegans, Kentia australis, K. Belmoriana, K. Foster-iana, K. Wendlandi, Areca lutescens, A. Bauerii, A. Verschaffeltii, Raphis flabelliformis, Phœnix rupicola, P. reclinata, P. tenuis, Corypha australis, Chamærops excelsa* and *Cocos Wedleyana.* Of *Dracenas : D. termin-alis, D. indivisia, D. Cooperii, D. fragrans, D. draco,* and *D. australis.* The " rubber plant," *Ficus elastica, Pandanus utilis, P. Veitchii,* are all much used. Plants used in fruit, such as : *Solanum Hendersonii, Ardisia crenulata ;* for flower, Chinese Primroses, Deutzias, Begonias, Cincrarias, Azaleas, Geraniums, Hyacinths and Tulips, Mignonette, Madam Plantier, or other white Roses, are all used for decoration at Easter, and other occasions for church work. For decoration at any date previous to January nothing is equal to well-grown plants of Chrysanthemums, which are now largely used for such purposes.

For the verandas of summer hotels, or those places where plants are used for decoration during the summer or early fall months, the fancy-leaved *Caladiums,* of which there is now a most extensive variety, truly wonderful in their leaf markings, a description of which it is useless to attempt, are finely adapted, as they are of the easiest growth during the hot months ; plants from three inch pots in May can be grown to a width of one and a half to two feet by September. The fancy kinds of *Caladiums,* though most of them are useless for planting in the open ground, are easily grown under glass or on

verandas, and make grand plants for summer or fall decoration, as their beautiful markings become fully developed as the season advances. *Begonia rex* is also well
adapted for verandas.

CHAPTER XLII.

GENERAL COLLECTION OF PLANTS GROWN UNDER GLASS.

The tender plants, grown under glass, in our climate
are divided into two classes—those styled " greenhouse
plants," which may be grown in a night temperature of
from forty to fifty degrees ; and those known as "hot-
house " or " stove plants," requiring a night temperature
from sixty to seventy degrees, with a day temperature, in
both cases, from ten to fifteen degrees higher. But the
line of temperature between greenhouse and hot-house
plants cannot be closely drawn ; still, it will help beginners to give a short list of each, until experience enables
them to make nicer distinctions. For a more extended
list, see special greenhouse catalogues.

GREENHOUSE PLANTS—NIGHT TEMPERATURE FROM FORTY
TO FIFTY DEGREES :

Abelia.	Bignonia.	Correa.
Abutilon.	Bonapartea.	Crowea.
Acacia.	Burchellia.	Cuphea.
Achyranthes.	Calceolaria.	Cyclamen.
Agapanthus.	Calla.	Cyperus.
Agave.	Camellia.	Daphne.
Ageratum.	Campsidium.	Dianthus.
Antirrhinum.	Centaurea.	Diosma.
Alonsoa.	Cereus.	Diplacus.
Aloysia.	Cestrum.	Epacris.
Ardisia.	Chorozema.	Echeverias.
Artemisia.	Cineraria.	Epiphyllum.
Asclepias.	Clethra.	Erica.
Azalea.	Clivia.	Erythrina.
Babiana.	Convolvulus.	Eugenia.
Beaufortia.	Coronilla.	Eupatorium.

Fabiana.	Manettia.	Pilogene.
Ferraria.	Mandevilla.	Rhynchospermum.
Fuschias.	Maurandia.	Ruellia.
Gardenia.	Metrosideros.	Scutellaria.
Gazania.	Mimulus.	Sedum.
Geranium.	Mesembryanthemum.	Senecio.
Hydrangea.	Myrsiphyllum.	Solandra.
Indigofera.	Mimulus.	Solanum.
Inga.	Myrtus.	Sollya.
Jasminum.	Nerium.	Sparmannia.
Kennedya.	Passiflora.	Stevia.
Lacheualia.	Pelargonium.	Streptosolen.
Lechenaulia.	Pentstemon.	Tradescantia.
Libonia.	Petunia.	Tremandra.
Lobelia.	Pilea.	Verbena.
Linum.	Pyrethrum.	Veronica.
Mahernia.	Primula.	

STOVE, OR HOT-HOUSE PLANTS,

Comprising such plants as should be kept at a night temperature ranging from sixty to seventy degrees :

Æchmea.	Dichorisandra.	Medinilla.
Æschynanthus.	Dieffenbachia.	Monochætum.
Allamanda.	Dipladenia.	Nepenthes.
Alocasia.	Dracæna.	Philodendron.
Alternanthera.	Echites.	Poinsettia.
Anthurium.	Eucharis.	Pothos.
Aphelandra.	Eranthemum.	Rogiera.
Aralia.	Euphorbia.	Rondeletia.
Ardisia.	Gesneria.	Ruellia.
Begonia.	Gloriosa.	Russelia.
Bertolonia.	Gloxinia.	Sanchezia.
Billbergia.	Goldfussia.	Sonerilla.
Bonapartea.	Goodyera.	Stephanotis.
Bouganvillea.	Heliotrope.	Tacsonia.
Brexia.	Hoya.	Tapina.
Caladium.	Imantophyllum.	Ticlanthera.
Centradenia.	Ipomœa.	Tillandsia.
Cissus.	Justicia.	Torenia.
Clerodendron.	Lapageria.	Tropæolum.
Coleu.	Lasiandra.	Tydæa.
Croton.	Maranta.	Urceolina.

For lists of hardy and tender annuals, see the seed catalogues.
For lists of hardy shrubs, see nurserymen's catalogues.
For lists of climbing plants, see nurserymen's catalogues.
For lists of hardy herbaceous plants, see lists of such as make a special business of growing them.

CHAPTER XLIII.

CONSTRUCTION OF BOUQUETS, BASKETS, ETC.

The greater part of the following chapter on making up flowers into bouquets, etc., descriptive of the various styles then in use in New York and vicinity, was written by James H. Park, of Brooklyn, L. I., in 1868. Since then there have been innovations made that render some of Mr. Park's instructions then given of little use. These portions I have stricken out, adding, to the best of my information, the flowers now most in use, with the present modes of construction. Mr. Park's taste and judgment in this business gave him an enviable reputation, and had the natural consequence of bringing to him the best customers of New York and Brooklyn, so that at the age of forty-five he was enabled to retire on a fortune of upwards of $100,000, made entirely from the profits of his business, begun on a capital of $3,000 fifteen years before, a better showing than any one within my knowledge has ever made under similar circumstances.

With the earliest civilization of our race, flowers began to be cherished and employed for decorative purposes ; nor is their arrangement in bouquets a modern art, although its practice is of comparatively recent and marvellous growth among us.

Many people decry the artificial arrangement of flowers ; but how shall we otherwise use them to advantage ? The moment we begin to tie them together we leave nature, and ought to do so only to study art. In their simplest arrangement, form and color must be studied to produce the best effect, and whoever best accomplishes this will surely succeed in displaying his flowers to the best advantage.

Bouquet making is (or at least ought to be) the art of

arranging flowers. Who has not seen bunches of beautiful flowers cut from the garden and tied up in the least artistic fashion with the most stupid result? And who that has attended fashionable weddings or parties has not occasionally seen a large bouquet or basket in which the quantity of good flowers was its only merit—where a mass of flowers was muddled together in a most incongruous fashion, equally removed from both nature and art? Nor is this fault that of the tyro in bouquet making only; many who practice it as an occupation have not learned the first principles of tasteful arrangement. Yet great allowance may be made for the bouquet makers, when we consider how much like labor their work becomes. No one, trying always to execute this work with taste, would ever accomplish the amount of work required of him in any thriving establishment, a great part of it being of necessity done hurriedly; and as the variety of flowers is so great and constantly changing with the seasons, and their colors so varied, it is only by trying them in various combinations that the best results can be obtained.

Probably the simplest, the easiest, and commonly the most desirable, method of using cut flowers is arranging them in vases. The more loosely and unconfused, the better. Crowding is particularly to be avoided, and to accomplish this readily a good base of greens is required, to keep the flowers apart. This filling up is a very important part in all bouquet making, and the neglect of it is the greatest stumbling-block of the uninitiated. Spiked and dropping flowers, with branches and sprays of delicate green, are indispensable to the grace and beauty of a vase bouquet. To preserve the individuality of flowers, which is of the greatest importance, the placing of those of similar size and form together ought to be avoided. Thus Heliotrope, Stevia, Eupatorium, or Alyssum, when combined lose their distinctive beauty;

but, if placed in juxtaposition with larger flowers and those of other forms, their beauty is heightened by contrast. It may be stated as a rule, that small flowers should never be massed together. Large flowers with green leaves or branches may be used to advantage alone, but a judicious contrast of forms is most effective.

Nothing is so strikingly beautiful on a refreshment table as a handsome centre-piece of flowers. All the airy castles of the confectioner are passed over by the eye, which is at once arrested and refreshed by the brilliant beauty of the products of the garden or conservatory; and we wonder how any person of taste, who possesses the means, should ever fail to have flowers on the table when entertaining friends. Considering the effect, flowers on the table, like plants in the garden, are certainly the cheapest of ornaments. There are those who would have nothing upon their table but what they can eat or drink—like a gentleman who once employed the writer of this to lay out a new garden, and objected to having roses planted by the fences, saying very earnestly : " Ah, yes ! I suppose they are very pretty ; but then, you see, we couldn't get anything to eat from them. Guess we won't have any of them things." Luckily for the well-being of poor humanity such desperately practical men are not very numerous. An épergne filled with flowers forms the most effective of table bouquets. For a large dinner table this bouquet holder ought to be from two to three feet in height, with three, four, or five branches ; and, if the table is very large, a small épergne at each end will add to the effect. For a less pretentious table an épergne twelve to eighteen inches in height may be used to equal advantage. The superiority of an épergne consists in its raising the flowers to a height sufficient to gain their full effect, whereas forms of flowers built from a lower vase lose much by the interference of surrounding dishes. With a handsome épergne and the flowers arranged in nearly semi-circular outline, pointed with two or more handsome flower-spikes, diversified with here and there a fine fern leaf and other sprays of lively green, with a few fine rose buds and spikelets of heath, acacia, or similarly formed flowers, projecting from the main body to give ease and grace, and with a profusion of bright green or variegated foliage and flowers in drooping sprays around, the best results may be attained. For

Fig. 48.—BASKET OF FLOWERS (IN FASHION 1867).

such a bouquet a fair proportion of large flowers is indispensable, and an excess of projecting points is to be avoided as confusing. Table bouquets made in the fashion of the confectioner's stiff pyramids of macaroons are wretched decorations, and very discreditable to all connected with them. Better, a thousand times, to have half the quantity of flowers decently arranged.

Baskets of flowers for decorating parlor tables, mantels, etc., ought to be somewhat in keeping with their surroundings; a rough bouquet, adapted to grace a rustic table at a picnic, would not be in as good taste here as

something finer and more neatly put together. Oval
and round are the only permissible forms for flower
baskets ; the flowers ought also to be rounding in form,
yet not too much so.   We give an illustration (fig. 48)
as the easiest method of conveying our idea of the best
outline.   The basket shown here is also one of the best,

Fig. 49.—BASKET OF FLOWERS (IN FASHION 1887).

but whether high or low, the open round or oval basket
is very effective. [I may here state that this formal
method of filling flower baskets is, at this date of writing,
completely ignored ; but it is well yet to let it be shown
here, for who can tell what may be the next fashionable
freak. This formal method of construction followed the
négligé style now in use, which was that of forty
years ago for what few bouquets or baskets were then

constructed.—P. II.]   The flowers used in the basket of
flowers shown at figure 48 are : For the center, scarlet
and white Fuchsias ; the next white line, Tuberoses ; the
next dark line, blue Violets ; the next line, white Camellias, the outer line surrounding these being *Bouvardia
elegans* (carmine), while the edging is Camellia leaves
over-laid by sprays of fern.   Handled baskets we deem
out of place for parlor ornaments, having doubtless
been originally designed to carry ; the handle invariably

Fig. 50.—HAND-BOUQUET (IN FASHION 1867).

interferes with the general effect, and can only be
tolerated when beautifully trimmed with flowers and fine
greens.   For parlor decorations, high stands, with or
without branches, small, pendant baskets, or hanging
baskets of flowers, or of plants with rich flower sprays
hung around them, are frequently used to advantage.
Balls of flowers, like hanging baskets, are best displayed
from the centre of an arch or folding doors, and with
festoons of flowers looped from centre to sides the effect
is greatly heightened.   Festoons of Smilax or other greens,
suspended chain-like from the top of a plain chandelier

to each light, with festoons of flowers from the center underneath to the same points, make one of the gayest of floral decorations.   Wreaths of flowers or of bright green leaves, or of both, around circular or oval framed pictures, may be used on especial occasions to advantage. A ball, or hanging bouquet, loosely arranged, suspended clear, in front of a high mirror and with rich festoons of flowers from the same point, looped to each side, makes a splendid display.

The circle must be taken as the line of beauty in all bouquet making, apart from those loosely arranged.

Fig. 51.—HAND-BOUQUET (IN FASHION 1887).

Whether it is a table or hand bouquet, or basket, there must be a certain rounding of outlines in the segment of a circle.   Hand bouquets admit of the most formal arrangement of flowers, and the tendency of all cultivated tastes in this direction must be admitted as proof that for this purpose something more than a mere bunch of flowers is required.   The American, French, or English lady never figures, even in a book of fashion, in evening dress, holding a bunch of flowers, or any odd shaped bouquet. Crude forms, pyramids, balls, etc., can never supersede the slightly rounding bouquet (fig. 50), which is likely

to continue for all time the true form, like the parasol,
which might have been its prototype. [The bouquet
shown is constructed in the formal style, and with the
flowers then most prized; its width is probably a foot of
rounded diameter; the ground work is a dozen white
Camellias, each surrounded by blue Violets, the further
filling being of Lily-of-the-Valley, and scarlet and white
Fuchsias.—P. H.] Ball bouquets would be handsome
enough but for the handles, which completely destroy
the line of beauty. As for those abortions of the same
form pointed with Rose-buds, they are only fitted to convey to moderns an idea of the ancient weapon of war
that was swung by a chain or thong, and which Sir
Walter Scott describes the Baron of Smailholm as
carrying:

> "At his saddle girth hung a good steel *sperthe*,
> Full ten pounds weight and more."

After form, the most important point in bouquet
making is the arrangement of colors. The incongruous
mixing of these in a great measure destroys the effect of
the finest flowers, while the more delicately the coloring
is blended and the more strikingly contrasted, the more
perfect and pleasing is the result. Let any one who
doubts this compare a bouquet of the best flowers, in
which many colors are freely used, with one made of pink,
shading delicately from the centre to blush and white,
or *vice versa*, and with a few tiny points of bright scarlet
or violet tastefully set amidst the white.

The arrangement of colors in simple geometrical forms
is greatly preferable to a succession of distinct rings in a
bouquet. The ribbon pattern is very pretty in a flower
bed, but in very questionable taste in bouquet making. [It
will be seen that Mr. Park's taste, in defiance of the
fashion then greatly prevalent, revolted against the
formal system now obsolete.—P. H.] A bordering of
white, blue, or pink, may be generally used with good

effect. Handsome leaves of the Geranium or Camellia (the latter is preferable for its brightness and durability) alternating with fine sprays of green, delicate flower scapes, or spikelets of heaths, or Lily-of-the-Valley, form a fitting edging for a hand bouquet. A fine hand bouquet may be made with smooth outline and relieved by delicate points of green or fine leaves. In filling out a hand bouquet, half-dried moss is preferable to bouquet

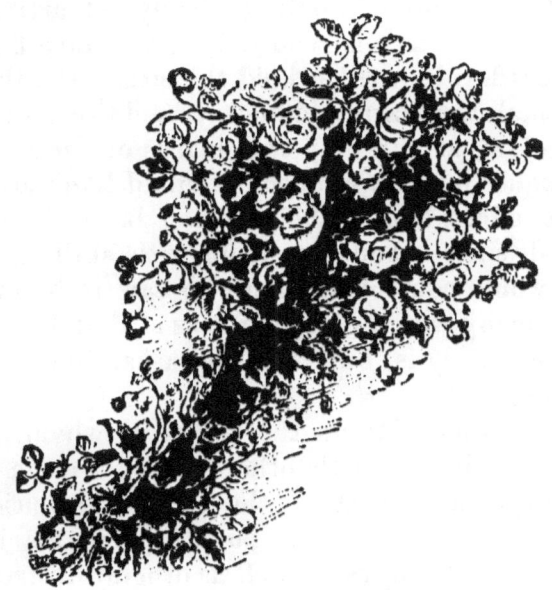

Fig. 52.—CORSAGE BOUQUET.

green, as it can be used more readily to keep the flowers apart without so much increase of weight and stem ; a light backing of green, concave underneath, finishes the bouquet. White lute-string ribbon, wound around the handle and tied in a bow, is preferable to tinfoil.

Judging the merits of bouquets, etc., has always been a very difficult point amongst gardeners and florists, nor is this to be wondered at when exhibitors and judges have each their own notions of excellence, various as the men themselves. It is only by comparison that the merits of any article can be well judged; and the best connoisseurs of arranged flowers are not to be found amongst gardeners, who have few opportunities of comparing such things, but amongst the lovers of flowers, the men and women of cultivated tastes who, having leisure and means, find pleasure in studying their merits, and thus set up for themselves a higher standard of excellence. An unskilled person set to judge a collection of Pansy flowers would probably not arrive at the same conclusions as one who judged the same flowers by the standard rules, which hold the circle, the thick and smooth petal, the sharply defined eye and the distinct division of colors, as the only true marks of perfection. A hand bouquet may have its colors inlaid like mosaic with very good effect, and if the coloring be well toned and contrasted, such a bouquet made with skill, like prize Pansies, would compel any one who saw it to admire it, although many would object to it as stiff and unnatural, which it certainly is, but it is also a handsome bouquet nevertheless.

There are some flowers the colors of which repel all close communication with others; such are the purple, ruddy purple and most of the striped carnations, all Roses with even a tinge of purple (and this includes most of the hardy Roses, as well as others), in fact, there is scarcely any shade of purple which can be used to advantage in bouquet making. Excepting blue like that of the Violet, there is scarcely any shade of blue, even, which can be advantageously used in a closely-arranged bouquet; and the Violet, beautiful though it be, is a very ineffective flower by gaslight. Still more so is the favorite Heliotrope. Many shades of yellow are harsh, yet some may be used with good effect in bouquets, particularly when toned with blue. For example, the racemes of *Acacia pubescens,* either in bud or blossom, as a bordering fringe are exceedingly beautiful and put to shame that over-fastidious taste which rejects all yellow flowers. [Fashion now gives preference to yellow flowers over all other colors.—P. II.] Even established rules on colors fail to guide us always in the arrangement of flowers. Artists tell us that blue and green should never come together, yet the Violet can have no more beautiful setting than its own green leaves, while dark blue flowers show to equal advantage in their darker green foliage. In Nature's own setting, all flowers are becoming ; it is only by placing them at a disadvantage that they can ever appear otherwise ; but so infinite are their shades and forms that their perfect arrangement in bouquets must ever be a work of taste and skill. We would not assert that bouquet makers, like poets, "are born, not made," yet we know that many in this, as in other callings, are and ever will be, utterly unfitted for the work they undertake.

Funeral flowers are now a very important part of the florist's trade. Ten years ago, ten dollars' worth of flowers were more rare at a funeral in New York than one hundred now, and sometimes one funeral demands a thousand dollars' worth. The wreath and crescent-wreath are undoubtedly the best forms for this purpose, and the cross is a favorite and beautiful emblem. An upright cross of flowers, solid on all sides, with a base of the same, is a very striking object, but unless well and richly made, were better left alone. Anchors, crowns, baskets and bouquets are all used for the same purpose. In any of these forms, the slightly rounding surface is the best ; that is to say, the flowers in the wreath, cross, etc., must neither be flat nor to highly rounded. [Funeral flowers are less used now than when this was written, owing probably to the fact that some dozen years ago it was carried to such an excess as to be a heavy tax on the poorer friends of the family in affliction. But the turning point in the tide of fashion was when one of New

York's biggest millionaires was dying, he requested that
no flowers should deck his bier.   Then the toadies to
wealth—the flunkies of fashion—took the cue, and there

Fig. 53.—FUNERAL DESIGN OF 1887.

was for years a standing protest against funeral flowers
from the fashionable world.   But the fiat was not sufficient to stop all use of flowers to deck the dead, for the
"common people" revolted.   The hearts of sympathiz-

ing friends could find no better way to express their feelings of veneration than by sending to those they have loved and respected a few flowers as a last tribute of remembrance.—P. II.]

It has ever been a matter of wonder to the workers in flowers how such a preponderance of white is required. Most of them have not realized (although often practising it) that the most beautiful colored bouquets have always a large proportion of white in their composition. When we consider that white flowers are used, in quantity at least, equally with flowers of all colors collectively, and add to this the large amount of white flowers used alone for funerals, weddings, church offerings, etc., we may more readily conceive how important the raising of white flowers is to all flower growers. We believe it is safe to affirm that no one in the flower business fairly discovered this necessity, until the vastly increasing demand for flowers in late years forced it upon his attention, and compelled him to the production of white flowers as the most important part of his business. [White flowers are no longer exclusively used in funeral pieces; subdued colored flowers, mixed with white, are now as often used as those entirely white.—P. II.]

Bouquet making is no longer a paltry business; the trade in flowers, in New York at least, has fairly outgrown that of flowering plants, and when so much of this work is required, and when that which is well done is so much more valuable, it becomes worthy of more study and attention.

Many people have little idea of the value set upon flowers by some of their fellow mortals. In New York, during winter, twenty-five cents is a common price for a handsome rose-bud [Many of the finest buds, such as American Beauty, Paul Neron, Magna Charta, and Baroness Rothschild are retailed at one dollar each from December 1st to February 1st; only a few years ago they sold for one-third more, but the greater quantity now grown has lessened the price.—P. II.], the same per dozen for Violets, while Camellias vary from one dollar each, when scarce, to twenty-five cents when plentiful. At Christmas and New Year's, 1866, Camellia flowers were frequently sold for two to three dollars each. [Now Camellias have no sale at all as individual flowers to be retailed, and sell very slowly at from five to ten dollars per hundred, to be used in mixing in large pieces.—P. II.] The price of hand bouquets varies from fifty cents upwards. What florists call good hand bouquets sell at about five dollars, extra fine from five to ten ; occasionally they bring still higher figures. This writer has sold not a few at fifteen, and, on rare occasions, has received twenty dollars for a hand bouquet; and that from men who knew well the usual prices of flowers. To give the uninitiated some idea how these things are used, we may mention having seen a belle at an evening party in New York, carrying a bouquet in each hand, while three others were strung from each arm as trophies of her prowess among the simpler, if not the softer, sex. Of course this display could not last long ; the very weight of her attractions would speedily compel her to surrender, for, be it remembered, those eight bouquets certainly contained about sixty Camellias alone. We have known rich and fashionable belles even more favored than this, and have heard of one having fifteen splendid hand bouquets sent for one occasion. We have never, however, heard of another showing such muscular prowess in their display. Baskets of flowers commonly sell for five to twenty-five dollars, stands from fifteen to fifty, extra large stands from fifty to a hundred. [Baskets of Orchid flowers are now coming into use, and of course, from their rarity and the expense necessary to produce them, the price can only be within the means of the wealthy. It is safe to say that a basket, costing ten dollars in Roses or other flowers, when filled with rarer Orchid flowers, to pay the grower would need to sell for one hundred dollars. —P. H.] Bouquets for refreshment and dinner tables range from five to fifty dollars each ; we have ourselves made one at one hundred. The prices of wreaths, crosses, etc., vary from five to twenty or thirty dollars ; from five to fifteen is a common range. On one occasion a New York florist is said to have supplied three thousand dollars' worth of flowers for a private entertainment, but two or three hundred is more common, and esteemed a very good order.

A business which in New York alone amounts to hundreds of thousands of dollars annually [It now reaches millions.—P. H.] will soon assert its own position, and it is for those engaged in it to make or mar it, as they conduct it more or less respectably. As Americans assuredly pay better prices for their bouquets than any other people, let the florist see to it that they get the finest and best arranged flowers.

We must apologize to the general reader for the minute description and the technical terms used in detailing the *modus operandi* of construction, but it is necessary to be thus particular to be properly understood by such as are interested in the subject. So many flowers have short or unmanageable stems, or grow so close to buds which the grower cannot afford to cut, that artificial stems must be largely used. Even where stems are available, the bouquet maker, in all good work, prefers having another added to hold the flower in position, the strength of the stem being proportioned to the weight of the flower it bears. Thick stems must be avoided, else the bouquet handle becomes clumsy,—a very objectionable feature, as amateurs speedily discover, particularly when using flowers on their own stems. The stems commonly used are of broom-corn or straw matting, cut in lengths as desired, from four to eight inches. With this and hair wire cut to three inches, the " stemmer " goes to work. By a rapid twist one end of the wire is fastened on the straw, and the flower is attached by a whirl of the stem between finger and thumb, as in figure 54. Stemming is a large part of the labor of bouquet making, and rather distasteful to the amateur. One bouquet maker requires two stemmers, and a very prosy business it soon becomes to both, and vastly less interesting than the growing of flowers. Strong spool cotton or shoe thread is used for tying up the flowers. Camellia stems being entirely unavailable, a wire the thickness of a pin is passed through the calyx of the flower, the ends being twisted together. It is then stemmed on a light, dried willow (wooden toothpicks are also much used for stems), which admits of bending to the required position. Flowers thus stemmed have

Fig. 54.

sufficient moss wound under the flower to prevent its outer petals being at all compressed, when set in the bouquet. Without some such provision it is impossible, either to attain the rounding outline of the bouquet, or to display the flowers in perfection.

With flowers prepared, let us take a Camellia [In the method of construction to-day, for Camellias, large Rosebuds are used.—P. H.] for the center of our bouquet, tie it securely to the bouquet stem (a piece of kite stick or stiff twig), and wind moss around it, as already described, to keep the flower from outer pressure, the moss running to a point about two inches below the flower. Six yellow Tea Rose-buds are now set at regular intervals around and on a line with the outer petals of the Camellia, and the spaces between these each filled with a small piece of

white Eupatorium, a very small Geranium leaf or point
of delicate green being set by each bud. A little moss is
wound lightly, close under the flowers, to prevent crowding, a pink Carnation set behind each Rose-bud, with
Tuberoses between, a speck of Eupatorium being inserted under the edge of each Tuberose, to fill out. Six
white Camellias of equal size and form, stemmed as
described, are now set at regular intervals around, particular care being taken to form with the face of these
flowers the correct outline of the bouquet, and their

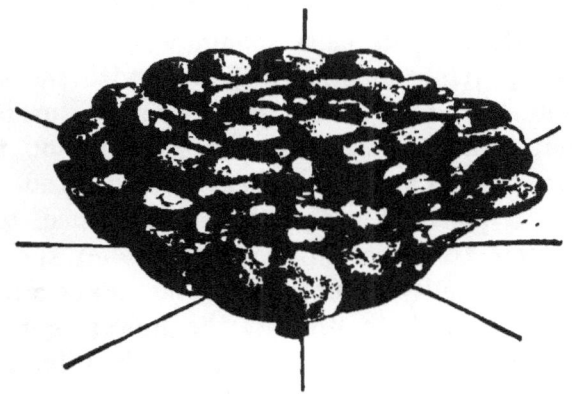

Fig. 55.—WIRING THE CAMELLIA.

stems tightly bound to prevent working out of place.
Between the Camellias on the inner side, another Tuberose is set, filled out with a speck of Stevia under each
side ; more moss is added, and a bright speck of crimson
Bouvardia forms the sole dividing line between the
centers of the Camellias—which nearly touch each other.
A yellow Tea Rose-bud follows, with a Violet set in Sweet
Alyssum on one side and a small Geranium leaf in the same
on the other ; a white Carnation is set behind each bud,
with a speck of Bouvardia in Eupatorium on each side.
A light border of Stevia is now set around the whole,
and with Camellia leaves of equal form stemmed on
willows, and projected nearly half their length, the bou-

quet is finished.   The handle is trimmed with bouquet
green, or fine leaves of any evergreen.   The handle is cut
to about three inches, and being a hand bouquet, is
wrapped with tin-foil, wound over, and neatly tied above
with a bow of white taffeta ribbon.

The outline of the bouquet must be carefully kept as
the work proceeds, and sufficient moss from time to time
packed lightly in front and immediately under the
flowers.   By this means the weight of the structure is
borne by the stems, the flowers being only allowed to
touch each other.   Moss not only serves well to keep the
flowers apart, but acts as a sponge when the bouquet is
set in water, giving moisture to flowers with the shortest
stems ; and bouquets thus made are more durable than
the casual observer—who gazes regretfully on the be-
headed flowers—is apt to imagine.   When, in addition to
the moss, a piece of wet cotton is stemmed to every
flower (as the writer has all good work done), the natural
stem is not unkindly superseded.   The maker must work
with a tight thread, to prevent the flowers getting out
of place, and keep a clean surface on the handle.   Another
method of bouquet making is to tie a ball of moss rather
loosely on the bouquet stick and insert the flowers (which
are stemmed to suit the work), drawing them down to
the desired position, and tying as the work proceeds.

Vase bouquets are made similarly, with more green
"backing" between and around the flowers, for loose
arrangement and to support the greater weight.   Flower
baskets are lined with tinfoil, or, if not likely to show
after filling, any tough paper will serve the purpose ;
they are then filled with sawdust, rounding above,
damped and covered with wet moss ; a border of arbor-
vitæ, bouquet, or other greens, is set around to support
the over-hanging flowers.   The flowers, stemmed on
twigs, are now inserted according to the taste of the
worker, with moss packed between them as the work

proceeds. Baskets thus filled and sprinkled with water keep well, but the more common method is to insert bouquet green (Lycopodium) over the whole surface, and arrange the flowers therein without any moss packing. Wreaths are commonly made on a stout wire, which has straw matting wound upon it, to enable the thread to hold ; a backing of green is laid for the flowers as the work proceeds. Both green and flowers must be wound on with points projecting to each side, the stems crossing like the letter X.   If laid straight along, the flowers are huddled together, and the arrangement seems thick-backed and clumsy.   When the desired length is attained the ends are firmly tied, and flowers and green together are pressed round on the wire, and by this means turned to face as required ; a bow of white silk bonnet string finishes the wreath.   Crosses are made on two pieces of thin wood ; the three upper points being made, the cross-stick is then tacked and tied in its place, the center filled, and so wound to the bottom.   Like wreaths, these may be finished with or without a bow of ribbon.   Wire frames have entirely superseded the old methods of winding flowers to sticks and wires,   These are made from half to three quarters of an inch in depth—that is with raised edges—and painted green, the breadth varying with the circumference.   The frame gives the florist at once the desired form, and makes it easy for any person of taste to arrange flowers in the shape of an anchor, star, etc., etc.   The frame is filled with damp moss, wound slightly to keep it in place, and the flowers, stemmed on short twigs, are inserted in the moss.

As has already been said, this chapter was written in 1868, by Mr. Park, who had the rare combination of being a clear and terse writer, as well as a practical florist.   But little can be added to the chapter, tho ground has been gone over so thoroughly, except to show briefly the changes in style that have taken place.

LEANING HORSESHOE

OVAL HANDLED

COTTAGE

CORNUCOPIA

SHEAF AND SICKLE

SCALE BASKET

FLAT SHEAF AND SICKLE

HIGH HANDLED OVAL

LOW OVAL HANDLED

GILT URN

GILT CHAMPAGNE

GILT PAN

GILT DOUBLE LID

Fig. 56.— DESIGNS IN STRAW AND WILLOW FOR FLORAL WORK.

The fashion in flowers and the mode of constructing designs now varies considerably, and I will endeavor to state wherein that difference now mainly exists. Since the rage for Roses began a dozen years ago, it is safe to say that nine-tenths of the whole bulk of flowers used are Roses. These are largely used in making up bouquets, baskets, and all kinds of floral ornaments for the table, and in a majority these are made exclusively of Roses; while corsage bouquets (little else is used in winter) often contain as many as two dozen Roses of one color. At present in the fall and early winter months the Chrysanthemums are perhaps used to a greater extent than any other flower. In the months of November and December nearly every other well dressed lady to be met with on the fashionable streets of New York, is found wearing a corsage bouquet of Chrysanthemums, and from their great range of color, almost every shade of dress can be matched except blue.

All Roses now are used with long stems; in fact since the use of loose bunches of flowers has come in vogue, replacing to a great extent the formal bouquets and baskets, flowers of nearly all kinds that can be cut with long stems are so gathered. One of the present fashions of using flowers for decorating rooms is to select colors of flowers to match the furniture; thus if the furniture is pink, the flowers used are as far as possible of that color; if of orange or yellow, flowers of yellowish tints are used; if of crimson, the flowers as near to that color as possible are employed, and so on.

A beautiful style of wreath for funeral work is formed from the pressed leaves of the Imperial Silver-tree (*Leucodendron argenteum*), which many of the enterprising florists are now importing. The leaves when pressed and dried glisten like silver, and form a most graceful circlet or wreath. There have been some attempts made, I believe, to grow the plant here, but as its leaves are valu-

Fig. 57.—DESIGNS IN WILLOW AND WIRE FOR FLORAL WORK.

able only when pressed and dried, it seems, if it is to come into general use, the cheaper way would be to still import the leaves in that state from Italy, where it is hardy enough to stand in the open air. The leaves of the Sago Palm, *Cycas revoluta*, are used largely for funeral work in all large cities, when they can be obtained.

Designs of every imaginable description are now made of flowers—shields, rainbows, canopies (under which the marriage ceremony is performed), etc. Mr. Wm. C. Wilson, the well known florist of New York, informed me that he has received $600 for the floral canopy supplied for the marriage of the daughter of one of New York's best known citizens, and the flowers used in the decoration of rooms in all footed up $5,000. These are rare occasions, however, though $500 and $1,000 are not unusual. The flowers for the balls of the Americus Club of New York in Tweed's palmy days often cost $6,000 for a single night.

DESIGNS IN STRAW, WILLOW AND WIRE FOR FLORAL WORK.

Most elaborate and beautiful designs for floral work are offered in straw, willow, and wire. Figures 56 and 57 show a few of the designs at present most in use, but new designs are being now offered each season, so that to keep pace with everything brought out, reference must be had to the catalogues of those making a business of such work.

Directions have already been given how to fill the wire designs in the preceding pages; the same will apply, with slight modifications that will be suggested to the operator while constructing, in the straw and willow designs.

CHAPTER XLIV.

HANGING BASKETS.

It is only of late years that the taste for hanging baskets has become so universal. The taste has extended to every town and hamlet throughout the land. The baskets are made either of wire-work, earthenware, or of rough and gnarled roots or limbs, to form "rustic" work. The wire and rustic baskets are the kinds in most general use.

Only certain kinds of plants are suitable for hanging baskets; such as are of low compact growth to cover the surface, and such as are of drooping or trailing habit, to hang over the sides. For a basket of one foot in diameter we name the following as suitable :

For center plants, either *Dracena terminalis, D. draco, D. indivisa* or the " Screw Pine " *Pandanus utilis.*

Coleus Verschaffeltii, well-known bronze foliage plant.

Coleus Golden Gem, clear yellow foliage plant.

Coleus Firebrand.

Centaurea candida, a plant with white, downy leaves, of compact growth.

Geranium, semi-double scarlet, or semi-double rose.

Sedum Sieboldii, a plant with light glaucous leaves and graceful habit, which is not only desirable on account of its foliage alone, but for its purplish rose colored flowers.   •

These are suitable for the upper surface of the basket. Those proper to plant near the edge of the basket are :

Lobelia Erinus Paxtoni, blue, drooping eighteen inches.

Tropæolum, Ball of Fire, dazzling scarlet, drooping two feet.

Lysimachia nummularia, bright yellow, drooping two feet.

Linaria cymbalaria, small flowers, graceful foliage, drooping three feet.

For a basket of two feet in diameter the below-named make a fine display. For the center plants the same as for the smaller basket :

Geranium, Mrs. Pollock, foliage crimson, yellow and green ; flowers, bright scarlet.

Alyssum dentatum variegatum, foliage, green and white, with fragrant flowers of pure white.

Alternanthera paronychioides major, leaves of pink and crimson.

Pyrethrum, Golden Feather, fern-like foliage, golden yellow.

For the drooping plants the following, which fall from two to three feet.

Maurandia Barclayana, white or purple flowers.

Vinca elegantissima aurea, foliage deep green, netted with golden yellow ; flowers deep blue.

Cerastium tomentosum, foliage downy white ; flowers white.

Convolvulus Mauritanicus, flowers light blue, profuse.

Solanum jasminoides variegatum, foliage variegated ; flowers white, with yellow anthers.

Geranium peltatum elegans, a variety of the Ivy-leaved, with rich, glossy foliage, and beautiful mauve-colored flowers.

Panicum variegatum, a procumbent grass from New Caledonia, of graceful habit of growth, with beautiful variegated foliage, striped white, carmine, and green. One of the most valuable plants for baskets or vases.

Although a few plants have been named as being suitable for hanging baskets, there is nothing arbitrary about using particular kinds ; it is a matter of taste in a great measure as to what kinds are used, though as a rule, it is best to use some graceful plant for the center, such as those already named.

In setting the plants in the hanging baskets, a layer of moss at least one inch in depth should be spread over the bottom and sides, so that the water may be held and prevented from washing through.

A very good plan to water hanging baskets where there are many of them, is to dip the whole basket in water until it is thoroughly soaked ; thus drenched it will stand quite as long as when watered in the usual way.

To have the plants bloom freely, they should be hung where they will be exposed to the sun at least two or three hours each day, and in dry weather copiously watered daily. If the surface of the basket between the plants is covered with moss, it will prevent the earth from drying out so soon, and will give a neater appearance to the basket. The soil used to plant in may be that suitable for potting ordinary plants, as described under the head of soils

---

CHAPTER XLV.

PARLOR OR WINDOW GARDENING.

To be successful in growing plants in the window of the parlor or sitting-room, it is of the first importance to begin with plants that are in a healthy state.

Experienced florists, with all their appliances for successful culture, often fail to bring health to a sickly subject. How, then, can amateurs, without experience, hope to recuperate the weakened energies of some petted plant in the less congenial atmosphere of an ordinary dwelling-house ? I well know the usual practice of our lady friends in this matter. In purchasing their supply of bedding plants from the florist in May, all are taken from the pots and planted in flower beds, to decorate the borders for the summer months. By the first appearance of frost in October, the plants of Bouvardias, Carnations, Fuchsias, Geraniums, Heliotropes, Roses, etc., etc., that were such tiny slips when planted out in May, are now, many of them, large plants, and in all their glory of bloom ; but Jack Frost shall not have them, they must be saved. Pots are sent for, soil of the most approved brand is procured from some florist high in the art, the plants are lifted up with all care and placed in the pots. Our amateur friend is in raptures ; as yet they look just as green and flourishing as when growing in the garden. But a day passes, and although they have been shaded and watered with all care, the plants somehow begin to show symptoms of collapse. The Geranium leaves, that looked so green and well, are now flabby. The Rose-buds, that held up their heads with such pride, now look abashed and hang down.

This state of affairs continues ; from the leaves being simply wilted they begin to get yellow and shrivel up ; by ten days many of the plants have died outright, and the remainder are in a sad looking condition, that is disheartening to the owner.

No other result than this will ever be obtained with plants treated in this manner. When florists wish to lift plants of this nature in fall, two-thirds of the shoots are usually cut off, and the plants put through a course of treatment to induce them to strike new roots, that is hardly ever in the power of the amateur to apply ; but even though we succeed in saving the plants, it is almost always at the expense of the bloom, for few plants can be lifted in bloom in October from the open ground, and continue to blossom through the winter. Now, having pointed out the errors, I will show the way to succeed in obtaining healthy plants that will grow and bloom freely in winter, provided they are supplied with the necessary moisture and heat. All plants that are intended for house plants in winter, when set out in May, should be first planted in pots six or seven inches in diameter. These pots should be planted, or, as we term it, "plunged" to the rim, or level with the surface; thus they are almost in the same condition as if they had been planted without the pot, only the roots are confined inside of the pot, so that when the plant is lifted in fall there is no mutilation of the roots, as must always be the case when the plant is put in the open ground without the pot, as then the roots ramify in all directions. One caution, however, is necessary: the hole in the bottom of the pot must be effectually stopped up so that the roots cannot strike through, or the pot should be turned two or three times during the summer, so as to break off the roots as they strike through the bottom. If this is not done, nearly the same difficulty will be experienced as if they had not been put in the pots. But if proper attention has been given to this, plants of every description that are suitable for winter will be in a fine state by the time of taking up—in this district, the 1st of October, as by this time there is danger of frost.

The following list comprises those plants most suitable for window culture, and such as are most easily managed and least expensive.

Abutilons,
Calla (*Richardia*),
Carnations—monthly sorts,
Cyclamens,
Chryanthemums,
Chinese Primroses,
Fuchsias,
Hyacinths and other Bulbs (See Bulb Culture),
Geraniums, Variegated, Zonale, Scented and Ivy-leaved.

Heliotropes,
Mahernias,
Pelargoniums,
Roses—Tea, Bourbon, and Bengal,
Solanums,
Stevias,
Camellias, Azaleas, etc., etc.

All of these will flower and grow freely in a green-house temperature, or at an average of not more than fifty degrees at night, with fifteen or twenty degrees higher during the day.

We add another limited list of plants requiring a higher temperature, some of them being in other respects more difficult of culture, besides being more expensive :

Allamandas,	Begonias,
Bouvardias of all sorts,	Euphorbias,
Coleus of all sorts,	Poinsettias,
Stephanotis,	Ruellia formosa,

Salvias, etc., etc.

All of the above will luxuriate best in a humid atmosphere, at an average of not less than sixty degrees at night, with fifteen or twenty degrees higher during the day. The best aspect for growing plants from October to April is due south. For the intermediate season east is preferable. Watering is a very important operation, but a little experience with plants, and ordinary care in observing will soon show when this is required. A good deal depends upon the condition of the plant ; if in vigorous growth there is but little danger of giving it too much. On the other hand, if the plant has been cut back or lost its leaves, water should be given sparingly. For example, you may take a vigorous growing apple or pear tree, and saw off its limbs to the trunk in mid-summer ; if its roots are kept saturated with moisture it will die, but if kept dry it will shortly again develop branches and leaves. This example teaches us a lesson

in more artificial culture, that in proportion to the vigor
of the subject should its food be supplied.   The practice
of placing the pots in saucers filled with water is destructive to the health of most plants, as, of course, so long as
the water remains in the saucers, the soil is absorbing it
and the roots of the plant are saturated ; it is well
enough to use the saucers to prevent the soil from washing through, but the water should be applied at the surface of the pot, and what little will pass through into
the saucer will do no harm.   Another source of annoy-
ance to those growing plants in rooms is the various
insects that attack them.   The most common and
injurious of these is the *Aphis* or Green-fly.   In our greenhouses we keep this little pest in check by continued
fumigation with tobacco, but as this would not be practicable in rooms, recourse must be had to immersing the
plant in tobacco water, made of a strength having about
the color of strong tea.   By dipping the plant in this
once in two weeks, or, when the plants are large, syringing them with it, *Aphides* will never be seen.   The Red
Spider and thrips are not so easily got rid of, but fortunately they are not so common or injurious, unless in a
very high temperature and dry atmosphere.   The only
way of arresting them is syringing or immersing as for
Green-fly.   For more particulars see chapter on Insects.

There are no special soils necessary for the amateur to
trouble himself about in cultivating parlor flowers.   For
our opinions on this head see chapter on soils.   Neither
should he tamper with guano or other fertilizers ; equal-
ization of temperature and moisture will secure the end
desired.

WINDOW-GARDENING IN LONDON—COTTAGE GARDENS.

One of the most refreshing sights to an American
arriving in London during the summer months is the
wonderful diversity and beauty of the flowers cultivated

in the windows and balconies of the houses. In some of the best streets, hardly a house can be seen that is not so adorned, and even the most squalid abodes of vice and poverty are often relieved by a miniature flower-garden on the window-sill. The most common style is the window-box, made to fit the window, usually from four to five feet long, and about six to eight inches wide and deep. It is made of every conceivable pattern, of terra-cotta, cork, and rustic design in endless variety. The plants used are not very numerous in variety, being selected of kinds suited to keep in bloom or to sustain their brightness of foliage. Now and then the ribbon-line planting is adopted on the balconies; a very handsome box in this style had first a row of Moneywort (*Lysimachia nummularia*), which formed a drooping curtain of four feet in length ; half-way down on it drooped blue Lobelia ; then upon the Lobelia fell a bright yellow Sedum (Stone-crop), then against the Sedum, for the top-line or background, a dwarf Zonale Geranium, a perfect blaze of scarlet. Hardly two of these window decorations were alike in the best streets, and varied from a simple box of Mignonette or Sweet Alyssum to cases filled with the rarest Ferns or Orchids. The effect as a whole is most pleasing, and one that cannot fail to strike the most indifferent observer as an agreeable change from the seemingly never ending brick and stone of the city. The window-gardening is not confined to private dwellings, but all the leading hotels are so decorated. In the dining-room of the Langham Hotel, a favorite resort of Americans, some hundreds of well-grown specimens of plants are placed in the windows, and kept in perfect order during the entire summer. The selection of plants is made regardless of expense, and in looking around the dining-hall it is with some difficulty that you decide if you are not dining in the midst of a vast conservatory, so redolent is the air with the perfume of flowers. The same taste for window-gardening is displayed, more or less, in all the English towns and villages, and even the humblest thatched cottage of the peasant by the wayside is given a look of quiet happiness by the bower of flowers in the window.   How different the look of those humble homes, where the occupant is receiving barely four dollars per week, from the squalid shanties in the suburbs of our great cities in America, where the " naturalized " American citizen is often earning three times that amount !   Grand effects may be produced in our climate by the use of climbing vines as window plants, which can be trained outside in summer on wire or strings.   Notable among these are : *Cobæa scandens, Ipomæa noctiluca,* or Moon-flower, *Maurandias,* purple and white, and *Lophospermums;* for inside, the Climbing Fern, Smilax, or Climbing Asparagus.

Here let me deviate from my text, but to a kindred subject, and tell how the English cottager works his garden in some of the old towns, such as Colchester. To each cottage, renting for about fifty dollars per year, is attached a garden of something more than an eighth part of an acre in extent.   In this little spot the tenant contrives to grow four to six kinds of vegetables, such as potatoes, cabbages, peas, turnips, etc., and of fruits, gooseberries, currants, raspberries, and strawberries. Every foot is made to produce something, and rarely a weed was seen in some scores that we saw ranged side by side.   The heavy work is done by the man of the house, " before or after hours," in his own time.   In the weeding and hoeing he is assisted by wife or children.   There is great rivalry among the different owners of these cottage gardens, and in many places liberal prizes are given by the horticultural societies to those that are best cultivated.

Prizes are also offered for the best window-grown plants, and in Hull and some other towns, plants are distributed gratis and printed instructions given for culture, to encourage the taste.

There may be, however, a reason for the neglect of their gardens by the mechanics and laboring classes here. There is no question that at the time when the bulk of the work should be done, in the hot summer weather, the laborer has greater need of rest here after his day's work is over than in the cooler climate of England; moreover, there is longer daylight in England in summer, all of which, together with greater necessity for thrift, may be the reasons why the English cottager's garden is so much superior to that of the same class in the United States.

WARDIAN CASES, FERNERIES, ETC.

The Wardian Case is usually made with black walnut base lined with zinc, in depth about six inches, and about two feet square on the sides; but it is made of various sizes. The covering is a glass case, made usually eighteen inches high; the top or lid, also of glass, is made movable, so that ventilation is provided, and undue moisture allowed to escape. The plants grown in Wardian cases are such as are selected for their beauty of foliage rather than for their flowers, plants whose natural habitat is shady woods; such as Ferns, *Lycopodiums, Dracenas, Caladiums, Marantas*, etc., etc. The soil used in such a case may be light peat or leaf-mould; nothing of a stiff or heavy nature of soil should be used. The case may be kept in any ordinary sitting-room, near the window, but not exposed to the direct sunlight. There is no trouble whatever in management; one moderate watering when the case is filled will keep it without further attention for six weeks, except an occasional ventilation when moisture lies heavy on the glass. In winter the temperature of the room may run from fifty to sixty degrees at night. The culture of

Ferns or *Lycopods* requires somewhat similar conditions as are found in the Wardian case when not grown in it ; they cannot be successfully grown unless in partial shade in a close, moist atmosphere. Hence it is useless to attempt the cultivation of such in the dry atmosphere of an ordinary sitting-room, unless they are enclosed in cases. The florist can easily adapt his greenhouse to the proper conditions when required, but the amateur must secure these by means of a closed case of some kind. For single specimens or a few ferns and the like, a glass shade with a proper base of metal or earthenware is frequently used, and is very ornamental. Ferneries of this kind are sold at the principal horticultural and seed stores.

CHAPTER XLVI.

FORMATION OF ROCK-WORK, AND PLANTS FOR ROCKS.

This feature of pleasure ground decoration is generally necessitated by circumstances ; if the ground which has to be chosen for that purpose is naturally stony, it often becomes the cheapest way to get rid of the stones, grouping them so that they become ornamental. They may often thus be used to advantage in forming breaks or screens, to hide the flower garden from the vegetable or fruit garden ; in this way they are laid up in rugged walls, the interstices filled with soil and covered with hardy perennial plants. Locations where rocks exist in their natural condition can often be made highly interesting and ornamental by setting out plants of a climbing habit to run up them, or a drooping or trailing habit to overhang them. Among those suitable for the purpose of climbing are the now popular species of Virginia creepers, *Ampelopsis quinquefolia, A. Veitchii,* and *A. Royallii.* The latter two are particularly valuable for climbing on rocks, and are now becoming much used by the principal railroad companies, not only to ornament but to "lace up" shaley rocks through which cuts are made. We sold a few years ago, to one of our leading railroad companies in one season five thousand plants of *Ampelopsis Veitchii,* which now in many places have attained a height of thirty feet, giving to slipping rocks not only great support, but covering them with glittering green leaves in the summer and tinting them in autumn with crimson and gold.

For drooping and the general covering of rocks the following list will be found useful:

Achilleas, of creeping growth,	Sempervivums, of all kinds,
Campanulas, of creeping growth,	Linnæa borealis,
Crucianella stylosa,	Lychnis grandiflora,
Cerastium tomentosum,	Lysimachia nummularia,
Phloxes, of creeping growth,	Orobus vernus,
Polemonium reptans,	Soldanella alpina,
Saxifragas,	Vinca major variegata,
Sedums, of all kinds,	Thymus vulgaris variegata,
	Violas of sorts.

All these are hardy.

Artificial rock-works are often formed thus : The shape and dimensions of the work being determined on, the clinkers from furnaces are collected, and dipped in hot lime wash, which gives a coloring of pure white to their fantastic shapes. With these the "rock-work" mound is formed of the height and shape desired, leaving at suitable distances cavities of six or eight inches deep, to be filled with soil in which to place the creeping plants. For this kind of rock-work a different class of plants is more appropriate,—such as are of bright colors and will contrast with the ground work of white. Scarlet or other high-colored Verbenas, Coleus, Gazanias, Scarlet

Geraniums, Blue Lobelias, Lysimachia, or Golden Money-wort, may be used with excellent effect. By the use of hydraulic cement instead of lime, the rock-work can be made of a pleasing drab color. A rockery so formed and planted, without having any pretensions to being " nat-ural," is always an interesting and attractive object on a well-kept lawn.

CHAPTER XLVII.

ARE PLANTS INJURIOUS TO HEALTH?

Even yet, with all the light of experience on the sub-ject, if physicians are asked if plants kept in rooms are in-jurious to health, three out of six will reply that they are.

They will generally follow up the reply by a learned disquisition on horticultural chemistry ; will tell you that at night plants give out carbonic acid, which is poisonous to animal life, and consequently if we sleep in a room where plants are kept, we of necessity inhale this gas, and sickness will follow. These worthies generally suc-ceed in their specious reasoning, and the poor plants, that have bloomed gaily all summer, are often consigned to the coal cellar for their winter's quarters, if given quarters at all. No theory can be more destitute of truth ; that plants give out carbonic acid may be, but that it is given out in quantities sufficient to affect our health in the slightest degree is utter nonsense.

No healthier class of men can be found than green-house operators, which makes me sometimes think that plants have a health-giving effect rather than otherwise. But doctors may tell us that our workmen are only at

work in the day-time, and that it is at night that the
carbonic acid is emitted.   Here we meet them by the
information that in most cases the gardener in charge of
greenhouses often has to be up the greater part of the
night in winter, and the greenhouse from its warmth,
is universally taken as his sitting-room, and sometimes
as his bed-room ; such was my own experience for three
winters.   I had charge of a large amount of glass,
situated nearly a mile from my boarding-house, too far
to go and come at midnight, with the thermometer
below zero.   Our means of heating were entirely inadequate, so that the fires had to be looked to every three
or four hours.   Disregarding all my kind-hearted employer's admonitions, I nightly slept on the floor of the
hot-house, which was rank with tropical growth.   The
floor was just the place to inhale the gas, if there had
been much to inhale.   It did not hurt me, however, and
has not yet, and that is now nearly forty years ago.
That plants are injurious to health in sleeping rooms is
one of the bugbear assertions that is willingly swallowed
by the gullible portion of the community, always ready to
assign effects to some tangible cause, and this, as the asser-
tion evinces some chemical lore, is very prevalent among
those disciples of Esculapius who are always willing to be
thought learned in the science so intimately connected
with their profession.

CHAPTER XLVIII.

THE INJURY TO PLANTS BY FORCING.

Under the head of Carnations I referred to a disease which was very destructive among many of the older varieties of monthly Carnations, or Pinks, which we have been forcing for the last twenty years. I assumed that the trouble was in consequence of this excessive forcing, which had so lessened the vitality of the plants, that disease followed whenever the conditions were slightly unfavorable, such as too wet or too dry a soil. Since then, our observations have shown that nearly all the varieties of Roses in use for forcing for winter flowers are similarly affected. About the first of May one season I planted out in the open ground young plants, that had been propagated in January, of Safrano, Bon Silene, Douglas, Maréchal Niel, and four other varieties, which had been used for forcing during the winter. At the same time we planted out young plants made from cuttings of over thirty varieties of other Tea Roses, that had been grown during winter in a cold house, without being forced. The plants of both lots were all seemingly in a fine healthy condition; but about July 1st, we found that the forced varieties had not only made a much weaker growth than the others, but probably twenty per cent. died outright. In a conversation on this subject with Mr. Miller, the well-known florist and landscape gardener of Germantown, Pa., he cited the case of a nurseryman in England, who sent out the Dahlia, "Beauty of Hastings"; the first year it was exhibited from the seedling plant, it was found to be so entirely double, as to have what is known as a "hard center." It has been freely exhibited, and being the finest of its class at that time, orders for hundreds

of plants were consequently received for it. To obtain
the plants to fill the orders from the limited stock, it
was forced in a temperature unusually high; other cuttings were taken from the cuttings already struck, so
that a dozen roots were made to produce nearly 3,000
plants. When these plants came into flower, instead of
producing the fine form and double variety that had
been exhibited, nearly all produced semi-double flowers.
This brought a storm on the head of the unfortunate nurseryman, who was charged with sending out a spurious
variety, and he had not only to refund the money which
he had received for the plants, but was seriously injured
in his business standing. That semi-double flowers were
produced in consequence of lessened vitality, was shown
by the fact that these self-same roots produced in the
succeeding year and afterwards, double flowers like the
original, and for many years the " Beauty of Hastings "
was known as a standard sort. Again, we remember
that in the day of the grape-vine fever, the " Delaware,"
and some other varieties, by being propagated in a high
temperature and from the young shoots year after year,
became so weakened, as to hardly be recognized as the
original variety. Plants of Rhubarb, after they have
been forced, are usually thrown away as useless, and
Hyacinths, Tulips, Lily of the Valley, and nearly all
other roots and bulbs used in forcing take years to recuperate in the open ground after they have been once
made to bloom in the hot-house. This is so well known
among florists, that nearly all throw away the bulbs that
have been forced in winter. If we consider that this
treatment of the natives of temperate latitudes is in
direct violation of their natural condition, we will not
wonder that they rebel against the abuse. Carnations,
Roses, Grapes, and bulbs of nearly all kinds, are hardy,
or nearly so, in northern latitudes, and their nature
requires a rest of three or four months. Our forcing

system, now so universally adopted to produce the
flowers of the Carnation and Rose in winter, subject
them to a treatment similar to that proper for tropical
plants ; and this continued violation of their natural
requirements of culture, results in the evil alluded to.   I
never like to refer to any disease or other trouble among
plants, without being able to suggest a remedy.   In the
Carnation we would advise that, instead of propagating them as usual from cuttings made in spring, from
plants that have been forced all winter, that cuttings
be taken at the time plants are lifted in fall ; after they
are rooted, the young plants may be kept in a cold
green-house or frame during winter.   The same plan
might be adopted with the Roses forced in winter, if the
plants are wanted for summer flowering in the open
ground.   I know it is not always convenient to do so,
but when it is, I think it will be found a good method to
maintain the vitality of the stock.   This is now our own
method and our stock both of Roses and Carnations have
been much benefited since we adopted it.

CHAPTER XLIX.

NATURE'S LAW OF COLORS.

It has long been a belief among students in vegetable
physiology, that, in certain families of plants, particular
colors prevail, and that in no single instance can we ever
expect to see *blue, yellow, and scarlet colors in varieties
of the same species ;* yet, undeviating as this law seems
to be, it is astonishing to see the credulity that there is,
even among intelligent horticulturists, some of whom
believe that we will yet have exceptions to this law,
which, as far as all our experience has gone, seems as un-

alterable as the law of gravitation. If we reflect, we will find there is nothing out of the usual order of nature in this uniformity. The coloring given to the plumage of birds is as unalterable as that given to the petals of a flower in particular families. The most enthusiastic poultry fancier will look in vain for the scarlet plumage of the Flamingo in his Dorkings or Brahmas, or the color of the Baltimore Oriole in the occupants of his pigeon-house. What more reason, then, has the florist to expect that Nature should deviate from her fixed course, and gladden his eye with a Rose or Dahlia of an azure hue, or that a Verbena or a Petunia should be produced of a golden shade ?

A knowledge of this subject is much needed by our amateur horticulturists, who are imposed upon year after year by itinerant dealers, who with flaming colored drawings of these impossibilities in floriculture extract largely from the pockets of their victims, and in addition expose them to the ridicule of their less credulous or more cautious neighbors. The audacity of these scamps is truly astonishing ; not a season passes but some of them have the impudence to plant themselves right in the business centres of the city of New York, and hundreds of our sharp business men have for the consideration of four or five dollars, *believed* themselves in the possession of veritable blue Roses. Need I say that they were no less humbugged than the rustic who falls into the hands of a mock auctioneer, and chuckles to think that he has become the possessor of a gold watch for a similar price ?

In Rand's "Flowers for the Parlor and Garden," page 101, in remarking on the colors of the Verbena, he says a good *yellow* Verbena has not yet been produced, but goes on to say that he, "by a curious process of watering and fertilization with a white Verbena, obtained a seedling which proved on blooming to be of a light straw color;

but the plant was *weakly* and *sickly*, and died before cuttings could be taken." This "weakly" and "sickly" condition was exactly why Mr. Rand obtained his straw color; had the plant been in health it, no doubt, would have been only an impure white.

There are few florists of any experience who have not raised hundreds of just such "straw colors" in Verbenas from white, that have been *weak* and *sickly*, for we all know that the want of vitality in the plant imparts a *jaundiced* hue to white flowers.

It is hardly fair in Mr. Rand to withhold from us what that " curious process of watering and fertilization " was, by which he succeeded in bringing into existence what De Candolle, Lindley, and Loudon, have said can never be. When a man writes a book for the information of the public, nothing should be held in reserve; his readers have a right to every "secret" he may possess connected with the subject, and this reservation of Mr. Rand in so very interesting a matter is tantalizing in the extreme. Who knows but if he had given us the *modus operandi* of his "curious process of watering and fertilization" our Verbena beds would have long since had a golden yellow flaunting side by side with scarlet and blue, or that the same "*curious* process of watering and fertilization" applied to the Rose, would have produced a color rivalling a blue-bird in April?

It is much to be regretted that Mr. Rand's yellow Verbena was lost, but we trust that the "curious process" by which it was produced is not among the lost arts. If an application of it can be made to produce a positively yellow Verbena, the gentleman will receive the honors of the whole horticultural world, and, if he chooses, can pocket some thousands of dollars.

Not only are *blue, yellow* and *scarlet* colors never found in *varieties of the same species*, but so far even pure yellow or pure scarlet is never found, nor ever likely to be found in certain families of plants. For example, although we have grand crimson shades in the Rose, there is yet no approach to scarlet as seen in *Salvia splendens* (Scarlet Sage), nor any yellow in the Geranium at all approaching to the yellow of the yellow Calceolaria. But there are yet some of our best florists, who watch, year after year, the seedlings they raise; with the hope— vain I much doubt—that their eyes will be regaled with the vision of a scarlet Rose or a yellow Geranium. The alchemists of old, in their endeavors to turn the baser metals into gold, by their experiments greatly benefited the science of chemistry. So do these sanguine florists benefit horticulture by producing improved varieties, though they are likely never to attain the object of their solicitude.

CHAPTER L.

WHAT FLOWERS WILL GROW IN THE SHADE?

The question "What flowers will grow in the shade?" is put to me every spring by scores of city people, whose little patch which they wish to devote to flowers is so walled up by neighboring houses, that the direct rays of the sun never touch it. But few plants will develop their flowers there, and none will do it so well as if it were lighted up by sunshine a part of the day. Fuchsias, Pansies, Forget-me-nots, Violets, Lobelias, Lily-of-the-Valley, Hollyhocks, Phloxes, and other herbaceous plants whose native habitat is a shady wood, will do best, but even these languish if denied all direct sunlight. The best effect in such situations is produced by ornamental-leaved plants, the beauty of which is not dependent upon their flowers. Among these may be ranked the Gold and Silver Variegated-leaved Geraniums, Achyranthes, Alternantheras, Begonias, Caladiums, Centaureas, Coleuses, etc., which, if planted so as to bring the various shades in contrast, produce a pleasing effect, which continues during the entire summer months, and is not surpassed by any display of flowers.

The cultivators of flowers in rooms should understand the necessity of sunlight to plants that are to flower, and endeavor to get these as close as possible to a window having an eastern or southern aspect. The higher the temperature the more plants suffer from want of light. Many plants might remain semi-dormant, in a temperature of forty degrees, in a cellar for example, away from direct light, for months, without material injury, while if the cellar contained a furnace keeping a temperature of seventy degrees, they would all die; such would particularly be the case with plants of a half-hardy nature, such as monthly Roses, Carnations, Fuchsias, Geraniums, etc.

In our greenhouse culture of flowers, direct sunlight is an all-important consideration; and a spell of sunless weather in midwinter is often a loss to us of hundreds of dollars by preventing the development of flowers. Hence, we use every means at command to dispose the plants to secure the greatest amount of light.

The debilitating effects of want of direct light on plants are well illustrated by taking a vigorous plant in full foliage and flower, that has been growing in the direct light of our greenhouse benches, and placing it under the bench. If the temperature is high, say seventy degrees, in forty-eight hours, the sickly signs, showing want of light, will be apparent to an experienced eye; in a week its condition would be such as to indicate sickness to the most common observer, and in a month it would most likely be dead.

In this respect there is some analogy between plant and animal life, and it teaches us the importance of light for our own healthy development. Certain it is that our greenhouse and garden operatives will compare favorably with any other class of workmen, so far as health is concerned. In the past thirty years I have had an average of fifty workmen daily. During that time but three have died, and six only have been seriously sick, and some three or four veterans who are growing grey in the service, have never lost an hour by sickness. I doubt if it would be easy to find the same number of workmen employed *out of the sunlight,* who could show such health as these sun-browned boys of ours.

CHAPTER LI.

SUCCESSION CROPS IN THE GREENHOUSE.

Whether the Florist's business is carried on in a small way or on the most extensive scale, to make it profitable it is essential to have the green-house benches filled as often as practicable with succession crops; simply taking one crop off the benches will result at the present rate of prices in very meagre profits indeed. In my own practice, we have for many years taken never less than two crops off of every foot of bench space, and in many of our houses three, and in some particular families of plants such as Coleus, Verbenas and Heliotropes, as many as six crops are taken off of every foot of space.

To get more than *two* crops one must have an order business, which runs over five or six months of the season, but even a florist who has only a local retail plant trade or the open market to sell in should always be able to use every foot of his green-house space twice. In most towns the sales of plants whether in market or locally, begin in April and extend to June, a period of eight or ten weeks. As soon as the greenhouse space gets emptied towards the end of April or first weeks in May, succession crops from seedlings or cuttings should be on hand to be potted and shifted on so that the green-house benches may be as full by the middle or end of May, as they were in the middle of April, so that the season may be lengthened with salable stock to the middle of June. Of course to do this extra labor must be had at the proper time. This is not always to be obtained at the time needed, but it is always profitable to pay employees for over time at that busy season of the year. Every season from April to June, we have from fifteen to twenty of our best men working by lamp-light until ten or eleven o'clock, which is equal to adding seven or eight effective hands to our force, which could not be procured at the busy season of the year. Our men always go at such work willingly, as every hour they work after six o'clock is paid for as over time, which any firm well established in business on a paying basis can well afford and should do, but beginners with only two or three men,—struggling to make ends meet—may reasonably expect to have their hands help them in emergency without extra pay for over time, particularly if they are men who are kept throughout the entire year. Where the florist be ginning has only his own hands to rely on, if he wants to make the business a success, he had better make up his mind to "burn the midnight oil" for at least three or four months in the spring. For the first fifteen years I was in business, I think it safe to say that either in the office, green-house or grounds, I averaged sixteen hours per day throughout the entire year. Such work will never hurt a healthy man, because it is certain to bring success if judiciously employed, and success, other things being equal, we all know conduces to happiness and health in a far greater degree than its opposite.

CHAPTER LII.

PACKING PLANTS.

As commercial floriculture is now becoming a matter of importance, it will be interesting for many to know the modes of packing for shipment. During February, March, April, and May last (1887), it is estimated that twenty tons each day were received at the different express offices in New York, of the products of the greenhouse only. These were to be distributed throughout the length and breadth of the land, shipments being now successfully made in all weather to the most extreme points in every direction. The system of packing adopted for even the most distant orders is of the simplest kind, differing entirely from that of the English or French, and is a result, like many other of our operations, of the necessities forced upon us by the higher price of labor. By the system of packing in our own establishment, we ship plants every day from January 15th to June 15th, throughout the coldest weather in winter, and the sultry days of summer, with hardly a case of injury, either from freezing or by heat. For the cold season we use close boxes, lining top, bottom and sides with thick paper, against that, as the best non-conductor we can find, we put two inches of sawdust on top, bottom, and sides of the box. Whenever the ball of roots is sufficiently firm, the plant is taken from the pot, and each plant wrapped in paper, or rather the ball or root of the plant is wrapped, leaving most of the top uncovered. This wrapping in paper not only serves to keep the ball from breaking, but it also, to some extent, prevents the pressure of the plants upon each other. In packing the plants in a box, they are placed compactly in layers, alternated with an inch or two of soft hay, or the new packing material "Excelsior," until the box is full. The utmost care is necessary to pack the box *entirely full,* so that no movement can take place in the plants should the boxes be roughly handled. The soil should be always rather dry than otherwise, as packed in this close manner the plants will not suffer for want of moisture. Boxes of medium size are best; we never like to use a box of greater capacity than the ordinary flour barrel, usually preferring such as are one-third smaller than that. If the box is too large, the plants may be injured by mutual pressure.

This is our method of packing as long as there is danger of frost, or until the middle of March. From the middle of March to the middle of April, we use a box of a different character, open on all sides to admit air, for now the danger to be avoided is from heat and not from cold. The manner of packing is in all other respects the same, except that no more hay or "Excelsior," is used around the inside of the box than necessary to make a soft bed for the plants. If the closely packed plants have any tendency to generate heat, it will be counteracted by the admission of air through the openings in the box. Again, we gradually make a change in our style of packing to suit the advancing season. For small orders, a light kind of chip basket is used, in which the plants are packed in the manner above described, and strapped over the top with hay or "Excelsior." We find a basket a most convenient and satisfactory article to pack in, as its open-work sides freely admit the air. In baskets weighing less than two pounds, we pack from 100 to 150 plants. Being annoyed at having frequently to pay for clumsy, heavy packages, in which our new importations were received from England, I took occasion to send over to a London nurseryman some fifty plants packed in one of these baskets, the whole basket and contents weighing about 15 lbs., and with two exceptions every plant was received alive. I implored the gentleman to pack the plants he was to send me in return in similar light baskets, as it would not only save freight but, what was far more important, save me the plants alive. He sent them in baskets, sure enough, each one weighing of itself 40 lbs.,—a shapeless, ponderous affair, that with its contents required two men to lift it into a wagon. This was not the worst of it ; three-fourths of the plants were dead—our usual experience in shipments of plants from Europe. This loss is, without doubt, in most cases occasioned by the cumbrous manner of packing.

When the weather becomes settled, so that all danger of plants being chilled is over, we change our mode of packing the plants, from laying them down, to standing them upright in the baskets or boxes, beginning with the heaviest plants at the bottom of the box or basket, and placing each succeeding layer, to the depth of three or four, one ball of roots on the top of the other. *After* packing, the box or basket is watered freely, each plant, or at least a portion of it, is exposed to the light, and thus packed they will remain ten or twelve days without injury.

CHAPTER LIII.

PLANTS BY MAIL.

Our postal laws permit plants, seeds, and bulbs, to be sent at a cost of 16 cents per pound, provided the package does not exceed four pounds in weight. This arrangement has been the means of sending seeds and plants into regions where they would not for many years have been procurable with other means of conveyance, and the projector of the idea deserves the gratitude of the nation for it. A number of different contrivances have been invented for packing plants to go by mail, including boxes of various styles and dimensions ; the main difficulty with all that we have seen is the weight.

Plants may be packed without using boxes at all by adopting the following method. Having selected the plants, choosing such as are small but well rooted, the soil is washed or shaken from each plant, leaving the fibres of the roots uninjured. A layer of moderately damp moss half an inch thick is then spread on two or three thicknesses of thick brown paper ; the plants are then laid on the moss, a similar layer of moss is laid over the roots, and the paper, moss, and plants, are *tightly* rolled up. The moss absorbs the water from the dripping roots, so that thus tightly enclosed, sufficient moisture is enveloped in the packages to keep the plants safe for a week, provided that the package has been firmly wrapped up. Another wrapping of oil silk paper follows—the final wrapping being of stiff brown paper. This process is so simple that any lady may transmit to another some favorite plant or cutting. a distance of 2,000 miles, if necessary, at little cost. The florists who make a special business of mailing plants now use a box specially made for the purpose, alternating the filling of the box with thin layers of moss—not too damp—with the layers of plants. Where moss is not procurable, raw cotton will answer the same purpose; the only danger to be avoided is in rolling up the package too loosely, in which case the dry air will penetrate and will be likely to shrivel up the plants.

Although it is a great convenience to be able to send plants by mail to points where there is no express office, yet we most emphatically protest against sending in this way wherever they can be sent by express. Not only is sending by a mail a slow and expensive method of packing, but the necessity to lighten the package, compels the soil to be taken from the roots and to compress the plants in the package so that they are often crushed to their injury. We, in our business, never send a plant by mail where it can be sent by express, unless at distinct request of the buyer.

CHAPTER LIV.

INSECTS AND DISEASES AFFECTING PLANTS.

There is no subject referred to in this volume, that I feel so incompetent to discuss as that of insects. Not that our experience with the pests has not been ample enough, but all the knowledge obtained from that expe-rience leaves us at times utterly helpless to prevent their ravages, particularly on plants grown out of doors. Un-der glass, we may say that they are entirely under control, and I have always considered that no better evidence of the incompetency or negligence of the person in charge of the greenhouse could be had, than to see the plants covered with insects.

The most annoying of all insects of the flower garden, is the

Rose Slug, *Selandria rosæ,* a light green, translucent little fellow, varying from one-sixteenth of an inch to nearly an inch in length. There are evidently two species or varieties, one of which confines its ravages to the lower side of the leaf; the other eats it entire. The first is by far the most destructive here. In a few days after the plants are attacked they appear as if they had been burned.

The best remedy we have found, is a preventive one, which, in fact, ought to be used against all insect life. Before the leaves of the roses appear, just as soon as the buds begin to develop, apply Whale-oil Soap, in the pro-portion of one pound to ten gallons of water; this, steadily applied for ten days, with a syringe or garden engine, has, in my experience, entirely prevented the at-tacks of the insect. But once let it get a foothold and it can hardly be driven off by this application, unless it be made strong enough to injure the foliage, making the remedy worse than the disease. A safe remedy when the insect has made an attack on the leaves, is to dust powdered White Hellebore or Pyrethrum over the leaves in the morning, when the dew is on; or if no dew, first wet the leaves by syringing, and then apply the powder. The species of Rose Slug that eats the entire leaf seems to confine its depredations more to young plants, and later in the season. We have found it quite troublesome in June and July among our young roses, which had been planted out in May and June, and as these were young and tender plants, the Whale-oil Soap remedy could not safely be applied, and it would hardly be practicable to apply the Pyrethrum or the Hellebore; so we have often had acres of young roses covered by myriads of these slugs, before they were observed, and nothing could be done except to shake the plants, and kill the insects when they fell to the ground. In the summer of 1866, we had some nine or ten boys shaking the plants and killing the slugs for upwards of a week, and by this means saved our crop of roses. In 1868 we had a whole army of volunteer exterminators, in the thousands of English Sparrows that had been imported some years previous, and which we yet feed and house with the greatest care during winter. We observed immense flocks of them actively engaged for days in picking up something in our rose beds, and had imagined it to be seeds obtained from the refuse hops, that we had used as a mulching. At times we felt inclined to believe that they would pick the tender leaves of the rose, to use by way of a salad, having always believed them to be strictly "vegetarians," or seed eaters. Finding, however, that we were less troubled with the Rose Slug that season than usual, it occurred to me that perhaps we were indebted to our noisy, feathered friends for the immunity. To test the matter, a victim was necessary; accordingly a plethoric looking fellow was shot, when, sure enough, his well-stuffed crop revealed seeds, Rose Slugs, and

Aphis, or Green Fly, in great abundance, demonstrating beyond all question the great value of these birds as insect destroyers.

The **Rose Bug** (*Macrodactylis subspinosus*), or Rose Chafer, as it is sometimes called, is so named from its attacking the buds or blossoms of the rose, in preference to anything else, although it is destructive to many other plants, particularly to the Dahlia, the flower of which it devours rapidly.   All the ordinary remedies seem to fall harmlessly on the Rose Bug, and if not destroyed by hand its ravages cannot be stopped, unless our feathered friends come to the rescue; whether they will be equally efficacious in destroying the Rose Bug, I am unable to say, although I am inclined to think they will. We have never yet been much troubled with them here, and so far have not had the opportunity of knowing whether the Sparrows feed on them or not.

The **Rose Bug**, (*Aramigus Fullerii,*) the larva of which is so destructive to the roots of roses grown under glass in winter, has no resemblance whatever to either the Rose Slug or the Rose Chafer, but is vastly worse than either of these in its ravages.   The perfect insect (that is not unlike the Curculio, which deposits its eggs in the fruit of the Plum tree) does little injury to the Roses, merely biting little circular pieces out of edges of the leaves, but it is by this cutting of the leaves that their presence is first known, as the insect, though larger than a common house fly, is not easily seen from its habit of keeping under the leaves or close to the stems of the plant.   So far all efforts to destroy this pest have proved futile, except to pick off the fully developed bug from the plants, and so prevent it depositing its eggs at the roots of the Roses.   These eggs quickly hatch into grubs, resembling meat maggots, which at once begin to feed on the roots, and thus quickly destroy the plants. Once a rose bed gets badly infested, there is as yet no known remedy. Nothing can be done but throw the plants out and the soil also, if Roses are again to be planted in the same house.

The first time I saw this Rose Bug was in 1872. I noticed that our Roses, though otherwise healthy, made nc growth. A friend coming along one day, who had sad experience with the insect, asked me to allow him to pull a plant up. At its roots hung scores of the maggots—the larvæ of the Rose bug. I at once threw out the whole—the plants, the soil, and even the bench itself, though the space it covered was ten feet by three hundred, containing nearly three thousand Roses. Fortunately its ravages were confined to that house, so I at once adopted the plan of paying our boys a dollar a hundred for what bugs they could find, working at their dinner hour. This soon subdued them, so that for years we have been free from the Rose bug, the greatest pest that the Rose grower has to fight against, particularly if he grows his Roses on the benches for two years.

The **Aphis** is one of the most common insects affecting plants. There are quite a number of kinds, showing different colors, on different plants. Thus, when it attacks the roots of plants, it is *blue;* on Roses and most other plants it is *green;* on the chrysanthemum and a few other plants it is *black*.

Hundreds of my amateur friends come to me year after year, with sorrowful tales of their verbenas, asters, etc., which were pictures of health and beauty, but now are one after another sickening and dying, apparently without cause. But there was a cause, and in most cases one cause only. The *Blue Aphis* is at the roots, and the only chance to save them is an application of tobacco water, about the color of strong tea, applied copiously and persistently to the roots, for at least a week.

We have occasionally saved all our stock by this remedy, when used at once, as soon as they were seen to be affected.

Many species of plants are attacked by this insect at the root. Asters, particularly, are much injured by it. In fact, when in excess, there is hardly a species of plant exempt from its attacks. We have often seen this Aphis clustering by thousands on the roots of melons, cucumbers, and of beets, to the very points of the roots, a foot below the surface.

The **Green Fly** (or Green *Aphis*) is *prevented*, (for I contend that it should never be seen, so that it need be destroyed), by fumigating with tobacco smoke, not less than twice each week. We do it in a manner much more simple and agreeable to the operator than is often practiced. Two or three times each week during the entire season at which our green-houses are filled with plants, we use a small handful of shavings, on top of which we place about half a pound of tobacco stems, previously made damp. The shavings are lighted, and the fire being on the cement flooring, is left to take care of itself. If the floor, however, is of wood, provision should be made against danger from fire. We use this quantity of tobacco to every five hundred square feet of glass; we burn thus five or six tons of tobacco stems every season, but we rarely see a green fly. We have occasionally seen this insect increase to such an extent in its different conditions, that fumigation was powerless to destroy it, or rather it would have required it to be applied so strong, to dislodge the vast number of the enemy, that the plants would have been injured. The safer way to treat a desperate case of this kind is to brush the insect off by hand, or with a soft brush; this is a slow process, but an effectual one. This condition of the plants can only be the result of utter neglect. The green fly sometimes injures plants which stand too near together, so that the leaves get matted so closely that the fumes of the tobacco cannot penetrate. This is a condition, where recourse must be had to brushing the insects from the leaves, and, if possible, spreading the plants so that the air can pass freely among them.

All Rose growers in winter now find that the best way to prevent the green fly is to strew tobacco stems under the benches or paths, two or three inches thick, renewing them every three or four weeks. Although the odor is hardly perceptible from the tobacco, yet it has the effect of entirely suppressing the *Aphis*. Of course, this plan would be equally effectual in destroying the insect on all kinds of plants, but is somewhat more expensive than smoking, and the reason of using it in the Rose houses is that the smoke injures the buds.

Another method, equally effective in destroying the Aphis, is to syringe the plants and then dust them over with tobacco dust. Still another, is to steep the stems until the water gets to be of the color of strong tea, and syringe it on the plants. These last two remedies are really the only ones that can be applied when the Aphis attacks plants out of doors, either method is effective against the *black Aphis*, which attacks the chrysanthemum as well as against the common green Aphis.

The **Red Spider** is rather a more insidious enemy than the Green Fly, and far more tenacious of life, and often does much mischief before its presence has become known. The experienced gardener, of course, should not only be able to detect its presence, but also to discover the atmosphere favorable to its production. A dry and hot atmosphere, so dry that few plants can long continue in health in it, is such as this pest delights to revel in. Such an atmosphere in hothouse or greenhouse is thus doubly hurtful to plant life, and therefore should never be allowed. The remedies are simple; if there is not time for syringing, let water be thrown copiously on the paths, under and on the benches, place pans filled with water on the flue or pipes, or use any other means that may suggest itself, to counteract the aridity of the air, due to heavy firing in winter, or hot, dry days in spring or summer. Therefore, as in the case of the Green Fly, if proper preventives are used, the Red Spider need never be seen in the greenhouse.

The red spider is an exceedingly minute insect, so small that it is a mere speck when seen by the naked eye, but when closely examined, may be seen moving with great rapidity. Though minute in themselves the presence of these insects may be quickly detected, by the upper side of the leaves becoming browned, though the ravages are confined to the under side of the leaf. Parlor plants are often subject to this insect, as it is not convenient to give the necessary moisture, and the only remedy in such cases, if the collection is not too numerous, is sponging the leaves. Florists who have a sufficient force of water, have but little trouble with the Red Spider, as forcibly applied daily it quickly destroys them. In the absence of city water, the force pump or hand syringe must be used.

We often have woeful complaints from inexperienced cultivators, that their plants all get brown and look sickly, and it requires but little thinking to divine what enemy is making the attack.

The aphis, from its size, is quickly seen, and means may be used at once to destroy it, but this minute red pest may be sapping the life of a plant for weeks before it is discovered. Amateur cultivators generally expect to see something more tangible in a spider, if they have heard of the red dragon at all, and are often hard to convince, that this minute insect is the cause of so much disaster.

I will relate a rather ludicrous incident, to show that some even of larger experience may become possessed of that notion.

Many years ago I had in my employment an active young Irishman, who, by showing more than ordinary energy, quickly passed through the different grades, until he was duly installed as foreman; at that time we had been firing a Camellia house, and by neglect of keeping a properly moist atmosphere, the red spider had made sad inroads. John was duly instructed to syringe the plants, night and morning, to destroy it, which he did; no doubt with a double object in view, as the sequel will show. John was on all occasions rather demonstrative, but one morning he came rushing towards me, his face radiant with triumph, with his hat off, but clasped in his hands, in a careful manner, evidently having something of no common value within it. Before I had time to inquire what was the cause of his excitement, he yelled out " I've got him! bedad! I've got him at last!" "What have you got," I enquired, expecting to see something in the way of a rat or mouse. " Arrah, the big devil himself, the blaggard that has been doin' us all the mischief, the *Reed* Sphider!" and opening his hat, a villainous Tarantula-looking fellow ran out, bigger than a thousand red spiders, which was quickly despatched by John's brogan. From that time John learned to know what the red spider was, but was never anxious to allude to it afterwards.

The **Verbena Mite,** the minute cause of the "black rust" so disastrous in its ravages on the Verbena, Heliotrope, Petunia, Pelargonium, and various other plants, is so small that it cannot be seen by the naked eye; but its ravages under certain conditions are so disastrous as to render the cultivation of the Verbena and some similar plants next to impossible.

Viewed by a powerful microscope, this insect, magnified 400 times, appears of the size given in Fig. 58; it moves with great rapidity, and can only be examined as it stops to feed. When this little pest has once got a foothold, all direct remedies to dislodge him seem to be powerless; the fumes of tobacco, so destructive to the aphis, or of sulphur, which is death to the spider, fall harmlessly on this microscopic insect.

There is hardly a doubt but that the fumes of sulphur or tobacco would destroy it, if it had not the power of imbedding itself in the leaf. This is evidently the case, as on subjecting affected plants to a severe fumigation with tobacco for thirty minutes no insects could be discerned on the leaves; but after a short time they again appeared on the field of the microscope, apparently unscathed. We also find that an excellent preventive against this insect is to syringe the plants twice a week with a weak solution of fir-tree oil; one-half pint to five gallons of water. This seems like tobacco smoke to check it somewhat, yet it is not a complete remedy and if plants are severely attacked, there is nothing for it but to throw those affected out—as there is but little doubt that it quickly spreads. Now, although we have no direct remedy against this insect, which produces the black rust, we have, I think, a preventive, by keeping the plants in that healthy condition which seems to be

Fig. 58.

repellant to its attack. For the means used to get that healthy condition, see chapter on the culture of the Verbena, which is, with slight modifications, equally applicable to all other plants affected by this insect.

The microscope reveals that this particular species, which is so destructive to our Verbena, Heliotrope, Petunia, and scores of other plants cultivated in the greenhouse or garden, is the same or one that closely resembles that which gives the roughness to particular parts of the cherry, plum, and peach trees, and no doubt is to be found on thousands of other kinds of plants, whenever a lessened vitality takes place. Corroborative of this view, I had a lot of about 500 plants of Heliotrope growing in two-inch pots in one of our greenhouses one

year, one-half of which were, in September, shifted into
three-inch pots, to be reserved for stock plants. They
were kept side by side and treated in all respects the
same. Those shifted, of course, with increased food,
grew vigorously and strong, while the unshifted remained
comparatively stunted, and on the following December
1st, the "black rust" showed itself on nearly every plant,
and the microscope revealed on every affected leaf hundreds of these insects, feeding like sheep on a pasture
field, while on the shifted plants none whatever were
found. This is only one of hundreds of cases which
yearly come under our observation, to prove that, from
whatever cause the vital action of a plant is impaired,
it is placed in the condition which in a greater or less degree invites the attack of parasitic fungi (mildew) or insects.

Mealy Bug, as it is familiarly termed, is a white, mealy
or downy-looking insect, belonging to the same family,
from which the cochineal of commerce is obtained. It
is an insect of the tropics, and is troublesome only among
hot house plants, or such as are grown at a high temperature. Fortunately we have now a complete antidote
against the ravages of the Mealy Bug by the use of fir-tree
oil, mixed at the rate of one pint to five gallons of water,
and syringed over the plants once a week. In fact the
use of fir-tree oil, mixed and applied as above, has kept
our greenhouses almost free from Mealy Bug and nearly
all other insects, since we began using it in 1884. The
great point, however, is its steady application, it being
applied weekly. The proportions above given we find
best for Dracenas, Crotons, etc., but for tender Roses,
Verbenas, etc., in delicate growth half a pint to five gallons of water is as strong as it can be applied with
safety.

Brown and **White Scale Insects.**—These are less injurious and less common to plants than any of the preced-

ing, and are generally found in dark or ill-ventilated greenhouses, adhering to the stems and under part of the leaves of hard-wooded plants. The best remedy is fir-tree oil, used as described for Mealy Bug.

Thrips is an active insect, varying in size from that hardly perceptible by the naked eye, to the size of the Green Fly, and varying in color from whitish-yellow to dark brown; it is a jumping insect, very active in its movements, and when it once gets a foothold is very destructive. It succumbs to tobacco smoke, but not so quickly as does the Green Fly. It luxuriates in shaded situations, and is generally found where plants are standing too thickly together, or where the ventilation or light of the greenhouse has been deficient. I think it may be safe to assert that in any well-regulated greenhouse or hot-house no injury from insects will ever become serious, if proper attention to *syringing* and *fumigating* has been given. Syringing, or other means of keeping a moist atmosphere, must never be neglected for a day, and fumigating by tobacco smoke should be done, at the least, once each week. The application of fir-tree oil will also quickly check Thrips or Aphis.

The "**Carnation Twitter.**"—This is an insect fortunately but little known, and called in this district only by its local name of "Carnation Twitter," given from its rapid and nervous motion. As seen by the naked eye it is about the twentieth part of an inch in length, and of a thickness not more than that of a cambric needle. It is of various shades of color, from green to black; it is never very numerous on the plants, but most destructive and evidently poisonous in its attacks on all varieties of the Carnation and Pinks.

Its effects on the Carnation somewhat resemble those of the Red Spider, except that when attacked by the "Twitter," the leaves have a cankered and twisted appearance, easily distinguishable from the browning effects of the Spider. When Carnations or Pinks get infested by this insect, all remedies to dislodge it seem futile. We have lost thousands of plants in a season by its attacks. It seems, however, to infest light or sandy soil more than heavy loam or clay, and seems, also, to be intermittent in its attacks, often not being seen for three or four years in succession, and again returning and destroying all in its path. In our light sandy soil at lower Jersey City we suffered from it, but for fifteen years, in our heavy, clayey soil on Jersey City Heights, it has rarely been seen. It generally attacks the plants in the open ground. We have not had it since we began the use of the fir-tree oil, and so have as yet had no opportunity to try it, but I am inclined to think it might be equally useful here, as it is against all other insects.

Slugs or Snails.—These are troublesome both in the open ground and in the greenhouse. Salt is certain death to them, even in smallest quantities, and when in the open garden, a slight sprinkling of salt over the ground is effectual; but the sprinkling, it must be remembered, must be very slight, as salt, if put on (even as thick as sand is usually strewn on a floor) will kill almost any kind of vegetation. In our greenhouses the snails usually feed at night, getting under the benches during the day. We have found a most effectual remedy in strewing a thin line of salt on edge of each bench;—this makes a complete "dead line" for the Slugs or Snails, for they cannot cross it and live. Another plan is to slice up potatoes, carrots, cabbage, or lettuce leaves, to feed on, for which they will leave all other plants. Examine these traps daily, and destroy the captives.

Ants are the most troublesome of all insect pests on lawns on sandy soils, and when these are on such large areas, any remedy as yet known is almost futile to destroy them. When on small areas, outside or in the greenhouse, we find about the best plans are to lay fresh bones, or paper covered with molasses, around their haunts. These they will come to in large numbers. They should be removed daily, and burned or otherwise destroyed. Another method that we have found more destructive to them than any other, is to puff Pyrethrum or Persian Insect Powder from a strong bellows among them. The smallest particle of this powder at once chokes and kills them, though it must strike them dry to be effective; for we find that when the powder lies *damp* on the floor, they will run over it, and even burrow in it with impunity. Nothing I have ever tried will "poison" Ants. Either their instinct causes them to avoid it, or else they are not affected by it.

Angle Worms probably do no harm to plants except to disturb and "glue up" the soil, but this is to some extent hurtful to plants grown in pots or on benches in greenhouses. A simple remedy is to slack one pound of lime in fifteen or twenty gallons of water; let the lime settle to the bottom, using only the clear water, which will be sufficiently impregnated with lime to destroy the worms. The same remedy can also be applied in the open ground; but Angle Worms do but little harm in the garden. In placing plants in pots out-doors or on an earth bench in the greenhouse, first sprinkle over with lime, which will prevent the worms entering the pots through the drainage holes.

CHAPTER LV.

MILDEW.

Opinions as to the cause of mildew are varied and somewhat contradictory. My view is, that mildew being a fungus growth, its seeds or spores are ever present in the atmosphere; and when a relaxed condition of the plant ensues, the minute germs find a suitable place for their development in the enfeebled leaf. Therefore I believe that anything that impedes the flow of the sap, places the plant in the condition fitted to develop mildew. Thus we often see our Roses without a taint of mildew during all the winter and early spring months, until the hot, dry weather of the middle or end of May dries the soil in the pots to such a degree that the plant wilts—the sap is impeded, and mildew follows. Or a door may be left open and the frosty air fastens on the stems and leaves, congeals the sap, enfeebles the plant, and though from an entirely opposite cause, the result is the same.

I once had a most marked example of this kind. Early in April we had an old-fashioned lean-to green-house filled with Roses in full leaf, in the very highest state of vigor. The house was some sixty feet in length and was ventilated by sliding down every alternate sash at the top. In ventilating on one occasion, the sashes had been neglected to be closed until so late in the evening that the Roses exposed to the air had become chilled by frost so that the young shoots hung down as if wilted; as the greenhouse got heated up they recovered, and to all appearance next morning looked none the worse for being frozen; but in a week after, mildew appeared in a clearly defined square space of about 3x3 feet, following almost exactly in the line where the plants had been frostbitten. It would here seem that the leaves thus enfeebled by the frost, simply afforded a congenial "soil," for the mildew germs, which probably are ever present in the atmosphere.

Had the sap been arrested by the roots getting dry in that condition of growth, no doubt the result would have been nearly the same.

Like most other diseases, mildew is best met by prevention rather than cure, and for this reason, all care should be taken to avoid the extremes referred to, as far as possible, to avoid great variation of temperature. Sulphur is applied in various ways to destroy mildew, but will often fail if the disease has gained much headway. The best way is to use it mildly as a preventive. This is done by boiling three pounds of sulphur and three pounds of lime in six gallons of water until it is reduced to two gallons; allow the liquid to settle until it gets clear, then pour it off and keep it in a jar, or bottle it for use. One gill of this is to be mixed in five gallons of water and syringed over the Roses in the evening. Applied in this weak state it does not injure leaves, and yet has the effect of preventing mildew, if perseveringly attended to, as the spores of mildew seemingly cannot vegetate in an atmosphere or in a soil impregnated with sulphur. The above preparation is Sulphite of Calcium.

Another method is, to dust the leaves very lightly with "Black," or "Virgin Sulphur"—the only reason this kind is used in preference to the ordinary yellow sulphur is, that it is more volatile and can be used to give a lighter covering to the foliage, answering equally well and being less unsightly. We use one or the other of these methods once a week during spring or summer on our Roses, and thus keep almost entirely clear of mildew on all Roses grown under glass.

But the most common and most efficient application of sulphur against mildew in the greenhouse, after firing has begun, is to paint the upper half of the hot-water pipes, with a mixture of sulphur and cow dung, sulphur and guano, or sulphur and lime. Either of these ingredients will do to mix with the sulphur, the object being to merely give a body to the mixture. We also paint our steam pipes with these mixtures, but care must be taken not to have more than *one-fourth* of the steam pipes painted, else the fumes of the sulphur might be strong enough to injure the leaves. For *Black Spot*, or *Black Mildew*, and *Club Root* or *Wart Root*, see chapter on " Rose Growing in Winter."

CHAPTER LVI.

DIARY OF OPERATIONS FOR THE YEAR.

The following diary of operations and observations of temperature was taken by my general foreman, at our greenhouses at Jersey City, N. J., from September 9th, 1867, to September 9th, 1868. It is here given with some additions from our operations taken from a diary running through the same months in 1885—86. Although it necessarily contains many repetitions and matters of minor interest, it will be found very valuable as a guide to the beginner, as well as for convenient reference to those of mature experience. We ourselves find such a diary an excellent monitor, as the importance of dates in all horticultural operations can not be over-estimated. The record of the thermometer taken in 1867—68 is placed at the end of the notes for each day, the first figure giving the temperature in the shade at 6 A. M., and the second that at 6 P. M.

SEPTEMBER.

9th.—From this date, once a week or oftener according to necessity, all plants grown under glass are syringed with a solution of fir-tree oil, to keep down mealy bug, scale, and other insects; it is also applied to Roses that are planted on benches for winter flowering, which are syringed every morning as soon as the sun strikes the glass, to keep down red spider, thrip, etc. We never syringe on dull days. Lifted and potted Bouvardias, preparatory to planting them out again on the benches for winter. It is of the utmost importance that Bouvardias should be potted early—not later than the middle of September, in this section. If left until cool weather sets it, they will not root freely in the pots, being plants that luxuriate in a high temperature. The plants are kept shaded and watered carefully, for a week or so after being potted, and it is better to keep them outside until they are placed permanently in the greenhouse. Also, put in cuttings of Variegated Geraniums of various kinds this day. Topped Carnations, for the purpose of producing suitable cuttings in October; it is now too late to cut back those that are wanted for winter flowers. Collected seeds of *Salvia patens* and *S. splendens*. Cleared off old plants of Pansies, to allow the self-sown seedlings light and air. Beginning to dry off Caladiums grown in six inch pots. 60°—62°.

10th.—Continued potting Bouvardias. Put in cuttings of Zonale Geraniums; also, a few cuttings of those Verbenas of which our stock is short. 61°—64°.

12th.—Repotted Primulas, for winter flowering. Sowed Cabbage, Cauliflower, and Lettuce seed in open ground, to be planted out under cold frames in October. 59°—55°.

13th.—Repotted Fuchsias for stock. Layered Strawberries in two-inch pots, to make a plantation next month, rather late, however. 54°—60°.

14th.—Began propagating general collection of Verbenas; cuttings in excellent order. Collected flower seeds of all kinds. 58°—59°.

16th.—Repotted Euphorbia, Poinsettia, and other plants for winter flowering. Lifted and potted stock Geraniums that we are short of to make cuttings during winter. 55°—59°.

17th.—Began propagating a general collection of bedding plants, and as the weather is getting somewhat hotter, precaution is taken to douse the walks, benches, and all parts of the propagating houses with water, to reduce the temperature. A little ventilation left on in all Rose houses at night—the object being to prevent a too tender growth, as colder weather must soon be expected. 65°—75°.

18th.—Collected seeds of Campanulas, Lychnis, Delphiniums, and other hardy herbaceous plants, and sowed at once; nearly all seeds of this character germinate better if sown as soon as gathered. 69°—74°.

19th.—Overhauled boilers and examined valves, preparatory for winter work, painted pipes with sulphur mixture to ward off mildew. See "Mildew."

20th.—Potted off in two-inch pots the Verbena cuttings that were put in on the 10th and 12th inst. Result excellent. No fire heat has as yet been used in propagating. 68°—70°.

22d.—Planted those Bouvardias that were potted on the 9th instant, on the benches of the greenhouse; also placed Poinsettias under glass. They are taken from the pots and planted in six inches of soil, at a distance of from eight to twelve inches apart, or near enough for the plants to touch. The distance apart is regulated by the size of the plants. Began to propagate second and largest lot of Verbenas, Heliotropes, and general collection of bedding plants, it being rather safer at this date than on the previous ones of the 10th and 12th, on account of a general lower temperature. Gathered Verbena, Salvia, and other flower seeds, that are in better state now than they were two weeks ago. 52°—52°.

23d.—Removed the slight shading from the glass that was put on in June.

24th.—Put in main crop of Verbena cuttings from open ground at this date. Fumigated greenhouses, in which bedding plants are kept for the first time this season; will continue to do so at least twice every week until the greenhouses are again empty of plants, the order being that Aphis or Green Fly must never be seen; placed fresh tobacco stems under the Rose benches.   43°—55°.

25th.—Lifted Carnations with balls of earth from the open ground, and planted them in five or six inches of soil on the benches of the greenhouses for winter flowering. We are enabled to lift them in this way from the peculiarity of our soil, which is stiff and clayey; on most soils this method would not be practicable; if the soil did not adhere to the roots it would be necessary to be more careful in shading.   Put in cuttings of Variegated and Zonale Geraniums for main crop.   58°—60°.

26th.—Continued putting in Verbena and other cuttings. First fires started. It is all important to watch for the first fall in temperature about this date. Many houses of Roses and other plants are ruined from the neglect to start slight fires when the thermometer quickly falls, as it often does at this date, fifteen degrees in twelve hours. In 1881, before this was generally understood, one-half of all the Rose houses in the vicinity of New York had their contents destroyed during a cold rain storm in September, where the thermometer fell twenty degrees in twenty-four hours.   40°—44°.

27th.—Planted out in the benches Eupatoriums, Stevias, etc., that have been kept in pots all summer.   42°—50°.

28th.—Put in cuttings of Coleus, Salvias, etc., from outside.   42°—49°.

30th.—Put all tender plants in the houses, as from about this date there is danger from frost. Lifted clumps

of double Neapolitan Violet, and planted them at distances of nine or ten inches apart, on the benches of cold
greenhouse, in the same way as the Carnations. The
same precautions necessary in shading and watering, if
the weather is dry and sunny. 42°—50°.

OCTOBER.

1st.—Lifted and potted Carnations and Pinks from the
open ground, that are wished for early flowering in spring.
42°—53°.

2d.—Potted off Petunias, Zonale Geraniums, and other
bedding plants that were put in as cuttings on the 17th
ult. Planted out *Stevia compacta* and other varieties on
benches of greenhouse, for winter flowering, as they
are too tall, they are planted by laying them on their
side, which answers well. Lifted up and planted Strawberry runners closely together in cold frames, so that they
can be conveniently got at in spring for early orders.
Planted early, they make root sufficient to stand the winter. 42°—52°.

3d.—"Top dressed" Rose beds, one inch in depth,
with a compost of two parts soil and two parts rotted
cow dung, to which is added about one-twentieth in bulk
of pure bone dust.

4th.—Potted off Verbenas put in on the 22d ult.; had
excellent success. 47°—50°.

5th.—Lifted from ground stock plants of Variegated
and Zonale Geraniums, and potted them. 49°—54°.

7th.—Operations same as Saturday. To-day shows the
first ice, and very tender plants outside are somewhat injured. *Dahlias uninjured.* 33°—48°.

8th.—Corrected and re-labeled Dahlias, in anticipation
of their soon being cut down by frost. Potted off Verbenas, and put in cuttings of Verbenas, and Rose and Zonale
Geraniums. 34°—46°.

9th.—The advancing season warns us to house Lemon

Verbenas, Geraniums, Roses, Chrysanthemums, and other of the more hardy plants that have yet been standing out-doors. Lemon Verbenas being deciduous (shedding their leaves), are put *under* the benches, as they can there be kept with safety until March, when they begin to start again; the temperature will average 45° under the bench. 46°—52°.

10*th.*—The same as yesterday.

11*th.*—Lifted Japan and other Lilies and placed them closely together, covered with four inches of sand, at the north side of a south wall, to retard them for spring sales; they are lifted for this purpose only, as nearly all Lilies are hardy, and will always do better if left out undis-turbed all winter where they grew; though if the situa-tion is very cold or exposed, a covering up with a few inches of sawdust, leaves, or manure, will be of benefit. 48°—61°.

12*th.*—Put in cuttings of Fuchsias, Heliotropes, and Carnations, that have been started from plants grown under glass; young shoots only.   49°—62°.

14*th.*—Lifted Tuberoses, and placed them in empty benches of greenhouses to dry. Tied down the flowering shoots of Tuberoses that are getting against the glass. 44°—52°.

15*th.*—The earlier kinds of Chrysanthemums, such as *Elaine* (white), *Red Dragon, Lance d'Or* (dark yellow), *Boquet Fait* (rose), *Geo. Glenny* (lemon color), *J. Collins* (bronze), are now coming in flower and selling well, other flowers being rather scarce at this date. We find it best to grow for flowers such Chrysanthemums as are *early* and *late,* and thus avoid the glut that always occurs in the latter part of November.

16*th.*—Put in cuttings of Carnations and Pinks of all kinds.   41°—58°.

17*th.*—Pricked out Cabbage, Cauliflower, and Lettuce

plants, (that were sown on the 12th of September,) in cold frames. 50°—61°.

18*th.*—Pricked out in shallow boxes seedlings of Delphinium, etc., sown on the 4th of last month. 50°—61°.

19*th.*—Planted Pansy seedlings from seeds sown on the 15th of September, in cold frames, four or five inches apart each way. 52°—68°.

21*st.*—Continued planting Pansies, and put in Verbena cuttings, taken from the open ground. Collected seeds of Verbenas, Salvias, etc., etc. 53°—55°.

22*d.*—Potted off the Verbenas put in on the 8th inst.; also, Coleus, Centaurea, Salvias, etc., that were put in on the 28th of September. Sowed Centaurea, Pyrethrum, etc., for ribbon line plants for spring. 54°—63°.

23*d.*—Lifted, divided, and potted Callas. 44°—46°.

24*th.*—Repotted Stock Giliflowers. First severe frost. Dahlias and all tender plants cut down. 24°—46°.

25*th.*—Made cuttings of a general variety of soft-wooded plants, of such as have yet stood uninjured in the open ground. 36°—44°.

26*th.*—Moved the first potted lots of Verbenas, to prevent them rooting through into the sand, and shifted about one-fourth into three inch pots, for stock plants for cuttings. 35°—41°.

28*th.*—Potted off Fuchsias, Heliotropes, etc., from propagating house. Lifted Roses from the open ground for shipment and for potting, to be kept in cold frames. 40°—56°.

29*th.*—Potted *Myrsiphyllum* (*Smilax*) *asparagoides*, from seed boxes, (sown on August 1st); cleaned up and top-dressed Primulas. 50°—50°.

30*th.*—Continued lifting Roses for shipment. 46°—54°.

31*st.*—Put in Carnations and Pink cuttings; we find greater success at this season than earlier, it being very important that Carnation cuttings are rooted at a low

atmospheric temperature. Caladiums completely dried
off taken from benches, and placed underneath them;
these must be kept dry until they are again to be started
in May.   41°—53°

NOVEMBER.

1st.—Potted Roses for spring blooming and sales, first
pruning off one-third of the shoots. This operation of
pruning should always be done before the plant is potted,
as it takes less than half the time, and the plant being
divested of its superfluous shoots is much more quickly
and easily handled in potting. The plants after potting
are freely watered *once*, to consolidate the soil, and if the
sun is bright and warm they are shaded by latticed shutters. The plants are placed in a cold greenhouse or cold
frame, care being taken to keep them as cool as possible,
and on no consideration to use fire heat unless to keep the
soil in the pots from freezing. Little fire need be used if
the pots are completely covered with dry leaves. If possible, Roses should never be kept at a higher temperature
than forty degrees by fire heat, until the young or
"working roots" are formed. See Chapter on the Rose
for more comprehensive details.   41°—53°.

2d.—Continued potting Roses, and put in Antirrhinum, Pentstemon, and other cuttings of half hardy
plants from the open ground.   45°—53°.

4th.—Cut down and placed *under* the benches the
Dahlias that have been grown during summer in pots.
47°—48°.

5th.—The Roses, Bouvardias, Carnations, Stevias, etc.,
are now blooming profusely.   33°—40°.

6th.—The cold weather warns us that everything must
soon be secured, so to-day we take up, divide, and pot for
spring sales, herbaceous plants of all kinds. Late Chrysanthemums grown in deep frames, must now be covered
up with straw mats every night, giving air freely in the

day time; also watch that they do not get dry at the roots. 31°—40°.

7th.—Last night's frost finally destroyed the Dahlias, so we lifted and secured them to-day, by drying on the empty benches of the greenhouse. Those to be started for cuttings in March are now placed at once in soil and kept there without water until they start; in this way every root can be saved. Cannas were lifted and placed under greenhouse benches. 30°—42°.

8th.—Planted in the open ground the Strawberry runners that were layered in pots, and covered them close up to the neck of the plants with rough manure. Put in Carnation, Begonia, Petunia, Verbena, and other cuttings, from plants that have been growing in the greenhouse. 41°—52°.

9th.—Put Tuberose bulbs that have been dried on the *top* of the benches underneath, to make room for plants needing light. 42°—50°.

10th.—The same. 42°—51°.

12th.—Again resumed the potting of the general collection of Roses, which had to be partially suspended for more pressing work. First snow, two inches deep. 34° —40°.

13th.—Potted Verbena cuttings and Roses. 33°—32°.

14th.—Lifted Violets from open exposure and placed them in a sheltered spot for planting out for stock in spring. 30°—45°.

15th.—Put in cuttings of Variegated and other Geraniums from plants that have been under glass since October 5th. 33°—34°.

16th.—Potted off cuttings of Geraniums that were put in the cutting bench in September. The cuttings were too soft, owing to the season, when they were put in, and in consequence have taken longer to root, yet have nearly all taken. 36°—40°.

17th.—Lifted and potted stock plants of Chrysanthemums and Phloxes. Roses and Azaleas imported from England and Germany, were received in fine order. 28° —25°.

19th.—Put in cuttings of Pelargoniums, Geraniums, Carnations, etc. 18°—25°.

20th.—Lifted Roses from the open ground and heeled them in under cover, as we were apprehensive they may yet freeze in the ground, and our potting of Roses is two weeks later than usual. An experience of over thirty years in the vicinity of New York shows us that we are never absolutely safe from having the ground frozen after November 20th. Hence all lifting of plants from the open ground, digging, or plowing should be finished by this date. 37°—39°.

21st.—The same. 33°—40°.

22d.—Received six cases of new plants from London, in fair order; we find this time of the year and March the safest months in which to import. Earlier in the season, the temperature is too high, and in the time intervening between November and March there is danger from frost. 32°—43°.

23d.—Put in cuttings of Roses made from ripened wood, and placed them in a cold frame, so sheltered as not to be frozen in winter. But the result from this method is far less satisfactory than in propagating Roses from cuttings of the young wood; here we lose an average of fifty per cent., while from the young shoots, if done at the time and in the manner described in the Chapter on Propagation, not even one per cent. need be lost. 39°—45°.

25th.—The same. 44°—49°.

26th.—The same. 50°—47°.

27th.—Cleared the ground of the remaining Roses and Shrubs, preparatory to plowing up for winter, though rather late. See remarks under 20th inst. 34°—43°.

28th.—The same as yesterday. 43°—48°.

29th.—Overhauled and arranged recently potted off plants. Tuberose flowers are now produced in quantity from bulbs that were planted in benches in greenhouse, on August 1st. 42°—50°.

30th.—Sowed large quantities of seed of Ampelopsis Veitchii in shallow boxes. Sown thus early they make fine plants for setting out in May; also seeds of *Dracena indivisa, Pandanus utilis* and *Latania Borbonica,* and other palm seeds were sown. 38°—24°.

DECEMBER.

2d.—Potted off cuttings of Carnations and Pinks that were put in on the 11th of October; loss heavy, as they have been put in two weeks too early. 27°—28°.

3d.—Potted off cuttings of Pentstemons, Antirrhinums, etc., which were put in a month ago. Very successful. 30°—35°.

4th.—Continued potting Roses, and putting in hardwood cuttings of Roses. 26°—30°.

5th.—Flowers of Bouvardias, Carnations, Heliotropes, Roses, and Tuberoses, are now produced in large quantities from the plantations previously made, as recorded. We find that in the planting out of Tuberose bulbs on the 15th of July, 1st of August, and 15th of August, those planted on the 1st of August give the most profitable results; the first date being too early, brings them in while the market is glutted, while by that of the 15th of August, the bulbs get too much exhausted by being kept dry too long out of season. Next season will put late bulbs in "cold storage vaults." 26°—28°.

6th.—Finished potting Roses in five and six-inch pots. The operation has occupied in the potting alone the time of three hands for about three weeks, the average work of each being eight hundred plants per day.

7th.—Put in cuttings of Verbenas, Carnations, Zonale and Variegated Geraniums, Pelargoniums, and soft wooded plants of all kinds, the condition of the temperature from this date to the middle of March being such that cuttings of every description are rooted with unerring certainty, if the simple conditions which we lay down in Chapter on Propagation are followed.

9th.—At this date, we number fifty thousand of our staple plant, Verbena. These we will multiply from ten to fifteen fold, until the first week in May, which is as late as the Verbena can be propagated, to make a plant of sufficient strength. 30°—26°.

10th.—Potted off Carnation cuttings, which were put in on November 8th, from plants grown under glass, which have done very well. Repotted and cleaned up Primroses. 27°—28°.

11th.—Put in green cuttings of Bouvardias, in bottom heat at eighty; top heat seventy. This mode of propagating the Bouvardia is not so good as by the root, but it is necessary sometimes to do so when we wish to increase new sorts rapidly. 27°—28°.

12th.—Put in cuttings of winter flowering Roses taken from the plants that are flowering. 20°—8°.

13th.—Again painted pipes with the sulphur mixture to counteract mildew; also put in fresh tobacco stems under benches to keep down *Aphis.* See "Insects." 4°—8°.

14th.—The same. 14°—12°.

16th.—Began staking Roses to-day. If stakes are provided, the average work for each hand is five hundred plants per day. Experienced hands should nearly double that number. 16°—24°.

17th.—Put in cuttings of the new Fuchsias, Chrysanthemums, etc., from the plants which were received from England on November 22d. 22°—28°.

18th.—Repotted Lantanas, Variegated Geraniums and other plants, kept in hot-house range. 23°—20°.

19th.—Potted off cuttings. 11°—10°.

20th.—Sowed Pansies, Daisies and Forget-me-nots for late flowering in spring. 8°—26°.

21st.—Put in root cuttings of Anemone. (See Propagation). 22°—26°.

23d. Shipped to-day large numbers of Verbenas, packed in close boxes. (See chapter on packing). 28° —26°.

24th.—Put in cuttings of Coleus, Lantanas, Fuchsias, Petunias, etc., etc. 27°—30°.

25th.—Christmas Day. 30°—36°.

26th.—Continued propagation of all kinds of plants, and shifted Geraniums, Heliotropes, Roses, etc., from two to three inch pots. 42°—38°.

27th.—The same. 44°—40°.

28th—Repotted Zonale and Variegated Geraniums, to induce growth to produce material for cuttings. 36°— 42°.

30th.—Cleared off the roots of Tuberoses that have done flowering (those that were planted in July and August). The last flowers sold at $8.00 per 100 florets on the 24th inst., (1867). Could they have been kept until January 1st, they would have sold one-third higher. Busy in cutting flowers to-day, in large quantities, to be made up into baskets and bouquets for New Year's Day. Late Chrysanthemums such as *Yellow Eagle, Cullingfordii,* (Crimson), *Christmas Eve,* (White), Moonlight, (Straw Color), *Mrs. Allen,* (Carmine), and *Fantasie,* (Pink), that have been kept in cold houses and matted up in deep pits—have done well and are very profitable when kept thus late. 26°—24°.

31st.—The same.

JANUARY.

2nd.—Sowed seeds of *Lobelia Paxtoniana,* Delphinium, and other plants suitable for bedding out for summer. 28°—22°.

3rd.—Repotted stock plants of Pelargoniums, Fuchsias, Lantanas, Petunias, etc., to encourage growth to
produce cuttings. 29°—34°.

4th.—The same. 24°—28°.

6th.—The same. 14°—26°.

7th.—Repotted Fuchsias, Pelargoniums, Heliotropes,
Petunias, etc., from two-inch to four-inch pots, to produce growth for spring sales. 20°—30°.

8th.—Large quantities of Verbenas, Heliotropes, Fuchsias, etc., are now put in the propagating benches, this
being, perhaps, the best season to root cuttings, to give
fine plants in May. 24°—32°.

9th.—Washed the soil from "pot bound" plants of
Heliotropes, Pelargoniums, and similar plants grown in
bench pots, and re-potted in fresh soil in pots of similar
size. For detail of this method see Potting of Plants.
28°—14°.

10th.—First sowing of Cabbage, Cauliflower and Lettuce in seed house. Night temperature, 55°. 4°—12°.

11th.—The same. 14°—18°.

13th.—First lot of Chrysanthemum cuttings put in
from general collection. 10°—12°.

14th.—Shifted Roses that are forcing to produce winter flowers. This date is not the best for this work—
nearer spring is better—but the plants required it. 10°
—20°.

15th.—The same 14°—22°.

16th.—The same. 18°—22°.

17th.—Pricked out in shallow boxes, one inch apart,
the seedling plants sown on the 2nd inst. 12°—20°.

18th.—Potted off from propagating house, struck cuttings of Petunias, Heliotropes, Variegated Geraniums,
Carnations, etc. 10°—22°.

20th.—Top dressed Roses with the same compost, and
in the same manner, as was done on October 3rd. Begun
grafting Roses. See Propagation. 20°—31°.

21st. The same. 18°—34°.

22nd.—The same. 20°—14°.

23rd.—Potted *Anemone Japonica* from root cuttings put in on the 21st ult. 22°—18°.

24th.—Again potted off Verbenas and Roses in large quantities, and filled up the place occupied by them in the bench with cuttings. 19°—24°.

25th. The same. 20°—18°.

26th.—Weather is steady and moderate, which is taken advantage of to ship plants to all parts of the country. Packing is done securely, so that almost every case is received in safety. See Chapter on Packing. 20°—22°.

28th.—All operations but firing and watering nearly suspended, in consequence of all hands being occupied in getting up orders and packing. 18°—24°.

29th.—Potted off *Passiflora cærulea* from root cuttings. Potted off in two-inch pots Delphiniums and Lobelias that had been pricked out in shallow boxes on the 17th inst. 22°—28°.

30th.—Continued to pot rooted cuttings of Verbenas, Geraniums, etc., filling up the space by fresh cuttings as soon as cleared. 16°—12°.

31st—Finished staking Roses to-day. Second sowing of Cabbage and Cauliflower in seed house. 8°—16°.

FEBRUARY.

1st.—" Plunged " Roses in greenhouse benches that have been taken from cold pits, in refuse hops to the rims of the pots. We find this a great saving in watering, besides keeping the roots in a uniform condition of moisture conducive to healthy growth. 8°—16°.

2nd.—The same. 8°—16°.

3rd. The same. 6°—4°.

4th.—The same. Zero—6°.

5th.—Cleared the benches of Eupatorium, Steria, Carnations, etc., which have become exhausted or are done flowering, and filled up with spring stock.   4°—18°.

6th.—The same.   22°—28°.

7th.   Put in cuttings of Roses, Lantanas, Fuchsias, Antirrhinums, Petunias, etc.   22°—28°.

8th.—The same.   1° below zero—12°.

10th.—Cleared off Bouvardias that have been forcing for flowers, cutting off the tops and planting the roots closely together in shallow boxes, and placing them under the bench.   These roots make splendid plants for next season, or the roots may be cut up for propagating.   12° —8°.

11th.—Pricking out Cauliflower and Cabbage into boxes one and one-half inch deep from the lot sown January 10th.   They are placed outside in cold houses or slight hot-bed and matted up.

12th.—Arranged plants on the benches where the Bouvardias and other flowering plants had been growing. Zero—26°.

13th.—Continued plunging Roses, as begun on the first inst., placing them, according to the size of the plants, at such distance apart as will allow the outside shoots to be an inch or so from each other.   A house full of Roses in the dormant state when the pots are placed close to each other should fill, when thinned out, just double the space, to give them sufficient room to grow. 20°—32°.

14th.   The same.

15th.—The same.

17th.—Put in cuttings of Phloxes and Chrysanthe. mums.   14°—32°.

18th.—Put in cuttings of Begonias, Stevias, Eupatoriums, etc., etc., to produce plants to grow in summer for next winter's flowers.

19th.—Cleared out Carnation plants that have been forced for flower.   As such plants are of but little use after they have been thus forced, we find it most profitable to throw them away and replace them by young and fresh stuff.   22°—30°.

20th.—Pricked out rooted cuttings of Carnations one inch apart in shallow boxes, to economize space; after being sufficiently rooted in the boxes, they are placed in cold greenhouses or frames. See Carnations for Cut Flowers. We find that thus treated and planted out in the open ground they do quite as well as if they had been potted, and nearly one-half the space is saved. 30° —34°.

21st.—Put in large quantities of the leading bedding plants, such as Verbenas, Petunias, Heliotropes, Geraniums, etc., for succession crops.   36°—30°.

22d.—Pricking out Cabbage, Cauliflower and Lettuce from the seed sown January 31st.   26°—30°.

24th.—The same.   24°—16°.

25th.—Put in first Rose cuttings from young wood, of some new sorts that are scarce with us. Finished thinning out and plunging Roses.   17°—22°.

26th.—Put in cuttings of Lantana, Variegated Geraniums, etc.

27th.—The same.   24°—30°.

28th.—The same.   28°—26°.

29th.—First sowing of Tomato, Pepper, and Egg Plant seeds in shallow boxes for spring plants, in a night temperature of 65°.   22°—20°.

MARCH.

2nd.—Put in first cuttings of Dahlias, new Chrysanthemums, new Fuchsias, etc. Sowed Chinese Primroses, Calceolaria, Cineraria, and seeds of other plants of this class, as we find it is better to sow now and carry them through the summer than to sow, as is often done, in August. See Chapter on Propagation by Seeds. 12° —10°.

3rd.—Pricked off seedling Petunias into shallow boxes one inch apart each way. Sowed Verbena seeds in shallow boxes; as they germinate slowly, care is taken to cover with finely-sifted leaf mould to the depth of half an inch, and sprinkle daily, so that they never get dry. See Propagation of Plants by seeds. Temperature at night 60° to 65°. Zero—4°.

4th.—Began to put in Rose cuttings in quantity, care being taken not to let the bottom heat exceed 65°, with an atmosphere of 10 or 15 degrees lower. See Propagation for further details. Zero—20°.

5th.—The same.

6th.—Potted off Pelargonium cuttings in good order; they will make fine, healthy plants by May. Sowed Zinnias, Asters, and all tender annual seeds. 16°—33°.

7th.—We are now shipping large quantities of all kinds of plants, mostly to florists. 32°—34°.

9th.—Put in cuttings of all sorts in large quantities. 30°—40°.

10th.—Second sowing of Tomatoes, Pepper, and Egg Plant seeds for succession. 32°—30°.

11th.—Put in Rose cuttings in large quantities. 36° —25°.

12th.—The same. 30°—30°.

13th.—Pricked out in shallow boxes, an inch to an inch and a half apart, the Tomato, Pepper and Egg Plants from seeds sown on the 29th ult. Average work for one hand is about 3,000 plants per day. 36°—42°.

14th.—The same.

16th.—Put in cuttings of Dahlias, Fuchsias, etc. 42° —44°.

17th—Potted off the Rose cuttings which were put in on the 25th ult. ; an entire success. 40°—46°.

18th.—Placed young Carnation plants out in cold frames, to harden them off, preparatory to planting them out in the open ground. 38°—42°.

19*th.*—The same. 30°—40°.

20*th.*—The same. 30°—34°.

22*nd.*—Continued putting in Roses and Verbena cuttings in large quantities. 28°—30°.

23*rd.*—The same. 30°—42°.

24*th.*—Pricked out in shallow boxes the Zinnias and Asters, which were sown on the 6th inst. 30°—42°.

25*th.*—Now shipping largely. 30°—28°.

25*th.*—The second sowing of Tomatoes and Egg Plants was pricked out in boxes. Continued putting in Rose cuttings in large quantities. 30°—26°.

27*th.*—The same. 40°—44°.

28*th.*—Pricked out in shallow boxes the seedling plants of Verbenas that were sown on the 3d inst. 32°—38°.

30*th.*—Putting in cutting. of Clematis and Azaleas, using the young wood partially firm. 30°—36°.

31*st.*—Potted off Rose cuttings that were put in on the 4th inst. 32°—48°.

APRIL.

1*st.*—The Pansy seedlings sown on 29th December and pricked out in boxes, were now pricked out in cold frames, and matted up on cold nights. These make fine plants by middle of May and bloom much better through the hot weather, than those sown in the fall. *Ampelopsis Veitchii*, from seeds sown January 1st, are now being potted in three inch pots. Selected and shifted stock plants of Verbenas, Geraniums, Fuchsias, Chrysanthemums, Roses, etc., to be reserved for stock.

2*nd.*—Began to plant in the open ground Carnations and Pinks that are to be kept for our own stock. (*Note.* —May 2nd. Since these have been planted, the ground has been frozen solid to the depth of four inches, or below the ball of roots, yet not a single plant is killed, or even injured. The Carnation, be it remembered, is almost a hardy plant, and if not raised too tender, will stand a great amount of cold without injury. Our lesson from this, then, is that, if we have plants in the necessary hardy condition, they may be planted out in spring just as soon as the ground is dry enough to work with advantage.)   32°—30°.

3rd.— Potted off Verbenas, and continued planting Carnations outside. 30°—32°. (*Note.*—May 2nd. Those planted from the boxes show quite as well as those that had been grown in pots.)

4th.—Put in cuttings largely of Alternantheras, Coleus, Lantanas, Bouvardia roots, and such cuttings as require the higher temperature that the brighter sunshine now gives. 30°—48°.

5th.—Began potting off a large quantity of Verbenas to-day; potted even at this date, they form splendid plants. 25°—34°.

7th.—Put in cuttings of Dahlias and Lemon Verbenas, the latter for next year's stock.

8th.—Continued making Rose cuttings and potting off such as are rooted. 45°—40°.

9th.—The same. 24°—36'.

10th.—The same. 28°—34°.

11th.—The same. 26°—32.

13th.—Put in cuttings of Lobelia, Pyrethrum, and similar plants, for baskets and vases. 25°—30°.

14th.—The same. 40°—44°.

15th.—Put in cuttings of Coleus, Verbenas, Pelargoniums, and Zonale, Variegated, and Rose Geraniums. It will be noticed that this date is later than plants are usually propagated by florists—but every years' business shows an increasing demand later in the season, and the plants from these late propagations make excellent specimens by June. See Succession Crops, page 261. 50°—60°.

16th.—The same. 48°—52°.

17*th.*—Continued putting in Verbena and Rose cuttings, and planted out Carnations in open ground. No Rose cuttings yet planted out, on account of a very wet spell. There would be no danger from frost now, were the ground sufficiently dry. 40°—44°.

18*th.*—Putting in large lots of Coleus cuttings.

20*th.*—Sowed Tomatoes for a succession crop. 44° —46°.

21*st.*—Put in cuttings of Double White Primula, for fall stock. 42°—48°.

22*nd.*—First planting of Roses in the open ground. Plants in very fine condition. They would have been planted ten days ago if the ground had been dry. 46° —52°.

23*rd.*—The same.

24*th.*—Put in to-day 20,000 Verbena cuttings. These will make very fine plants by the end of May. 32°—44°.

25*th.*—Put in cuttings of Dahlias and Double Geraniums. 40°—36°.

27*th.*—Selected the best Pansies, and planted them out for seed for stock. 40°—48°.

28*th.*—Planted out Roses. 36°—42°.

29*th.*—The same. 42°—46.

30*th.*—Rose cuttings made to-day, later than this, it is rather uphill work propagating Roses, owing to the increased heat of the advancing season. 42°—60°.

MAY.

1*st.*—Planted out Lilies, Pæonies, and other hardy plants, in open ground, divided Caladium Bulbs and potted into two inch pots in leaf mould and sand ; also, potted and started Tuberous rooted Begonias and Gloxinias, find these tropical bulbs should not be started much earlier than this date. 42°—60°.

2nd.—Planted out in open ground seedling Verbenas from the boxes in which they have been pricked out, at distances of eighteen inches between the rows, and four inches between the plants, also, stock plants of named Verbenas. They are put thus close to admit of rejecting inferior sorts as they flower. 46°—52°.

4th.—Pricked out Egg Plants from third sowing, (April 10th) and also potted those previously pricked out in boxes. Egg plants being rather difficult to transplant, we prefer to pot them, but there is no such reason for putting Tomato or Pepper plants in pots. 46°—54°.

5th.—Potted off root cuttings of Bouvardia in large quantities. 48°—52°.

6th.—Planted out in the open ground stock plants of Variegated and Zonale Geraniums, the ones we have been propagating from all winter, also the young plants shifted for new stock. 50°—53°.

7th.—Put in cuttings of Dahlias, Coleus and Alternanthera, and potted off such as are rooted. 50°—44°.

8th.—Put in cuttings of Lemon Verbenas for next season's stock, and potted off the last of Verbena cuttings for the season. 42°—52°.

9th.—Potted off a general assortment of bedding plants mostly new, for our own stock. 46°—54°.

11th.—Planted out Roses largely. 48°—56°.

12th.—Potted off Rose cuttings. 46°—50°.

13th.—Potted off the Lemon Verbenas that were put in on the 7th ult. ; found them too largely rooted, but had no room to pot off until now. They should have been potted off ten days ago. 52°—56°.

14th.—Put in cuttings of Chrysanthemums, Phloxes, and Lantanas, for plants for next fall and winter sales, we find that Chrysanthemum cuttings from healthy stock, put in now, make plants large enough for six or seven inch pots by October, if properly shifted. 54°—55°.

15th.—The same. 50°—58°.

16th.—Budding Roses on Manetta stock, grown in three-inch pots.

18th.—Potted off Geraniums, etc., etc. As we are running short of Egg plants, have put in 2,000 of the tops as cuttings, as it is too late to sow seed—but the plan is not advised if it can be avoided. 54°—56°.

19th.—Potted off Dahlias and Lemon Verbenas. 50° —54°.

20th.—The same. 52°—56°.

22nd.—Put in cuttings of Pelargoniums for fall and winter stock. 52°—56°.

23rd.—The same. 54°—64°.

25th.—Potted off Double White Primulas put in on the 21st ult., with a loss not exceeding one per cent. 58°—66°.

26th.—Planted out stock plants of Petunias, Calceolarias, Pentstemons, etc. 57°—68°.

27th.—Planted out Roses in large quantities to-day. 58°—56°.

28th.—Shifted winter flowering Roses from three to four inch pots. 54°—60°.

29th.—The same. 58°—64°.

30th.—The same. 62°—68°. Divided and planted out Canna roots in open ground, also Dahlias from green cuttings together with stock of Coleus, Alternanthera, etc.

JUNE.

1st.—Planted out in shallow benches (having four inches of soil) stock plants of Roses from four inch pots, ten inches apart, these are the plants from which our summer propagation of Roses is made. The soil used in the benches is good loam, without manure. 62°—66°.

2nd.—Potted off cuttings of Egg Plants that were put in on the 18th inst. 62°—66°,

3rd.—Potted Chrysanthemums, Phloxes, and Lantanas, that were put in on the 14th ult. 60°—64°.

4th—Continued to put in Dahlia cuttings. 64°—68°.

5th.—Planted out our collection of hardy Herbaceous Plants. 66°—70°.

6th.—Shaded all glass very slightly by syringing it with Naptha and White Lead; using only enough to sprinkle it like rain drops, over such plants as Roses. 68°—72°.

8th.—Topped Carnation plants that were planted out on April 2nd, to keep them dwarf and bushy. 60°—64°.

9th.—Potted off Roses, Dahlias and double White Primroses. 62°—66°.

10th.—Repotted stock plants of Double White Primroses. They are kept under glass during summer, and rather lightly shading the glass from May 1st to November 1st, heavier shading being given during the months of July and August. 54°—60°.

11th.—Shifted the Lemon Verbenas that were potted on May 13th from two inch to three and four inch pots, in which they will remain all summer. Shifted Caladiums potted May 1st into three and four inch pots. 64°—68°.

12th.—Washed the soil entirely from the roots of stock Pelargoniums, which have been exhausted by excessive cutting for propagation, and potted in a size *smaller* pots. 66°—68°.

13th.—Planted out Bouvardias in open ground, at a distance of nine inches each way. 68°—70°.

15th.—Finished planting out Roses on benches for propagation began on the 1st inst. 64°—66°.

16th.—Repotted Roses, to be kept in pots during summer and fall, to force for flowers in winter. 62°—66°.

18th.—Planted out stock Dahlias. 66°—72°.

19th.—Have continued budding Roses from May 16th to this date with excellent success.

20th.—Planted out large Roses that had been left unsold. 78°—82°.

22d.—Still propagating Chrysanthemums largely. 60° —62°.

23d.—First lot of cuttings taken from the Roses planted on benches on the 1st. 60°—72°.

24th.—Planted out what remained of stock plants. 58° —64°.

25th.—Carnations have been much injured by continued rains; we observe that they are more susceptible of injury from wet than almost any other plant grown, consequently all soils on which they are planted should be well drained, either naturally or artificially. 60°—68.

26th.—Shifted Chrysanthemums, Roses, Bouvardias, Carnations, Solanums, Geraniums, Primulas, Cyclamens and such plants as are being grown for fall flowers or for the sale of plants; all are placed in beds outside and exposed to full sunshine except Primulas, Cyclamens, Cinerarias and similar plants, that we find are benefitted by being shaded with the protecting cloth "sashes"—(see chapter on Cloth Frames)—or shutters made by tacking lath on light frames, at an inch and a half apart. These are placed over the plants in bright, hot days, from ten to four o'clock. 60°—66°.

27th.—Repotted different kinds of plants that are kept in pots for winter, such as Chrysanthemums, Eupatoriums, Roses, Poinsettias, Heliotropes, etc. 64°—76°.

29th.—Potted off last lot of Pelargonium cuttings, for the season. 66°—74°.

30th.—Sowed seeds of Hollyhocks, Carnations, etc.

JULY.

1st.—Repotted Roses for winter flowering. Planted out Roses from five inch pots on benches for winter. See chapter on Rose Growing in Winter. 68°—70°.

2d.—Potted off Dahlia cuttings, the last for the season; later than this, the roots would hardly ripen sufficiently. 66°—68°.

3d.—Planted out Chrysanthemums on solid greenhouse borders, at one foot apart, for fall flowering. Chrysanthemum cuttings put in at this date will yet make fine young plants to flower in fall, or to keep over for spring sales. 72°—72°.

6th.—Shifted Dahlias from two to three-inch pots, where they will now remain for the season, care being taken, however, to thin out the shoots and lower leaves, to admit sufficient air to the roots to ripen the tubers. 72°—76°.

7th.—The same. 70°—70°.

8th.—The same. 72°—78°.

9th.—The same. 74°—76°.

10th.—Shifted Roses for winter flowering. 76°—80°.

11th.—Putting in Rose cuttings, largely from stock plants, planted in benches in June.

13th.—Topped Carnations, to induce a dwarf growth and prevent them from exhausting themselves now by flowering, as the flowers are required only in winter. 82°—88°.

14th.—Weather exceedingly hot; nothing done but to water the plants and clean up. 76°—88°.

15th.—Planted out Roses from five inch pots on raised benches for winter flowering. See chapter on Rose Growing in Winter. 80°—90°.

16th.—The same. 88°—88°.

17th.—The same. 76°—80°.

18th.—The same. 88°—88°.

20th.—The same. 70°—74°.

21st.—The same. 72°—72°.

22d.—Shifted Heliotropes, Chrysanthemums, Roses, etc., for winter flowering. 74°—76°.

23d.—The same. 72°—74°.

24th—.Putting in Rose cuttings, largely; have had excellent success on the first lots, unless in a few cases where stock was unhealthy. 72°—72°.

25th.—Planted out dry bulbs of Tuberoses on benches, in five inches of well-prepared, rich soil; these we expect to flower in December. Every alternate sash is removed from the eleven feet wide greenhouse, so that they have almost full exposure to the open air. The same plan is adopted in those greenhouses where Chrysanthemums are now planted out from five inch pots, at one foot apart, for fall flowering. 76°—80°.

27th.—Repotted *Stevia compacta* and other winter-blooming plants. 74°—76°.

28th.—Layered in two-inch pots Roses of some new sorts that are scarce. There is little loss in layering Roses if it is done in small pots sunk in the soil. The practice is now nearly done away with in all large establishments. 66°—74°.

29th.—The same.

30th.—Shifted Cyclamens and Primroses, and thinned out the Primroses, spreading them over a larger surface, to admit air around the pots. 68°—74°.

31st.—Pinched out the points of the shoots of Chrysanthemums that were planted out on the 3d and 25th inst., to make them bushy. 70°—74°

AUGUST.

1st.—Second planting of Tuberoses in the manner done on the 25th ultimo. Will endeavor to retard this lot by keeping the soil as dry as possible, the great object being to delay the flowering until January. 72°—78°.

3d.—The same.

4th.—The same. 72°—78°.

5th.—To-day we pot dry roots of Tuberoses, placing them in a cool shed and keeping them *dry*. They can be thus kept in a shed for ten or twelve days, after which they must be exposed to the open air, but will still be kept as dry as possible until they begin to grow. They will be thus kept in pots (two roots in a six-inch pot,) until there is danger of frost, when they will be planted out in soil on the benches as the others are. The object of potting them at all is, that their removal to the benches can be done without injury to the roots, which could not be effected unless they were first potted. If we had planted them at once on the bench we do not think we could keep them back so well, as by placing them in a partially shaded place in the open air.—Cut over for the last time this season those Carnations that are wanted to produce flowers in December and January. 70°—76°.

6*th.*—Shifted winter-flowering plants of all kinds. Began to withhold water from Hybrid Roses grown in pots, so that they can be started in October, to flower in January. See Rose Growing in Winter. 70°—78°.

7*th.*—Removed Hybrid Tea Roses, such as Bennett, La France and American Beauty, that have been grown in eight-inch pots, outside in open air, to the shelter of the greenhouse. 70°—76°.

8*th.*—Continued to put in large lots of Rose cuttings, from stock plants grown in benches. 72°—74°.

10*th.*—Potted off cuttings, and shifted into larger pots, *Chrysanthemum laciniatum* (the winter-flowering variety). 72°—76°.

11*th.*—Continued to pinch back late kinds of Chrysanthemums. 74°—78°.

12*th.*—The same. 60°—64°.

13*th.*—Put in green cuttings of Bouvardia, Cissus, etc. 54°—60°.

14*th.*—Shifted for the last time this season Roses that are to be used for winter flowering. 55°—62°.

15*th.*—Put in largely, at this date, cuttings of the leading kinds of Alternantheras; it is most important to do so *now*, if a large stock is wanted as, unless under very high temperature, this plant cannot be grown, so that it can be propagated in winter. It is easily propagated in May, but it is then too late.

17*th.*—Shifted Eupatoriums, Stevias, Poinsettias, and other winter-flowering plants, for the last time this season.

The next shifting will be from the pots to planting out in the benches. 66°—74°.

18*th*.—Washed the soil from the roots of Roses that have become "pot bound," and repotted in new pots with fresh soil. This practice we find very effectual to recuperate all plants that have been stunted by any cause whatever. 64°—72°.

19*th*.—Topped Bouvardias, to keep them dwarf and delay the flowering until the winter months. 70°—80°.

20*th*.—Put in cuttings of Abutilons, Begonias, Hibiscus, Moonflowers, Passifloras, Salvias, Trapæolums, Ivy, Geraniums and several assortments of bedding plants; also cuttings of Crotons, Dracenas and tropical plants grown inside. 75°—72°.

21*st*.—The same. 72°—70°.

22*d*.—The same. 68°—70°.

24*th*.—Put in green cuttings of Bouvardias, Cissus, Clerodendrons, and other plants of a tropical nature. (*Note.* — September 5th. This resulted successfully). 70°—76°.

25*th*.—Cut down stock plants of Pelargoniums, and put in the shoots as cuttings. The Pelargoniums have been kept under glass all summer, slightly shaded, and have ripened their shoots finely, so that, no doubt, nearly every cutting will grow. Great difficulty is always found with the rooting of Pelargoniums that have been planted out. The cut down plants will, of course, receive no water until they begin to grow. 68°—74°.

26*th*.—Stirred up the surface of the Rose benches to the depth of about one inch. 68°—74°.

27*th*.—Repotted Poinsettia, Heliotrope, Eupatorium elegans, and stock plants of Lantanas, for the last time until they are placed in winter quarters. 64°—72°.

28*th*.—Shook out and overhauled stock Fuchsias that have been injured by exposure outdoors to heavy rains. 72°—75°.

29th.—Cut back and top dressed Verbenas, to induce healthy growth of cuttings. See chapter on Verbena. 70°—74°.

31st.—Cut down stock Heliotropes and put in the cuttings. 70°—74°.

SEPTEMBER.

1st.—Potted off cuttings of new Bouvardias that were put in on the 13th instant, only about one-half of which have rooted, owing to too high a temperature. 72°—80°.

2d.—Shifted Roses thus early, so that they may become sufficiently rooted in the pots to force for winter flowers. 65°—70°.

3d.—Cut back Petunias, shrubby Calceolarias, etc., to produce young shoots for cuttings, which they will do by the end of the month. The hard growth of the flowering shoots, or even the ordinary growth of the blind shoots made in summer, is too hard for the purpose. See the necessary condition of the cutting in chapter on Propagation. 56°—60°.

4th.—Continued to stir up the surface of the Rose benches. 50°—61°.

5th.—Lifted and potted Bouvardias from the open ground and placed them against a north wall outdoors. Careful attention is necessary in shading and watering until they begin to root. 55°—58°.

7th.—The same. 64°—62°.

8th.—Put in cuttings of Mrs. Pollock and other Golden tricolored Geraniums in propagating house. The propagation of all classes of Geraniums will be continued from the plants growing outdoors, from now to the end of the month. The plants of such as are wanted for stock are lifted and potted, as soon as cut down for cuttings. 60°—61°.

CHAPTER LVII.

THE CULTURE OF GRAPE VINES UNDER GLASS.

In the previous editions of this work I have included
a chapter on Hothouse Grape Culture, and though it is
outside of the legitimate scope of the book, yet I have
found that not only are quite a number of florists themselves, (particularly in the vicinity of the large summer
resorts), find it profitable to combine the growing of
Grapes with their flower business, and in addition, in
many sections of the country the patrons of the florists
often desire to add a Grapery to their establishment, and
look to the florist for information on this subject, which
he does not often possess.

It is many years since I have had personal experience
in the growing of grapes under glass, and this was so
limited that I feel incompetent to do justice to the subject,
even in the short treatise that my restricted space here
will permit. For this reason I have called in the assist-
ance of my life-long friend, Mr. Hugh Wilson, of Salem,
Mass., whose knowledge of the subject is, perhaps, equal
to that of any one in this country.

THE LOCATION OF THE VINERY.

As with all glass structures, the vinery should, whenever practicable, be in a situation sheltered from the
north and west, and if the ground is gently sloping towards the south-east so much the better.

THE BORDER

or soil in which the vines are to be planted, is an all important matter. It is rarely that the natural soil is of
such a character as would serve the purpose, and hence,
in nearly every case, it is necessary to prepare the ma-

terials for the "border." The usual rule laid down is, to take of the top spit (or spade's depth), from an old pasture, as the main material of the border—say three parts; lime rubbish, charcoal, scrapings from a paved street, or oyster shells broken up, one part ; rotted stable manure one part, with perhaps one ton of crushed bones added to every twenty tons of this border compost. Something depends upon the soil of the pasture from which the top spit is taken; if it is a heavy, adhesive loam, more in proportion of the lime rubbish or street scrapings should be added, as it is all important that when the organic substances of the manure or fibers of the sod are rotted away, that the material forming the border should not become sodden or solid, so that it would be retentive of water and impervious to air. For this reason, when choice can be made, the pasture from which this turfy top spit is taken, should be of a shaly or calcareous character. If the whole material for the border can be prepared a year before using so much the better ; let it be repeatedly turned so as to mix the different ingredients thoroughly. This is not indispensable, however, as we have often used the compost fresh with nearly as good results.

THE EXCAVATION FOR THE BORDER

should be made from 16 to 20 inches deep, and of the width of the grapery itself ; that is, if the grapery is a span roof, 20 feet wide—the border on each side should not be made less than 10 feet wide to begin with—and in two or three years should be extended to double that width. If the house is a "leanto, " 15 or 20 feet outside. For a span roof, make it the same distance on each side outside. Above everything, it is indispensable that this excavation be thoroughly drained—it should be formed so that the bottom slopes about one foot in twenty to the outside of the border, and there a drain should be placed of sufficient capacity as to quickly carry off all surplus from

the rains that may fall on the border.   Perhaps the safest
and simplest plan to prevent the roots getting through
into the cold subsoil is to cement the bottom of this excavation.   One inch of thickness of cement is enough.
When this is done the border material may be thrown in,
filling it up five or six inches higher than the general
level to allow for settling.   Be careful never to handle
the materials for the border in wet weather.

OF THE CONSTRUCTION OF THE VINERY

little may be here said, as there are now architects in
every large city, fully competent to give plans.   I will
simply say that for early forcing, or perhaps in all
graperies where artificial heat is used, the lean-to or one-
sided structure is preferable, or what is more sightly and
will answer equally well, is the two-third span greenhouse now considered the best model for Rose forcing.
(See Greenhouse Structures.)   While for cold graperies,
or those not heated artificially, the curvilinear or span-
roofed is the best. (See Green-house Structures.)   The
"lean-to" or "two-third span" may be 18 or 20 feet
wide, and of any desired length, giving a length of rafter
from 20 to 24 feet.   When the curvilinear span for cold
vineries are used, the base width may be 25 feet, which
will give about 15 feet of rafter on each side.

PLANTING THE VINE.

Amateurs planting graperies, commonly desire to produce vines that are two or three years old, but such as
have had much experience with stocking new graperies,
know that a one-year-old vine that is well ripened, better
answers the purpose than those of greater age; in fact it
is a question whether a vine started from an eye in February or March, and planted in June, will not by September make as fine a cane as one of any greater age.
As such vines are not very easily transportable or even
procurable at all by beginners, the best thing they can do

is to procure well-grown one-year-old vines and plant them in spring, but not too early—say May in this latitude, or just when their buds are beginning to start if kept, as they should have been, in a cool place. It is best to shake the soil from the ball of the young vines that have been grown in pots, although the disentanglement or spreading of the roots, to which so much importance is by some attached, is of no consequence. In planting it has ever been my practice to set the roots outside, drawing the tops through the apertures formed in the wall, a little higher than the border inside the house (if there is one). The distance apart at which the vines should be planted is three feet. Strong galvanized wire should be run horizontally fifteen inches across the rafters and fifteen inches from the glass, on which to train the vines.

I may here state to such as may object to outside planting for hot house or forcing graperies, that I have grown vines so planted for twenty years in succession, and never failed to have a satisfactory crop. And do not think it of any importance to prepare borders inside of the house where the exclusion of the light when the vines are in full leaf, must render the value of the roots inside of but little importance. In *early* forcing of course, sufficient leaves or manure must be used to cover the border to exclude all frost.

Firing begun about the first of February. But for earlier forcing, say that beginning in December or January, it is necessary to heat such a border by the use of hot manure or leaves, which must be in sufficient depth to ferment; and it must be covered with boards in winter so as to throw off rain. The treatment of

VINES THE FIRST SEASON

is very simple, presuming they have been planted in May and were cut back to two or three buds inside the front wall. Select the strongest growth from one of these buds, tying it to the wires as it grows, and pinching off to one leaf the laterals or side shoots which it will throw out above the first joint, until it reaches the top of the house, after which let it revel at will.

THE SECOND SEASON.

After planting, this single shoot or cane should be cut down to the foot of the rafter, from which a shoot will be allowed to grow as on the previous season. Vines are not allowed to fruit in their first year's growth. When the vines, however, are strong and well ripened, instead of cutting them down as above stated, I have adopted the following plan of fruiting the shoot, with good success:

On well-grown vines the shoot or cane will be well ripened, seven or eight feet from bottom of the rafter; this shoot is "layered" by being twisted once round (in order to check the flow of sap), in a twelve-inch pot, which is filled up with vine border compost; roots will be emitted from this "layer" sufficient to sustain and mature the fruit, and as good a shoot will grow from *below* the layer as if it had been cut down, as is usually done; and if the young cane has been well matured the previous season, a good crop will be secured with no injury to the part of the vine relied on for permanent use. The layer after fruiting may be thrown away or cut off and used as a plant.

[The plan is often adopted by those planting new graperies to use the space that otherwise would be useless by fruiting vines in pots, so that from the first erection of the grapery, fruit can be obtained. Such vines are specially prepared for this purpose and can usually be obtained from those who make a specialty of growing hothouse grape vines. They should be such as are grown in ten-inch pots, and should have the canes thoroughly ripened, and not less than an inch in circumference.

. Such shoots should be cut back to four or five feet, and be allowed to bear from four to eight pounds of grapes, according to their strength. They should be fruited in the pots in which they are grown; not shifted; but when well started into growth, may be fed with manure water. Such vines cost from two and a half dollars to five dollars each, according to size. The Black-Hamburg is the best to use for this purpose.—P. H.]

THE THIRD SEASON.

At the pruning of the ripe wood, instead of cutting the vine down to a third of its length, or five feet on a fifteen foot rafter, I think it preferable to leave two-thirds, and if the vine is strong and well-matured it will break freely, but allow it to bear only a light crop. By doing this, I have found the strength of the vine better equalized, as a strong vine when shortened to five feet, is apt to make a stronger growth on the following season, leaving the lower part comparatively weak.

THE FOURTH SEASON.

A full crop may be taken, which should be about eighteen or twenty pounds to each rafter of fifteen feet in length.

TRAINING THE VINE.

In this short series I will confine myself to the "spur system," which is the easiest to be comprehended by those beginning the culture of the vine. It is done in this way: presuming that the vine has reached its "third season," and has been cut back to say ten feet from the foot of the rafter, the cane is allowed to branch or spur at each joint or eye, a shoot from the upper part of the cane is allowed to run to the top of the house, which completes the length of the cane. The side shoots, or bearing wood, are cut back, or spurred to one eye. The vine is now complete. The upper part will bear its first crop on its next season's growth; the bearing wood when next pruned will be cut back as before to one eye, and so on annually the side branches or bearing wood to be cut back to one eye, the bunches of fruit being borne on the spurs annually.   •

IN FORCING VINERIES.

The temperature to start with should be from fifty to fifty-five degrees at night, with a day temperature of ten or fifteen degrees higher, increasing ten degrees when the buds are fairly broken, which will be in about a month from time of starting; in six or seven weeks more, the fruit will be set and the temperature may be raised ten degrees more, and so continued. Next in importance to temperature is

MOISTURE.

The vine luxuriates in what gardeners call a "tropical atmosphere," and during the whole period of its growth, particularly in our arid climate, the grapery should be copiously syringed twice a day with water of the temperature of the house, until the first young leaves are formed. Besides this, evaporating pans placed on the pipes should at all times be kept full of water. In cold vineries, where there are no pipes, water should be freely dashed all over the floor; this necessity for moisture occurs during the whole period of the growth of the vine until the fruit is beginning to ripen, *except* that at the time the vines are in flower, it must be discontinued, as a dry atmosphere is best fitted for the proper fertilizing action of the pollen. I have long believed the cause of

RUST ON THE GRAPE,

Is an excess of moisture at the time of the "setting" of the fruit; the "flower," the cup of petals, instead of dropping off will, in a moist atmosphere, adhere to the forming berry, and while being forced off by the growth of the latter, it leaves its impression on the tender skin, which increases in size as the berry grows and results in the well known mark on the matured fruit called from its appearance "rust."

It is a good plan to jar the wire or trellis to which the vines are tied, when they are in flower, so as to cause a movement of the pollen through the house. This will be found to greatly assist in "setting" the fruit of such varieties as Muscat of Alexandria, which does not sometimes set freely.

THINNING.

Only one bunch of grapes should be left on each spur or shoot, if large bunches are desired. The berries should be thinned when they are not larger than peas; if left until the bunches are crowded, the process of thinning is not only much slower but the berries are more apt to be bruised. I have long been guided in thinning grapes by the fact (and one I think not generally noticed), that the flowers of the grape are produced in sets of three. In cases where each of the three flowers form a berry, two may be safely cut out in thinning; but in many instances two only are formed, and sometimes only one, which the operator must take into consideration in thinning. With large clusters it is necessary to cut away entirely from the heart of the bunch many of these sets of three alluded to. The large bunches of some of the varieties ought to be "shouldered," that is, the shoulders, or loose and overhanging portions of the clusters, are to be tied up from the main body of the bunch, giving opportunity for fuller development. This is especially necessary with Hamburgs and Muscats.

SUMMER PRUNING

Should commence just before the vines are in flower. The shoot may be shortened to one joint above the bunch intended to be left. The laterals which grow below the bunch must be rubbed off, while that which grows by the bunch and above it is to be left and shortened to one joint. When the laterals have again made a few leaves they need to be again shortened in the same way, all through the season while the vine continues to grow.

MULCHING THE BORDER

Is always beneficial if not indispensable to the well-being of the grapery, not only to protect the roots from being frozen in winter, but also because when such fertilizing materials as stable manure is used, the roots are drawn to the surface of the border, which greatly conduces to the health of the vine and the quality of the fruit.

PROTECTING THE VINES IN COLD GRAPERIES

Is of great benefit. About the simplest way to do so is to run a board along eighteen inches or so from the front wall. After pruning the vines (which may be done at any time after they drop their leaves), they are to be taken down from the wires and laid down between this boarding and the front wall, and the space entirely filled up with soil or sand. It is necessary, though, to watch that ground mice do not get to the vines, as they might destroy them by eating the bark. We have found that vines so covered up keep admirably, and that the plan is less liable to draw vermin than when they are covered with straw or hay. They are usually covered up about the middle of December, and are not uncovered or otherwise disturbed until the first of May, when they are lifted up and tied to the wires, and started as before described. In cases where it is not practicable to cover with sand or soil, the vines can be laid down snugly along the front wall and covered up with mats or bagging; but in either manner of covering up the grapery must be freely ventilated during the warm part of the day, unless in extremely cold weather.

VARIETIES.

The varieties that I consider to be best suited for a cold vinery of fifty feet in length, requiring twenty-one permanent vines, would be: twelve Black Hamburgs, two White Frontignac, two Forster's White Seedling, two Purple Constantia, two Muscat Hamburg, one Royal Ascot.

For Vines for Forcing.—Ten Black Hamburg, two Grizzly Frontignac, two Victoria Hamburg, two Golden Hamburg, one Buckland Sweetwater, two Muscat of Alexandria, two Cannon Hall Muscat; the last two at hottest end.

I regret the necessity of being compelled to compress these notes into so limited a space, being well aware that many of the points alluded to should have been more fully treated. But I trust what has been said may be of some benefit in guiding beginners who are entirely without any knowledge of grape culture under glass. To the experienced grape-grower it contains few facts but those he already knows, and is, no doubt, wanting in many that he is familiar with.

INDEX.

Mushrooms: How to Grow Them.

Any one who has an ordinary house cellar, woodshed or barn, can grow Mushrooms. This is the most practical work on the subject ever written, and the only book on growing Mushrooms published in America. The author describes how he grows Mushrooms, and how they are grown for profit by the leading market gardeners, and for home use by the most successful private growers. Engravings drawn from nature expressly for this work. By Wm. Falconer. Cloth. Price, postpaid. 1.50

Land Draining.

A Handbook for Farmers on the Principles and Practice of Draining, by Manly Miles, giving the results of his extended experience in laying tile drains. The directions for the laying out and the construction of tile drains will enable the farmer to avoid the errors of imperfect construction, and the disappointment that must necessarily follow. This manual for practical farmers will also be found convenient for references in regard to many questions that may arise in crop growing, aside from the special subjects of drainage of which it treats. Cloth, 12mo. 1.00

Allen's New American Farm Book.

The very best work on the subject; comprising all that can be condensed into an available volume. Originally by Richard L. Allen. Revised and greatly enlarged by Lewis F. Allen. Cloth, 12mo. 2.50

Henderson's Gardening for Profit.

By Peter Henderson. The standard work on Market and Family Gardening. The successful experience of the author for more than thirty years, and his willingness to tell, as he does in this work, the secret of his success for the benefit of others, enables him to give most valuable information. The book is profusely illustrated. Cloth, 12mo. 2.00

Henderson's Gardening for Pleasure.

A guide to the amateur in the fruit, vegetable and flower garden, with full descriptions for the greenhouse, conservatory and window garden. It meets the wants of all classes in country, city and village who keep a garden for their own enjoyment rather than for the sale of products. By Peter Henderson. Finely Illustrated. Cloth, 12mo. 2.00

Johnson's How Crops Grow.

New Edition. A Treatise on the Chemical Composition, Structure and Life of the Plant. Revised Edition. This book is a guide to the knowledge of agricultural plants, their composition, their structure and modes of development and growth; of the complex organizations of plants, and the use of the parts; the germination of seeds, and the food of plants obtained both from the air and the soil. The book is a valuable one to all real students of agriculture. With numerous illustrations and tables of analysis. By Prof. Samuel W. Johnson of Yale College. Cloth, 12mo. 2.00

Johnson's How Crops Feed.

A Treatise on the Atmosphere and the Soil, as related in the Nutrition of Agricultural Plants. This volume—the companion and complement to "How Crops Grow"—has been welcomed by those who appreciate the scientific aspects of agriculture. Illustrated. By Prof. Samuel W. Johnson. Cloth, 12mo. 2.00

Market Gardening and Farm Notes.

By Barnet Landreth. Experiences and Observations for both North and South, of interest to the Amateur Gardener, Trucker and Farmer. A novel feature of the book is the calendar of farm and garden operations for each month of the year; the chapters on fertilizers, transplanting, succession and rotation of crops, the packing, shipping and marketing of vegetables, will be especially useful to market gardeners. Cloth, 12mo. 1.00

Forest Planting.

A Treatise on the Care of Woodlands and the Restoration of the Denuded Timber-Lands on Plains and Mountains. By H. Nicholas Jarchow, LL. D. The author has fully described those European methods which have proved to be most useful in maintaining the superb forests of the old world. This experience has been adapted to the different climates and trees of America, full instructions being given for forest planting on our various kinds of soil and subsoil, whether on mountain or valley. Illustrated, 12mo. 1.50

Harris' Talks on Manures.

By Joseph Harris, M. S., author of "Walks and Talks on the Farm," "Harris on the Pig," etc. Revised and enlarged by the author. A series of familiar and practical talks between the author and the Deacon, the Doctor, and other neighbors, on the whole subject of manures and fertilizers; including a chapter especially written for it, by Sir John Bennet Lawes of Rothamsted, England. Cloth, 12mo. 1.75

Truck Farming at the South.

A work which gives the experience of a successful grower of vegetables or "truck" for Northern markets. Essential to any one who contemplates entering this promising field of Agriculture. By A. Oemler of Georgia. Illustrated, cloth, 12mo. 1.50

Sweet Potato Culture.

Giving full instructions from starting the plants to harvesting and storing the crop. With a chapter on the Chinese Yam. By James Fitz, Keswick, Va., author of "Southern Apple and Peach Culture." Cloth, 12mo. .60

Heinrich's Window Flower Garden.

The author is a practical florist, and this enterprising volume embodies his personal experiences in Window Gardening during a long period. New and enlarged edition. By Julius J. Heinrich. Fully illustrated. Cloth, 12mo. .75

Greenhouse Construction.

By Prof. L. R. Taft. A complete treatise on Greenhouse structures and arrangements of the various forms and styles of Plant Houses for professional florists as well as amateurs. All the best and most approved structures are so fully and clearly described that anyone who desires to build a Greenhouse will have no difficulty in determining the kind best suited to his purpose. The modern and most successful methods of heating and ventilating are fully treated upon. Special chapters are devoted to houses used for the growing of one kind of plants exclusively. The construction of hotbeds and frames receives appropriate attention. Over one hundred excellent illustrations, specially engraved for this work, make every point clear to the reader and add considerably to the artistic appearance of the book. Cloth, 12mo.   1.50

Bulbs and Tuberous-Rooted Plants.

By C. L. Allen. A complete treatise on the History, Description, Methods of Propagation and full Directions for the successful culture of Bulbs in the garden, Dwelling and Greenhouse. As generally treated, bulbs are an expensive luxury, while, when properly managed, they afford the greatest amount of pleasure at the least cost. The author of this book has for many years made bulb growing a specialty, and is a recognized authority on their cultivation and management. The illustrations which embellish this work have been drawn from nature, and have been engraved especially for this book. The cultural directions are plainly stated, practical and to the point. Cloth, 12mo.   2.00

Henderson's Practical Floriculture.

By Peter Henderson. A guide to the successful propagation and cultivation of florists' plants. The work is not one for florists and gardeners only, but the amateur's wants are constantly kept in mind, and we have a very complete treatise on the cultivation of flowers under glass, or in the open air, suited to those who grow flowers for pleasure as well as those who make them a matter of trade. Beautifully illustrated. New and enlarged edition. Cloth, 12mo.   1.50

Long's Ornamental Gardening for Americans.

A Treatise on Beautifying Homes, Rural Districts and Cemeteries. A plain and practical work at a moderate price, with numerous illustrations and instructions so plain that they may be readily followed. By Elias A. Long, Landscape Architect. Illustrated, Cloth, 12mo.   2.00

The Propagation of Plants.

By Andrew S. Fuller. Illustrated with numerous engravings. An eminently practical and useful work. Describing the process of hybridizing and crossing species and varieties, and also the many different modes by which cultivated plants may be propagated and multiplied. Cloth, 12mo.   1.50

Parsons on the Rose.

By Samuel B. Parsons. A treatise on the propagation, culture and history of the rose. New and revised edition. In his work upon the rose, Mr. Parsons has gathered up the curious legends concerning the flower, and gives us an idea of the esteem in which it was held in former times. A simple garden classification has been adopted, and the leading varieties under each class enumerated and briefly described. The chapters on multiplication, cultivation and training are very full, and the work is altogether one of the most complete before the public. Illustrated. Cloth, 12mo.　　1.00

Henderson's Handbook of Plants.

This new edition comprises about fifty per cent. more genera than the former one, and embraces the botanical name, derivation, natural order, etc., together with a short history of the different genera, concise instructions for their propagation and culture, and all the leading local or common English names, together with a comprehensive glossary of Botanical and Technical terms. Plain instructions are also given for the cultivation of the principal vegetables, fruits and flowers. Cloth, large 8vo.　　4.00

Barry's Fruit Garden.

By P. Barry. A standard work on Fruit and Fruit Trees; the author having had over thirty years' practical experience at the head of one of the largest nurseries in this country. New edition revised up to date. Invaluable to all fruit growers. Illustrated. Cloth, 12mo.　　2.00

Fulton's Peach Culture.

This is the only practical guide to Peach Culture on the Delaware Peninsula, and is the best work upon the subject of peach growing for those who would be successful in that culture in any part of the country. It has been thoroughly revised and a large portion of it rewritten, by Hon. J. Alexander Fulton, the author, bringing it down to date. Cloth, 12mo.　　1.50

Strawberry Culturist.

By Andrew S. Fuller. Containing the History, Sexuality, Field and Garden Culture of Strawberries, forcing or pot culture, how to grow from seed, hybridizing, and all information necessary to enable everybody to raise their own strawberries, together with a description of new varieties and a list of the best of the old sorts. Fully illustrated. Flexible cloth, 12mo.　　.25

Fuller's Small Fruit Culturist.

By Andrew S. Fuller. Rewritten, enlarged, and brought fully up to the present time. The book covers the whole ground of propagating Small Fruits, their culture, varieties, packing for market, etc. It is very finely and thoroughly illustrated, and makes an admirable companion to "The Grape Culturist," by the same well known author.　　1.50

Fuller's Grape Culturist.

By A. S. Fuller. This is one of the very best or works on the Culture of the Hardy Grapes, with full directions for all departments of propagation, culture, etc., with 150 excellent engravings, illustrating planting, training, grafting, etc. Cloth, 12mo. 1.50

Quinn's Pear Culture for Profit.

Teaching How to Raise Pears intelligently, and with the best results, how to find out the character of the soil, the best methods of preparing it, the best varieties to select under existing conditions, the best modes of planting, pruning, fertilizing, grafting, and utilizing the ground before the trees come into bearing, and finally of gathering and packing for market. Illustrated. By P. T. Quinn, practical horticulturist. Cloth, 12mo. 1.00

Husmann's American Grape Growing and Wine-Making.

By George Husmann of Talcoa vineyards, Napa, California. New and enlarged edition. With contributions from well know grape-growers, giving a wide range of experience. The author of this book is a recognized authority on the subject. Cloth, 12mo. 1.50

White's Cranberry Culture.

Contents:—Natural History.—History of Cultivation.—Choice of Location.—Preparing the Ground.—Planting the Vines.—Management of Meadows.—Flooding.—Enemies and Difficulties Overcome. —Picking.—Keeping.—Profit and Loss.—Letters from Practical Growers.—Insects Injurious to the Cranberry. By Joseph J. White, a practical grower. Illustrated. Cloth, 12mo. New and revised edition. 1.25

Fuller's Practical Forestey.

A Treatise on the Propagation, Planting and Cultivation, with a description and the botanical and proper names of all the indigenous trees of the United States, both Evergreen and Deciduous, with Notes on a large number of the most valuable Exotic Species. By Andrew S. Fuller, author of "Grape Culturist," "Small Fruit Culturist," etc. 1.50

Stewart's Irrigation for the Farm, Garden and Orchard.

This work is offered to those American Farmers and other cultivators of the soil who, from painful experience, can readily appreciate the losses which result from the scarcity of water at critical periods. By Henry Stewart. Fully illustrated. Cloth, 12mo. 1.50

Quinn's Money in the Garden.

By P. T. Quinn. The author gives in a plain, practical style, instructions on three distinct, although closely connected branches of gardening—the kitchen garden, market garden, and field culture, from successful practical experience for a term of years. Illustrated. Cloth, 12mo. 1.50

Roe's Play and Profit in My Garden.

By E. P. Roe. The author takes us to his garden on the rocky hill-sides in the vicinity of West Point, and shows us how out of it, after four years' experience, he evoked a profit of $1,000, and this while carrying on pastoral and literary labor. It is very rarely that so much literary taste and skill are mated to so much agricultural experience and good sense. Cloth, 12mo. 1.50

The New Onion Culture.

By T. Greiner. This new work is written by one of our most successful agriculturists, and is full of new, original, and highly valuable matter of material interest to every one who raises onions in the family garden, or by the acre for market. By the process here described a crop of 2000 bushels per acre can be as easily raised as 500 or 600 bushels in the old way. Paper, 12mo. .50

The Dairyman's Manual.

By Henry Stewart, author of "The Shepherd's Manual," "Irrigation," etc. A useful and practical work, by a writer who is well known as thoroughly familiar with the subject of which he writes. Cloth, 12mo. 2.00

Allen's American Cattle.

Their History, Breeding and Management. By Lewis F. Allen. This book will be considered indispensable by every breeder of live stock. The large experience of the author in improving the character of American herds adds to the weight of his observations and has enabled him to produce a work which will at once make good his claims as a standard authority on the subject. New and revised edition. Illustrated. Cloth, 12mo. 2.50

Profits in Poultry.

Useful and ornamental Breeds and their Profitable Management. This excellent work contains the combined experience of a number of practical men in all departments of poultry raising. It is profusely illustrated and forms a unique and important addition to our poultry literature. Cloth, 12mo. 1.00

The American Standard of Perfection.

The recognized standard work on Poultry in this country, adopted by the American Poultry Association. It contains a complete description of all the recognized varieties of fowls, including turkeys, ducks and geese; gives instructions to judges; glossary of technical terms and nomenclature. It contains 244 pages, handsomely bound in cloth, embellished with title in gold on front cover. $1.00

Stoddard's An Egg Farm.

By H. H. Stoddard. The management of poultry in large numbers, being a series of articles written for the AMERICAN AGRICULTURIST. Illustrated. Cloth. 12mo. .50

Stewart's Shepherd's Manual.

A Valuable Practical Treatise on the Sheep for American farmers and sheep growers. It is so plain that a farmer or a farmer's son who has never kept a sheep, may learn from its pages how to manage a flock successfully, and yet so complete that even the experienced shepherd may gather many suggestions from it. The results of personal experience of some years with the characters of the various modern breeds of sheep, and the sheep raising capabilities of many portions of our extensive territory and that of Canada—and the careful study of the diseases to which our sheep are chiefly subject, with those by which they may eventually be afflicted through unforseen accidents—as well as the methods of management called for under our circumstances, are carefully described. By Henry Stewart. Illustrated. Cloth, 12mo.   1.50

Wright's Practical Poultry-Keeper.

By L. Wright. A complete and standard guide to the management of poultry, for domestic use, the markets or exhibition. It suits at once the plain poulterer, who must make the business pay, and the chicken fancier whose taste is for gay plumage and strange, bright birds. Illustrated. Cloth, 12mo. $2.00

Harris on the Pig.

New Edition. Revised and enlarged by the author. The points of the various English and American breeds are thoroughly discussed, and the great advantage of using thoroughbred males clearly shown. The work is equally valuable to the farmer who keeps but few pigs, and to the breeder on an extensive scale. By Joseph Harris. Illustrated. Cloth, 12mo.   1.50

The Farmer's Veterinary Adviser.

A guide to the Prevention and Treatment of Disease in Domestic Animals. This is one of the best works on this subject, and is especially designed to supply the need of the busy American Farmer, who can rarely avail himself of the advice of a Scientific Veterinarian. It is brought up to date and treats of the Prevention of Disease as well as of the Remedies. By Prof. Jas. Law. Cloth. Crown, 8vo.   3.00

Dadd's American Cattle Doctor.

By George H. Dadd, M. D., Veterinary Practitioner. To help every man to be his own cattle-doctor; giving the necessary information for preserving the health and curing the diseases of oxen, cows, sheep and swine, with a great variety of original recipes, and valuable information on farm and dairy management. Cloth, 12mo. 1.50

Cattle Breeding.

By Wm. Warfield. This work is by common consent the most valuable and pre-eminently practical treatise on cattle-breeding ever published in America, being the actual experience and observance of a practical man. Cloth, 12mo.   2.00

Dadd's American Cattle Doctor.

A complete work on all the Diseases of Cattle, Sheep and Swine, including every Disease peculiar to America, and embracing all the latest information on the Cattle Plague and Trichina; containing also a guide to symptoms, a table of Weights and Measures, and a list of Valuable Medicines. By George H. Dadd, V. S., twenty-five years a leading Veterinary Surgeon in England and the United States, and author of the "American Reformed Horse Book." Cloth, octavo. Illustrated. 2.50

Cattle and Their Diseases.

By A. J. Murray, M. R. C. V. S. Breeding and Management of Cattle. This is one of the very few works devoted exclusively to cattle diseases, and will be particularly valuable to cattlemen for that reason. It is written in plain, simple language, easily understood by any farmer, while it is learned and technical enough to satisfy any veterinary surgeon. Cloth, 12mo. 2.00

Silos, Ensilage, and Silage.

A practical Treatise on the Ensilage of Fodder Corn, containing the most recent and authentic information on this important subject, by Manly Miles, M. D. F. R. M. S. Illustrated. Cloth, 12mo. .50

Manures.

How to Make and How to Use them. By Frank W. Sempers. The author has made a concise, practical handbook containing the latest researches in agriculture in all parts of the world. The reports of the agricultural experiment stations have furnished many valuable suggestions. Both commercial and home-made manures are fully described, and many formulas for special crops and soils are given. Price postpaid, paper 50 cents, cloth. 1.00

Potato Pests.

No farmer can afford to be without this little book. It gives the most complete account of the Colorado Beetle anywhere to be found, and includes all the latest discoveries as to the habits of the insect and the various means for its destruction. It is well illustrated, and exhibits in a map the spread of the insect since it left its native home. By Prof. C. V. Riley. Paper. .50

Your Plants.

Plain and Practical Directions for the Treatment of Tender and Hardy Plants in the House and in the Garden. By James Sheehan. The work meets the wants of the amateur who grows a few plants in the window, or has a small flower garden. Paper covers. .40

Pedder's Land-Measurer for Farmers.

A convenient Pocket Companion, showing at once the contents of any piece of land, when its length and width are unknown, up to 1500 feet either way, with various other useful farm tables. Cloth, 18mo. .40

Hop Culture.

Plain directions given by ten experienced cultivators. Revised, enlarged and edited by A. S. Fuller. Forty engravings. .30

Wheat Culture.

How to double the yield and increase the profits. By D S. Curtiss, Washington, D. C. Importance of the Wheat Crop. Varieties Most Grown in the United States. Examples of Successful Wheat Culture. Illustrated. Paper covers. .50

Starr's Farm Echoes.

By F. Ratchford Starr, Echo Farm, Litchfield, Ct. This handsome little book tells how the author turned from a successful business career to agricultural pursuits, and has achieved health, happiness and prosperity upon his broad acres near Litchfield. Cloth, 12mo. Illustrated. .50

The American Merino. For Wool or for Mutton.

A practical and most valuable work on the selection, care, breeding and diseases of the Merino sheep, in all sections of the United States. It is a full and exhaustive treatise upon this one breed of sheep. By Stephen Powers. Cloth, 12mo. 1.50

Coburn's Swine Husbandry.

New, revised and enlarged edition. The Breeding, Rearing, and Management of Swine, and the Prevention and Treatment of their Diseases. It is the fullest and freshest compendium relating to Swine Breeding yet offered. By F. D. Coburn. Cloth, 12mo. 1.75

Tobacco Culture: Full Practical Details.

This useful and valuable work contains full details of every process from the Selection and Propagation of the Seed and Soil to the Harvesting, Curing and Marketing the Crop, with illustrative engravings of the operations. The work was prepared by Fourteen Experienced Tobacco Growers, residing in different parts of the country. It also contains notes on the Tobacco Worm, with Illustrations. 8vo. .25

Keeping One Cow.

A collection of prize Essays and Selections from a number of other Essays, with editorial notes, suggestions, etc. This book gives the latest information, and in a clear and condensed form, upon the management of a single Milch Cow. Illustrated with full page engravings of the most famous dairy cows. Cloth, 12mo. 1.00

Guenon's Treatise on Milch Cows.

A treatise on the Bovine Species in General. An entirely new translation of the last edition of this popular and instructive book. By Thomas J. Hand, Secretary of the American Jersey Cattle Club. With over 100 illustrations, especially engraved for this work. Cloth, 12mo. 1.00